JIMI HENDRIX

sessions

ALSO BY JOHN McDERMOTT

Hendrix: Setting the Record Straight

JIMI HENDRIX

The Complete Studio Recording Sessions, 1963–1970

sessions

JOHN McDERMOTT

with Billy Cox and Eddie Kramer

LITTLE, BROWN AND COMPANY

BOSTON NEW YORK TORONTO LONDON

First Paperback Edition

ISBN 0-316-55549-5 (hc) 0-316-55546-0 (pb)

Library of Congress Catalog Card Number 95-77932

Frontispiece: see page 52

10 9 8 7 6 5 4 3 2 1

RRD-OH

Designed by Barbara Werden

Published simultaneously in Canada by Little, Brown &
Company (Canada) Limited

Printed in the United States of America

contents

Preface　ix

■

The Early Years: 1963–1965
Recording Sessions for Little Richard, King
Curtis, and the Isley Brothers　3

■

1966
Recording sessions for "Hey Joe" and
"Stone Free"　15

■

1967
Recording sessions for "Purple Haze," "Little
Wing," *Are You Experienced?*, and *Axis:
Bold as Love*　25

■

1968
Recording sessions for "Voodoo Chile," "Gypsy
Eyes," and *Electric Ladyland*　49

■

1969
Recording sessions for "Izabella," "Stepping
Stone," and the "Star Spangled Banner"　91

■

1970
Recording sessions for "Freedom," "Dolly
Dagger," and *Cry of Love*　133

Discography　181

Acknowledgments　195

THE purpose of this book is to examine, in detail, Jimi Hendrix's remarkable catalog of recordings, both released and unreleased. Having attempted in *Hendrix: Setting the Record Straight* to detail the myriad of personal and professional concerns under which Jimi thrived, I have set out in *Jimi Hendrix: Sessions* specifically to profile Hendrix's unique approach to composing and recording.

The model for this book, and indeed all books of this sort, is Mark Lewisohn's superb, richly detailed *The Beatles Recording Sessions*. I cannot claim, as that book did for the Beatles, to have documented and detailed every known Jimi Hendrix recording session, as it is unlikely such a task can be done. Unlike the meticulously detailed log sheets, technical data, and billing information kept by EMI for the Beatles, Jimi Hendrix's recording sessions were never tracked in a consistent and organized manner. Unlike the Beatles, who recorded the great majority of their sessions at EMI's fabled Abbey Road Studios—a facility owned and operated by their record company—Hendrix ventured from studio to studio until May 1970, when he opened Electric Lady Studios, his own state-of-the-art facility in the heart of Greenwich Village.

The recording studio, as Billy Cox would later describe, was Jimi Hendrix's laboratory. As a result, Hendrix left behind hundreds of reels of multitrack recording tape filled with unfinished ideas, spontaneous moments of inspiration, and countless hours of unrealized ideas—in addition to the handful of albums whose release he authorized. Nothing speaks louder, or more impressively, about his unique talents than the music he created during a career that lasted less than four years.

While Jimi's authorized masterworks remain accessible to consumers, far too many Hendrix multitrack masters have unfortunately been lost or stolen in the years since his untimely death in September 1970. Other essential recordings remain in legal limbo, as bitter arguments—some now entering their third decade—over credits, and, more frequently, missed royalties, render them unavailable for release or even research. Worse still was the arguably shortsighted approach initially adopted by Alan Douglas. During production of *Crash Landing* and *Midnight Lightning,* the first two posthumous compilations he prepared, he actually erased original performances in favor of new overdubs from musicians who had never played with Hendrix. Other original master tapes were edited without safety copies having been made, while other Hendrix multitrack master recordings, deemed unsuitable for commercial issue by Douglas, were simply destroyed. Such actions have done little to diminish the notion that 'lost' recordings, which might further clarify Hendrix's magnificent talent, actually still exist.

To present a balanced perspective from both the control room and the studio, Billy Cox and Eddie Kramer joined forces with me in writing this book, sharing their many recollections of the sessions that created Hendrix's recorded legacy.

Billy Cox was one of Hendrix's closest associates, their friendship dating back to a shared stint in the U.S. Army. After their discharge, the two formed a group, the King Kasuals, in Nashville and set out to establish their respective reputations. Career opportunities ultimately pulled them in different directions, but not before a deep bond had been established. Before the two parted, they vowed that as soon as one "made the big time," he would look up the other. Hendrix made good on the promise in April 1969, reaching back to his old friend at a time of deep inner turmoil. Despite the tremendous popularity of the Jimi Hendrix Experience, this vehicle, by which Hendrix had finally emerged from the ranks of nameless session guitarists, was coming apart at the seams. During these dark times, Cox supplied his old friend with encouragement and stability. Furthermore, Cox's arrival revived the creative arrangement Jimi had successfully employed with his first producer, Chas Chandler: a private sounding board for concepts and ideas he wished to develop. Empowered by Hendrix, Cox, in turn, began to develop his capabilities, improving not only as a bassist but also displaying a budding ability as a songwriter.

Eddie Kramer played a major role in shaping Hendrix's recorded legacy, engineering all the guitarist's authorized recordings, from *Are You Experienced?* to *Band of Gypsys.* Kramer also supervised the production of the first four posthumous albums.

Kramer's technical knowledge and passion for sonic exploration perfectly complemented Chandler's production skills. Jimi thrived on such interaction, and Kramer's special rapport with Hendrix was founded on such experimentation. Kramer was also an integral member of the guitarist's hand-picked team entrusted to construct Electric Lady Studios. Kramer was named director of engineering at the new facility and continued his work with Hendrix there until the guitarist's death.

To detail Hendrix's amazing catalogue of recordings, Cox, Kramer, and I drew upon multiple sources. We reviewed original multitrack recordings whenever possible, supplemented by research gathered from evaluating hours of unreleased recordings held in private collections. Additional recordings not referenced here no doubt exist, but to provide as comprehensive a perspective as possible, we incorporated testimony from musicians such as Cox, Buddy Miles, and Noel Redding, who played beside Hendrix, along with the many engineers who shaped his sound and worked under his direction.

Dates for individual sessions listed herein were taken directly from the original tape boxes. However, these dates do not definitively represent all the various recording and mixing dates or even the final date of completion for any song, as Jimi—especially from the recording of *Electric Ladyland* forward—regularly returned to masters in an effort to improve his own performances. Many such tracks, ranging from "Gypsy Eyes" to "Dolly Dagger," were regularly revisited, with Jimi either adding or rejecting overdubs he considered.

Unless otherwise noted, the roles assumed during recording sessions were as follows: Jimi on guitar and vocals, Mitch Mitchell on drums, and Noel Redding on bass. These lines of distinction began to blur as early as the October 1967 sessions for *Axis: Bold as Love,* where Jimi would substitute bass lines originally recorded by Redding with new performances of his own. Long before the Band of Gypsys was formed during the fall of 1969, Buddy Miles was a frequent participant in Jimi's many jam sessions. Jimi's friendship with Miles and the various members of his band, the Express, often resulted in the participation of guests such as Duane Hitchings, Bill Rich, and Jim McCarty.

Beginning in the spring of 1969, Jimi began to rely more on Miles and such Express alumni as Roland Robinson and Bill Rich for bass, until Billy Cox arrived in May 1969. While Noel Redding did not formally leave the Experience until after its June 29, 1969, performance at the Denver Pop Festival, his role in Hendrix's studio recordings had gradually diminished. Redding's efficient approach to recording clashed with Hendrix's philosophy. As Jimi began to use the studio more as a venue for writing, rather than recording finished masters, the two ceased to function effectively.

With the Experience disbanded, Hendrix's sound continued to evolve. The recordings made during the late summer of 1969 featured the expanded ensemble with which he performed at Woodstock. This group featured Hendrix,

Mitchell, and Billy Cox, bolstered by guitarist Larry Lee and percussionists Juma Sultan and Jerry Velez. The shortcomings of this outfit were initially revealed at the Woodstock festival and then confirmed during the recording sessions that followed at the Hit Factory and the Record Plant.

Hendrix's next group, the Band of Gypsys, was made up of Hendrix, Cox, and Buddy Miles. Unless otherwise noted, all sessions from September 25, 1969, through February 16, 1970, feature this lineup.

After the demise of the Band of Gypsys, Jimi reformed the Experience, retaining Cox and reuniting with Mitch Mitchell. Using this lineup, Hendrix made impressive strides toward the completion of his long-overdue fourth studio album. Beginning in late May 1970, Hendrix began recording at Electric Lady Studios, using that facility exclusively until his death in September 1970. His tragic death came before this crucial project had been completed, leaving Eddie Kramer and Mitch Mitchell the painful task of assembling the posthumous *Cry of Love*.

JIMI HENDRIX

sessions

IMMEDIATELY upon his discharge from the U.S. Army in 1962, the nineteen-year-old Jimi Hendrix set his musical career in motion. Teamed with his former Army buddy Billy Cox, he settled in Nashville and struggled to establish his reputation and earn a living.

It was Cox who organized Hendrix's first known recording session. Cox had been hired as a bassist for King/Starday Records. The producer on the date was none other than legendary disc jockey Bill "Hoss" Allen. Cox had already been hired for the session when Allen asked if he knew a guitar player who could also take part. Cox suggested Hendrix, and Jimi came to the studio eager to impress. Allen's requirements were simple, and Jimi was given a modest role in the song's arrangement. Unfortunately, Allen grew so unnerved by Jimi's loud, wild playing that he simply faded his guitar out of the final mix.

In late 1963, sometime after his failed session for Hoss Allen and King/Starday Records, Jimi's recorded debut came as a session guitarist for saxophonist Lonnie Youngblood. Four spirited R&B tracks were later issued on Fairmont Records. These recordings, "Go Go Shoes" b/w "Go Go Place," and "Soul Food (That's What I Like)" b/w "Goodbye Bessie Mae," were up-tempo, dance-oriented numbers not unlike similar efforts marketed by such competing labels as Atlantic and Stax. Neither of these two singles, however, made any kind of chart impact.

Hendrix, nonetheless, did maintain a friendship with Youngblood, electing to record with him again. That batch of recordings was as unsuccessful as the first. Despite this, in the years following Hendrix's death, *hundreds* of albums have been fashioned from these master tapes. Just as other unscrupulous manufacturers misrepresented Hendrix's role and level of participation — if any — with Little Richard and, later, Curtis Knight & the Squires, these various compilations are routinely mislabeled in order to exaggerate Hendrix's participation. The liner notes — if any are supplied — are often maddeningly incomplete or blatantly inaccurate. To cash in on the posthumous sales bonanza created by Jimi's death, producers flocked to these early session tapes looking for product. Worse still, new overdubs specifically created to *sound* like Hendrix were recorded after his death to try and fill out additional releases. Perhaps the most notorious example was 1971's *Two Great Experiences Together*. In addition to copious amounts of echo added to tracks like "Wipe the Sweat," other tracks were enhanced with new stereo overdubs performed by a pathetic Hendrix soundalike. The album's cover, a photograph of Jimi jamming with Youngblood during the reedman's performance at Harlem's Small's Paradise in 1969, bore no connection with the music contained therein. Nonetheless, *Two Great Experiences Together* arrived in record shops almost simultaneously with Reprise's *Cry of Love*. Issued on Maple Records, the album managed to climb to number 127 on the *Billboard* Top 200 album chart before it quickly exited and was replaced by a steady stream of dubious compilations drawn from the same source material.

Hendrix's next known recording session took place in Los Angeles, where he befriended Rosa Lee Brooks, a Los Angeles–based R&B artist. "Jimi and I had met at the California Club in Los Angeles," explains Brooks. "Neither of us were onstage — we were there watching the Ike and Tina Turner Revue. It was love at first sight, and we spent three beautiful months together. We were scouting around looking for work and trying to get gigs at different clubs in Hollywood and L.A."

Shortly after the two met, Jimi cowrote "My Diary" with Brooks at the Wilcox Hotel on New Year's Day, 1964. Brooks explains: "Jimi sang the first verse, 'I know that I will never love again, I know that I will be my only friend,' as he started playing what he called a 'love note.' The rest of the words were written by me. Jimi and I felt that we had an Ike & Tina or Mickey & Sylvia thing happening. We were Jimi and Rose, and this song was our baby."

With their new song completed, Brooks introduced Hendrix to Billy Revis, who ran Revis Records, a local R&B label. "Jimi and I were at the California Club one night, and Billy Revis was there. I told Jimi who he was, and we both went to him and told him we had a song we would like him to hear. Billy gave us his home address and asked if we would come by the following day, which we did. We played the song for him there, and he loved it. He asked if we could get some other musicians together, and we said yes. At that time, Major Lance's band was in town, performing at Ciro's on the Strip. Jimi was the kind of guy who would walk backstage and introduce himself. We wound up partying with them that night, and Big Francis the drummer and Alvin the bass player agreed to come and do it."

In addition to sidemen from Major Lance's touring ensemble, another notable Los Angeles–based artist was involved with the recording, as Brooks recruited her friend and future Love front man Arthur Lee to contribute background vocals. "I knew Arthur before I met Jimi," she explains. "He really didn't have that much going for him musically at that time. Arthur and Pat, my singing partner, had a little thing going on back then. I arrived to pick him up at his mother's house on 29th and Arlington Street on the day of the session. When Jimi saw him, he became very jealous. Jimi hardly spoke to Arthur, thinking that he and I had something more than a friendship going on. Arthur got into the back seat of my 1959 Chevy Impala, and Jimi was up front. All was quiet during the trip, except for when Jimi spoke to me."

Produced by Billy Revis, who also organized the horn section, "My Diary" and "Utee" were recorded in a converted garage in March 1964.

"Utee," the song's spirited B side, was a spontaneous effort developed entirely at the session. As Brooks explains: "Alvin, the bass player, had told us about a dance that was popular in Detroit called the 'U.T.' He even demonstrated how to do it, and Jimi and I had the steps down pat." Billy Revis said, 'We need a B side.' So Jimi took off on a rhythm, and I just started singing."

While Hendrix's playing on these two sides clearly highlights Curtis Mayfield's considerable influence on his style, "My Diary" stands as perhaps the finest example of Jimi's pre-Experience work, showcasing his emerging sound and identity. "People have tried to claim that Jimi's rock roots didn't start until he got to London, and that's just not true," argues Brooks. "If you listen to Jimi's rhythm and lead guitar on 'Utee,' you hear that he was way ahead of his time. He was playing his own style of rock music long before he went to England."

Revis did release the single, but apart from some modest interest in Los Angeles, the song faded from view. "Jimi left Los Angeles shortly after we recorded our song," Brooks recalls. "When I turned twenty-one, I started dancing at the Club LaRouge in L.A. At that time, I received a letter from Jimi. He was living in New York and calling himself Maurice James. He had joined the Isley Brothers and asked me to send him sixty dollars to get his guitar out of the pawn shop."

With dogged assistance from his girlfriend in New York, Faye Pridgeon, herself a fixture on the Harlem music scene, Hendrix struggled to find a gig. His fortunes turned when Tony Rice, a former associate of soul giant Joe Tex, recommended Hendrix to Ronnie Isley of the Isley Brothers. The group needed a guitarist. An audition was staged, and Jimi earned a position with the I. B. Specials, the group's touring band. The Isleys quickly befriended Jimi and were impressed by his raw talent. Jimi's first recording session with the group followed shortly thereafter, resulting in the fiery "Testify (Part One)" and "Testify (Part Two)."

Later that year, the Isley Brothers signed with Atlantic Records. A session was soon organized to record their label debut at Atlantic's in-house facility. With some behind-the-scenes assistance from a young Dionne Warwick, the Isleys recorded the aching ballad "The Last Girl" as well as "Looking for a Love" on September 23, 1964, at Atlantic Studios in New York. "Rudy (Isley), Kelly (Isley), Jimi, Dionne Warwick, and I did that," explained Ronnie Isley

in 1971. "We all put it together. It was a lot of fun." Hendrix's third and final session with the group came on August 5, 1965, yielding the up-tempo "Move Over and Let Me Dance" and "Have You Ever Been Disappointed?" Despite their merits, neither of the group's two Atlantic singles enjoyed any notable chart success. After Hendrix had departed the group to pursue other opportunities, the Isleys moved from Atlantic to Motown's Tamla affiliate. Their debut single there, "This Old Heart of Mine (Is Weak for You)" provided the

group with their most successful crossover single to date, peaking at number 12 on *Billboard*'s Top 100 chart in February 1966.

Though Hendrix and the group had parted ways, Ronnie Isley recalled that they maintained a friendship. In 1969, with the Isleys riding high on the strength of their smash hit "It's Your Thing," the group extended an invitation to Hendrix to jam onstage during a performance at New York's Yankee Stadium. Hendrix wanted to accept, Isley recalled, but schedule conflicts forced

Jimi spent parts of 1965 and 1966 touring and recording as a member of Curtis Knight & the Squires.
(Michael Ochs Archives)

him to decline. That same year, when the group established T-Neck Records, their own recording label, Isley states that Jimi, upon learning that the group planned to reissue their recordings with him, even offered to rerecord his original parts if necessary. "We had always stayed friends," said Isley. "He used to ask us if we had any copies of the records we made together. We didn't, because of contracts. But we knew the tapes were coming back to us, and when we told him about it, he said, 'If there is any stuff I played that isn't right, let me know and I'll come in and do it over.' I told him not to worry about it. Jimi never played anything wrong."

In 1971, the Isley Brothers issued *In the Beginning*, a compilation featuring Jimi's recordings with the group. Hendrix's performances were remixed, with his guitar placed more prominently in the mix than it had originally been, usually at the expense of the original saxophone parts. "We remixed it so that Jimi was more up front," Isley admitted when the album was released. In addition to these remixed versions, an alternate take of "Testify (Part One)" was included.

Sandwiched between his sessions with the Isley Brothers, Hendrix was also involved in two separate sessions at the famed Stax Records studio in Memphis. Jimi's first experience at Stax came as a result of a chance meeting with Booker T & the MGs' guitarist Steve Cropper. During the conversation that ensued, Hendrix spoke of his desire to record an original song he had composed. Intrigued, Cropper invited him to the studio so he could hear Hendrix's ideas. Nothing resulted from the demo recordings, but Hendrix's ability seemed to have struck a chord with Cropper. "It was very strange," Hendrix told *Rolling Stone* in 1968. "We messed around the studio for four

or five hours doing different little things. He turned me on to lots of things. He showed me how to play lots of things, and I showed him how I played 'Have Mercy' or something like that."

Despite the warm reception Cropper had accorded him, Hendrix's second visit to Stax was entirely unsuccessful. Without Cropper present, Jimi's unique style met with derision from the other studio musicians. "The first time I met Jimi Hendrix was when he was with the Isley Brothers and I was playing with Eddie Floyd," recalls Stax and future Buddy Miles Express bassist Roland Robinson. "He was at the Satellite Record Shop outside of the Stax Recording Studio, dressed in a white suit, with his hair all processed. He had come over to Stax wanting to play with Steve Cropper and the guys at the studio. Cropper wasn't there, but Jimi hooked up his stuff in the studio. He started playing a bit in his wild style and those guys just kind of laughed and walked out of the studio. Jimi packed up his stuff and left town."

After a variety of short stints backing such artists as Gorgeous George, Hendrix joined the Upsetters, Little Richard's touring ensemble, in January 1965. Despite Little Richard's shameless claims to the contrary, Hendrix recorded only one single during his brief tenure as Richard's guitarist. The single, "I Don't Know What You Got but It's Got Me (Part One)" b/w "I Don't Know What You Got but It's Got Me (Part Two)" was issued by Vee-Jay Records in November 1965. Indicative of Richard's withering pop following, the single reached number 92 on *Billboard*'s Top 100, lasting a single week before it fell from the chart. The song enjoyed far greater success on *Billboard*'s Rhythm & Blues chart,

where it ultimately peaked at number 12.

After leaving Little Richard, Hendrix briefly reprised his position with the Isley Brothers, joining the group in July 1965 for a series of New York dates prior to taking part in the recording of "Move Over and Let Me Dance" and "Have You Ever Been Disappointed?" at Atlantic Studios on August 5, 1965. Legendary record producer Juggy Murray, whose Sue Records was the home of such R&B greats as Ike & Tina Turner and Baby Washington, witnessed Hendrix performing with the Isley Brothers at Small's Paradise in Harlem. "I thought he was great," Murray remembers. "He came down to my studio [Juggy Sound] a couple of times before he signed a management and recording contract [July 27, 1965] with me." While Hendrix's ability as a guitar player was obvious, incorporating that talent into conventional Top 40 R&B proved difficult for Murray. "At that time, Jimi wasn't playing the way that he ended up playing," recalls Murray. "But I knew this guy was going to be great, so I signed him. Jimi would go up into the studio and rehearse, but how the hell do you record a guy who is a great guitar player without a hit single? I had to find a way to do it."

Despite Murray's impressive stable of artists, Hendrix did not serve as a session guitarist for the label. "He could make more money playing on the road," admits Murray. "Let me tell you, at Juggy Sound we used to cut four sides in three hours in those days. All those great Baby Washington sides like 'That's How Heartaches Are Made' and 'Only Those in Love'? They were recorded during three-hour sessions, and sometimes with big orchestras. No overdubbing — everything was done live, all on four tracks."

Jimi's massive fingers grip the fretboard of his
Stratocaster. The tone of Hendrix's string
bends was entirely unique and a crucial
element of his sound.
(Michael Ochs Archives)

With Hendrix forced to return to
working as an itinerant sideman, his career at Sue Records stalled without ever
starting. "He just wasn't around that often," admits Murray. "When he was
around, we would rehearse different
things with him. We were trying to find
a way to get over with him, but we
never completed anything. Then he'd
get lost, and you wouldn't see him for
two or three months. But that was Jimi.
All this guy did was play his guitar for
anybody and everybody — from when
he woke up in the morning to the last
thing he did before he went to bed.
He'd put that guitar down to go to
sleep, and it would be the first thing he
would pick up in the morning. He was a
guitar freak, but he was also the nicest
human being on earth. He was kind,
friendly and would play for anybody."

Having left the Isley Brothers for
good, and with marginal progress at Sue
Records, Hendrix joined Curtis Knight
& the Squires, an R&B outfit that enjoyed a modest following throughout
New York and New Jersey. Hendrix enjoyed a larger role than he had in previous stints, with Knight according much
more of the spotlight to Jimi than any
other performer he had backed to date.
In September 1965, Hendrix and
Knight were introduced to a record producer named Ed Chalpin. Knight & the
Squires had been recommended by a
friend who thought Chalpin would be
interested in the group. Working out of
Studio 76, his own recording facility in
Manhattan, Chalpin's PPX Industries
had achieved remarkable success by recording cover versions of U.S. Top 40
hits for worldwide release. Over these
newly recorded backing tracks, foreign
singers would overdub translated lyrics.
These "cover" records were extremely
profitable, and Chalpin had developed
a large clientele who licensed his recordings on a regular basis. In addition

to creating remakes for foreign markets, Chalpin tried his hand at breaking into the American singles charts. He auditioned the Squires at Studio 76 and, after the group recorded a number of finished songs, signed both Knight and Hendrix to separate recording contracts. These one-page agreements were signed at Studio 76 on or about October 15, 1966. At no time did Hendrix ever mention to Chalpin that he had already signed an exclusive contract with Juggy Murray's Sue Records just three months earlier.

The Squires recorded a number of original songs at Studio 76 in October and December 1965. While much of their stage repertoire was comprised of such popular fare as "Sugar Pie, Honey Bunch" and "Hang On Sloopy," under Chalpin's direction the group experimented with a wide variety of musical genres in an effort to develop an effective formula for chart success. While Knight's brooding "Don't Accuse Me" showcased the group's firm grasp on the blues, "Simon Says," "Welcome Home," and "Gotta Have a New Dress" were dance-oriented rhythm-and-blues efforts whose structure was based largely on superior Stax and Motown recordings.

On March 15, 1966, Chalpin secured a licensing deal with Jerry Simon's RSVP Records. Simon released two singles in 1966, "How Would You Feel" b/w "Welcome Home," followed by "Hornet's Nest" b/w "Knock Yourself Out." "How Would You Feel," which Knight would later call the first black rock protest song, was based largely on Bob Dylan's "Like a Rolling Stone," a massive hit the previous summer. As co-composer of both "Hornet's Nest" and "Welcome Home," Hendrix, named "Jimmy Hendrix" on the disc, received his first label credit. Both these efforts, however, missed the charts entirely.

Despite the modest progress Hendrix had made with Knight & the Squires, economics forced him back out onto the road, first as a member of Joey Dee's Starlighters and then as a member of King Curtis's Kingpins. On January 21, 1966, under Curtis's direction, Jimi added guitar to Ray Sharpe's "Help Me (Part One)" and "Help Me (Part Two)," which was subsequently issued as a single on Atlantic's Atco subsidiary later that year. Hendrix's last known session with King Curtis yielded three songs, "Linda Lou," "Baby How About You," and "I Can't Take It," recorded at Atlantic Studios on April 28, 1966. These recordings were not issued at that time, however, and have remained unreleased. Years later, a fire ravaged Atlantic's master tape library. These particular masters were among those destroyed in the blaze. Sadly, no safety copies are known to exist.

While Hendrix may privately have nurtured a desire to lead his own group, his modest efforts to date had been entirely unsuccessful. With his financial status dire, Hendrix briefly reprised his duties with Curtis Knight, joining the Squires in May 1966 for an extended engagement at the Cheetah, New York's hottest nightspot. While performing with Knight & the Squires, Hendrix caught the attention of London fashion model Linda Keith, the girlfriend of Rolling Stones guitarist Keith Richards. Keith, sitting with friends Roberta Goldstein and Mark Kauffman, was taken by the group's lead guitarist. Keith explains, "I was sitting near the back of the Cheetah when I noticed a guitarist in the back line of Curtis Knight's band whose playing mesmerized me. After the set, I had Mark check him out to see if he wanted to come have a drink with us. Fortunately, he did."

Hendrix was taken with Linda's sincerity, and the two quickly became friends. With her encouragement, Hendrix combed Greenwich Village's folk-pop scene for musicians willing to join a group he would head. Billing his group as Jimmy James & the Blue Flames, Hendrix set out to establish himself as a bandleader. While their lineup was never firmly established, the Blue Flames featured guitarist Randy California, who would later star as the lead guitarist for the popular group Spirit, second guitarist Randy Wolfe, and Chas Matthews, a black bassist who would occasionally handle drum chores. To further the meager earnings generated by the Blue Flames, Jimi sat in with blues guitarist John Hammond Jr. on a number of occasions, most notably at the Cafe Au Go Go. "When we were backing up John Hammond, we used to run back and forth between the Cafe Wha? and the Cafe Au Go Go," says California. "We'd play his two sets *plus* our five sets. Those were tiring nights!"

Shortly after their formation, Jimmy James & the Blue Flames established a residency at the Cafe Wha?, one of the many tiny nightspots that dotted the Village. "We used to play about five sets every night at the Cafe Wha?" remembers guitarist Randy California. "We were mostly doing cover stuff like 'Hey Joe,' 'Wild Thing,' 'Shotgun,' and 'High Heel Sneakers.' We used to jam a lot, and some of the songs would turn out to be pretty long." It was during these extended sets that Hendrix began to incorporate original material he had begun to develop, including embryonic versions of songs that would later appear on *Are You Experienced?* "Jimi had fragments of that first album in his set," explains guitarist Bob Kulick, whose group Random Blues frequently performed at the Cafe Wha? "He definitely had 'Hey Joe,' and he used to play a rough version of 'Third Stone from the Sun.' " Ragamuffins guitarist Ken

Pine echoes Kulick. "He may not have had all of the songs together as they were on *Are You Experienced?*, but when I later heard the album, I remembered him playing around with those riffs and melodies."

Performing in the Village served to expand Jimi's musical horizons, introducing him to many other talented but struggling artists trying to establish themselves. One such musician was

Paul Caruso: "I had been playing harmonica for a few years and was looking for people to play with," recalls Caruso. "I first saw Jimi at the Cafe Wha? in the Village and thought, 'My God, isn't this an opportunity!' He was playing with the Blue Flames and had Randy California in the band with him. It was the most powerful blues playing I had ever heard. The scene was pretty liberal at that time, and people could jam and get

Chas Chandler *(second from left)* recording with the Animals at RCA Studios. (Chuck Boyd/Flower Children Ltd.)

to know one another easily. We used to hang out with Linda Keith and run around the city and talk about Bob Dylan. He was a Dylan freak, and we talked about Dylan a lot, the symbolism and poetry of his lyrics and just how brilliant he was. Jimi was very self-conscious about his lack of education and his speech. He was impressed by people who could speak well. That's one of the reasons why he got into Dylan, because it was very literate rock n' roll."

Before his performances with the Blue Flames at the Cafe Wha?, Hendrix often took refuge at the Nite Owl, frequently joining the club's afternoon jam sessions. Musicians who participated were given free lunch, a policy which, considering the miserable state of Jimi's finances, proved a tempting draw. Hendrix's financial condition hamstrung his development, forcing him to rely on the kindness of friends and girlfriends just to survive. He often resorted to pawning guitars, and even an article as seemingly minor as a guitar string was regarded as a precious commodity. "He broke a guitar string during his show and he threw a fit afterwards," recalls Bob Kulick. "I couldn't understand what the problem was. I figured he just didn't have the particular string he needed, so I opened up my case and gave him one. His eyes lit up, and it was only then that I realized how badly off he was."

Though unable to afford even an hour of time in a recording studio, Hendrix was determined to monitor his progress. When he could borrow a tape machine, Jimi would make primitive live recordings of his club performances. Ken Pine remembers one such instance. "One night he had set up a Roberts reel-to-reel tape machine which never seemed to run correctly. I had seen him try it once before and it

didn't work, but on this night, Mark Klingman, who later worked with Buzzy Linhart and Bette Midler, sat in with him. The playing was great, but afterwards, when he tried to play back the tape, the machine had failed him again."

A similar effort was made by Linda Keith, who was determined to showcase Hendrix's abilities. Keith wanted to document one of the Blue Flames performances to use as a résumé on Jimi's behalf. "We were trying to record a demonstration tape live from the Cafe Wha?" Keith remembers, "but it was a very amateur effort. We couldn't afford to bring Jimi into a studio." Despite the good intentions, the demonstration tape idea — as well as the tape itself — was scrapped.

Determined to advance Jimi's struggling career, Keith next decided to trade on her friendship with Andrew Loog Oldham. Oldham, producer and manager of the Rolling Stones, had developed a reputation as one of the brightest young music entrepreneurs and had already launched Immediate Records, his own recording label. Keith hoped that Oldham would recognize Hendrix's considerable talents. Oldham, however, did not share her enthusiasm. After witnessing a performance at the Cafe Au Go Go, Oldham passed. A similar rejection was handed down by Seymour Stein, another record industry executive.

Having exhausted Linda Keith's best resources, Keith and Hendrix were forced to regroup. One evening, Keith was introduced to Animals bassist Chas Chandler at Ondine's, a popular nightspot. Chandler mentioned his desire to withdraw from the Animals and try his hand at record production. Hearing this, Keith implored Chandler to come and see her friend Jimmy James perform at the Cafe Wha? Intrigued,

Chandler agreed to do so the following day.

In July 1966, the Animals had gathered in New York, preparing for their final tour of North America. "I had gone there about a week ahead of time to see some friends," recalls Chandler. "The night before we were to play in Central Park, someone played me Tim Rose's version of 'Hey Joe,' which had been out for about nine months in America. I was so taken by it that I vowed, 'As soon as I get back to England, I'm going to find an artist to record this song.' Later that evening, we went out to a club called Ondine's. As we walked in, Linda Keith came walking out, and we stopped to talk. She told me she was going out with this guy in the Village that I had to see. It hadn't been public, but all of my close friends knew that I was getting into record production after the Animals' impending split, and Linda suggested that her friend might be just the guy to start with. So I made arrangements to meet her the next afternoon. I went down to the Village again and saw Jimmy James & the Blue Flames perform at the Cafe Wha? It just so happened the first song Hendrix played that afternoon was 'Hey Joe.'" By chance, Ken Pine was seated next to Chandler during Jimi's set. "Chas was so excited that he kept hitting me with his elbow. I thought he was going to crush me," laughs Pine. "I didn't think he was going to survive the set." "Chandler was so excited by Jimi's performance that he spilled some of the milk served to him on his lap!" adds Bob Kulick.

After his show, Keith introduced Chandler to Jimi. "We just sat and talked for about an hour," recalls Chandler. "I told him that I was going off on a tour with the Animals, but I would be back in a week or so. I left then, saying, 'I'll come back to New York, and if you

still feel like it, I'll take you to England and we'll start.' He agreed."

While Hendrix's raw potential struck a chord within Chandler, the same could not be said for Hendrix's support group, the Blue Flames. "I wasn't impressed with the Blue Flames at all," remembers Chandler. "They were a pickup band who sounded as if Jimi had met them that day. I didn't bother to make a recording of any of their performances, because the drummer was lousy. Randy California, the other guitar player, was a nice young kid, but all he wanted to do was play blues, and I didn't think that just play-

Chas Chandler *(left)* talking to Hendrix press agent Michael Goldstein.

(Chuck Boyd/Flower Children Ltd.)

ing blues was the way to make a hit with Jimi Hendrix."

"Jimi asked me to sit in on that first meeting with Chas," remembers California. "Jimi wanted to take me along and be part of it, so I was suggesting that we do more traditional Delta blues. Chas wasn't interested in me at all, he was just interested in Jimi. It was obvious that I was only there because Jimi had asked me to come along. I couldn't have gone along anyway, because I was only fifteen at the time. I asked my parents if I could go with Jimi to England, but they said no."

In addition to Jimi's obvious ability, his powerful renditions of "Hey Joe" and "Like a Rolling Stone" convinced Chandler of his promise. "That afternoon at the Cafe Wha?, Jimi was just an explosive kid whose potential struck me," he explains. "As much as his version of 'Hey Joe' impressed me, what convinced me of his talent was another song that he did that first day — 'Like a Rolling Stone.' I knew Dylan well and loved his material, but 'Like a Rolling Stone' was the first of his songs which I didn't quite get. It was something about the way Dylan had sung the song. I never felt he expressed it properly. When Jimi sang the song, he did it with tremendous conviction, and the lyrics came right through to me. My initial impression, having heard him play 'Hey Joe' and 'Like a Rolling Stone,' was that I couldn't see his career going in any other way but the place between those two songs. That was where it had to go."

As impressive as Hendrix's abilities seemed, Chandler couldn't help but think that Hendrix had already been spotted and signed to another label. He explains, "I was astonished to hear that nobody had ever signed him, apart from some small labels, where he felt he was actually under contract as a session man. I remember him telling me that

he viewed those agreements as a guarantee of session work — not as a recording contract. To that extent, I immediately sat with him and got a list of people he had signed agreements with. I started going around buying them up, including his agreement with Sue Records. Unfortunately, the one he didn't mention was with Ed Chalpin and PPX. Jimi thought it was nothing more than another session man agreement."

Enthused by his discovery, Chandler returned to the Animals to complete the group's remaining tour dates. As he quietly plotted his strategy, Chandler initially kept word of his plans close to his vest. His solo career was about to begin, and Chandler wished to embark on this new journey with a minimum of distractions. Immediately following the group's last scheduled appearance, his quest began in earnest. "The last gigs the Animals did were at the Steam Pier in Atlantic City [August 6, 1966]," Chandler explains. "Michael Jeffery had come to the show, and afterwards the two of us drove to Philadelphia. I never mentioned anything about Jimi to him, I simply asked him to drop me off at the parents of Bobbi Shore, a girlfriend of mine at that time. I took the train to New York the next morning, checked into the Gorham Hotel, where Hilton Valentine and I shared a suite, and began running around the Village trying to find Jimi."

Chandler's pursuit was further complicated by Jimi's tenuous living arrangements. His protégé-to-be had neither a working phone number nor a permanent address. "Jimi was very vague about his living situation," remembers Chandler. "I knew that he had a room in a place on Broadway, but he never seemed to stay there." Hendrix was something of a nomad, but Chandler was determined to find him.

Fortunately, the Blue Flames were

still performing at the Cafe Wha?, and Chandler located Jimi there. That evening, Chandler reaffirmed his interest in producing and managing Jimi's career. Hendrix accepted Chandler's offer as genuine and agreed to travel to London with him.

With relatively few contacts in New York, Chandler knew that his experiment would have to be staged in London — so that he could, if necessary, trade on favors in order to organize a backing group for Hendrix. Eager to begin, Chandler took immediate measures to meet all Jimi's pending commitments in New York, closing out old contracts and having Hendrix fill any final engagements at area clubs. "At the same time that I was buying all of his contracts up, I was thinking to myself that we had to get some musicians together. I was determined, however, to do this in London — not New York. Hendrix wanted to know why we couldn't use Randy California. Randy was fifteen years old. I was exasperated. The first thing that would happen was that we would be arrested! Jimi genuinely wanted to bring Randy to England, but I was adamant that he make space between them. I said, 'Jimi, how the fuck am I going to get a visa for a fifteen-year-old runaway? Do you understand what implications there are with something like that? You just can't do it.' I told him frankly that there was nothing in the Blue Flames which had interested me. There was an occasional blues solo from Randy, yes, but the rest was utter chaos. The bass player was a jerk, and the drummer couldn't play. The way I looked at it was, 'Hey, you've been playing this and nobody's fucking signed you. What's the point in carrying on?'"

While loyal to those who had supported him initially, Hendrix was unwilling to squander his opportunity. He consented to Chandler's requests and fulfilled his remaining gigs with the Blue Flames.

With the help of Animals attorney Lee Dicker, Chandler made his final preparations to take Hendrix to London. "The first thing I did was to get his papers together so that he could get a passport," he explains. "He had nothing, as he hadn't been home in so long. Finally, when Hilton Valentine left for London, Jimi and I used the suite we had shared as an office to send letters and telegrams back to his father to get all the details. All Jimi had was an address, but he didn't even know if his father was still living there. Following that, I went down and found Scott English, a songwriter from the Brill Building who was a big mate of mine. To help us get Jimi's passport, Scott agreed to say that he had known Jimi for years."

With his passport in hand, and nothing more to go on than Chandler's reputation and pledge of unwavering support, Hendrix left for London on September 24, 1966.

UPON his arrival in London Chandler immediately set his plan in motion. Despite his inexperience as a producer, Chandler had a firm understanding of the sound and style he wanted his new protégé to showcase. His belief in the commercial prospects of "Hey Joe" was resolute — so long as Hendrix could record a version as forceful and convincing as the performance that had grabbed Chandler's attention at the Cafe Wha?

Chandler understood that Hendrix, in addition to recording "Hey Joe," would need to tour Britain and Europe aggressively to develop a following. His concept was to market Hendrix as a star of the first magnitude, a genuine bluesman imported directly from America. To create a supporting act, auditions were staged at the Birdland club in London. "I was looking for drummers and bass players, even though I didn't know what the band was going to be or what kind of lineup it would have," says Chandler. "We were just looking for musicians." Hendrix's criteria were just as simple. "I was thinking of the smallest pieces [instruments] possible with the hardest impact."

The first musician selected was guitarist Noel Redding, who had arrived at the audition with the hope of landing a spot in the new Animals. Alerted by an advertisement in *Melody Maker*, Redding traveled by train from his home in Kent. Though the Animals position had been filled, Chandler suggested that he sit in with Jimi Hendrix, a guitarist he was now managing. Armed with Chandler's bass, Redding sat in with Hendrix, pianist Mike O'Neill, and drummer Aynsley Dunbar. After completing a series of simple chord sequences, Hendrix took Redding aside and asked him to join his group. Choosing a drummer proved more difficult, as Hendrix and Chandler were forced to decide from a pool that included Dunbar, John Banks of the Merseybeats, and Mitch Mitchell, formerly of Georgie Fame & the Blue Flames. Days after their auditions, a coin flip decided the issue, with Mitchell coming up the winner. The new group, Chandler decided, would be known as the Jimi Hendrix Experience.

Unlike Mitchell, Redding had enjoyed fleeting experience in the recording studio. His first opportunity had come in 1962, when the Lonely Ones, of which he was a member, recorded four songs in the living room of a local friend. Twelve copies of a four-song extended-play disc were pressed for local jukebox play. This was followed by similar local efforts before the Loving Kind, guided by songwriter Gordon Mills, was signed to Pye Records in January 1966. At Pye, the group issued three singles, none of which sold in excess of a thousand copies.

To make their recorded debut, Chandler booked time at London's DeLane Lea Recording Studios. "That was where the Animals had done almost all of their recording," explains Chandler. "I knew the studio well; that's why I took them there."

Limited cash reserves forced Chandler to complete much of the necessary preproduction at his London flat. Still, he considered such an arrangement an improvement on his stint with the Animals. "The Animals had no say on matters like studio time," says Chandler flatly. "When time was available, the studio was booked. Then we went off to a rehearsal room to work our butts off. If we couldn't get time in a rehearsal room, we would come early to a gig and jam for an hour or so. When I started with Jimi, we were sharing the flat and doing all of our work there. That was a luxury the Animals never had. The flat was Jimi's rehearsal room. That was such an advantage. When we took the Experience into rehearsals, Jimi had already developed the song to the point where he could indicate the chord sequences and tempo to Mitch, and I would work with Noel about the bass parts. Then everything would come together."

While the comfortable confines of the apartment may have afforded Chandler the privacy to refine Jimi's sound and style, invitations to either Mitchell and Redding were rarely extended. However exclusive this may have seemed to Mitchell or Redding, Chandler was unsympathetic. His goals were twofold: establishing himself as a producer and making good on his promise to make Jimi Hendrix a star. "I wasn't concerned that Mitch or Noel might feel that they weren't having enough — or any — say. Their say was a bit of a nuisance, really. I didn't need the confusion. I had been touring and recording in a band for years, and I'd seen everything end as a compromise. Nobody ended up doing what they really wanted to do. I was not going to let that happen with Jimi."

■
Sunday, October 23, 1966
London, DeLane Lea Studios. Producer: Chas Chandler. Engineer: Dave Siddle.

Having presided over a series of rehearsals, Chandler now deemed the group ready for their initial recording session. Hamstrung by his dwindling savings, the focus of the session would be "Hey Joe," the song on which Chandler had based this grand experiment. "I had only enough money to cover the cost for 'Hey Joe,'" remembers Chandler. "I couldn't even think of recording a B side until I had more cash."

As the session date at DeLane Lea loomed closer, Hendrix had increasingly questioned the range and quality of his singing voice. Unsure of his ability as a vocalist, Hendrix grew edgy in the days prior to the session, fearing that a poor performance might doom the progress he had made since arriving in London. To Chandler, Jimi's reservations represented little more than a heightened case of nerves. "Jimi was paranoid about his voice from the very first day I met him," says Chandler. "From my first day in the studio with him to my last, he would always want his voice buried, and I would want to place it more forward in the mix."

At the session, another battle manifested over the volume of Jimi's guitar. Chandler explains: "When Jimi first came to London, his visa had been restricted. I had received an extension, one that carried us through the date I had scheduled for us to record 'Hey Joe.' The day we were recording 'Hey Joe,' I had gone over to the immigration office in the morning to get some papers completed for a three-month extension of his passport. It took so long that I came straight from Immigration to DeLane Lea. Right after we started, Jimi threw a tantrum because I

wouldn't let him play his guitar loud enough in the studio. It was a stupid argument over sheer volume. He was playing through a Marshall twin stack, and it was so loud in the studio that we were picking up various rattles and noises. He said, 'If I can't play as loud as I want, I might as well go back to New York.' In my pocket, I had his passport and immigration papers. I took them out, threw them down on the console, and said, 'Well, here you go. Piss off!' He looked at them, started laughing and said, 'All right, you called my bluff!' and that was it."

While Chandler had labored to minimize any chance of delays caused by a lack of preparation, capturing the Experience's unique sound required a series of experiments with microphone placements and amplifier settings.

In the two hours afforded by Chandler's slim budget, the Experience managed to complete an effective backing track. While additional work remained, principally a finished lead vocal from Hendrix and a chorus of female backing vocals, Chandler was pleased with what had been accomplished. Hearing the group's sound on tape made Jimi's potential seem much more tangible.

According to Noel Redding, Chandler had the group complete more than thirty different takes before the song's basic track met his approval. With that in hand, a considerable investment was then required to capture Jimi's modest, appealing lead vocal on tape. A number of attempts were recorded at different studios before Chandler felt Hendrix had successfully completed the task. Hendrix, however, still harbored some reservations. "It was the first time I had ever sung on a record, actually," Jimi later confessed. Chandler expressed no such doubts. "Chas was sure it would be a hit," Hendrix explained.

Recording a lead vocal.

(Willis Hogans, Jr./Bill Nitopi Collection)

studio and see how they worked," explains Chandler. "Although we had completed the backing track, we still weren't finished, because we couldn't get the girls' vocals right. I ended up going from one studio to another, trying to get different girls to put the vocals on. Initially I went to DeLane Lea, but they were booked, so I had to go elsewhere. I nearly screwed it all up, because my master tape was one-inch four-track [most London studios used half-inch four-track tape], and it took sessions at three different studios to complete." Chandler finally added backing vocals by the Breakaways, and "Hey Joe" was complete.

With "Hey Joe" completed to his satisfaction, Chandler's next task was to produce a B side. Apart from the handful of cover tunes the group had rehearsed to establish their repertoire, Hendrix had no other original material prepared. "When we discussed what was going to be on the B side, Jimi said that he could record a version of 'Land of 1000 Dances,' " Chandler recalls. "I said absolutely no way. If anyone was going to make publishing money, it was going to be him. I told him that he was going to sit down that night and write a new song. That's how 'Stone Free' came about, the first Experience song he ever wrote."

■

Wednesday, November 2, 1966

London, DeLane Lea Studios. 6:00 P.M. to 12:00 midnight. Producer: Chas Chandler. Engineer: Dave Siddle.

With little money available for experimentation, recording "Stone Free" was decidedly less complicated than "Hey Joe." " 'Stone Free' was recorded and mixed in one day," Chandler explains with pride. "I couldn't afford to have

The recording sessions for "Hey Joe" served a dual purpose for Chandler and Hendrix, who used them as a gauge to measure the compatibility and talents of Mitchell and Redding. "Jimi and I literally used the recording session as a test, to take Mitch and Noel into the

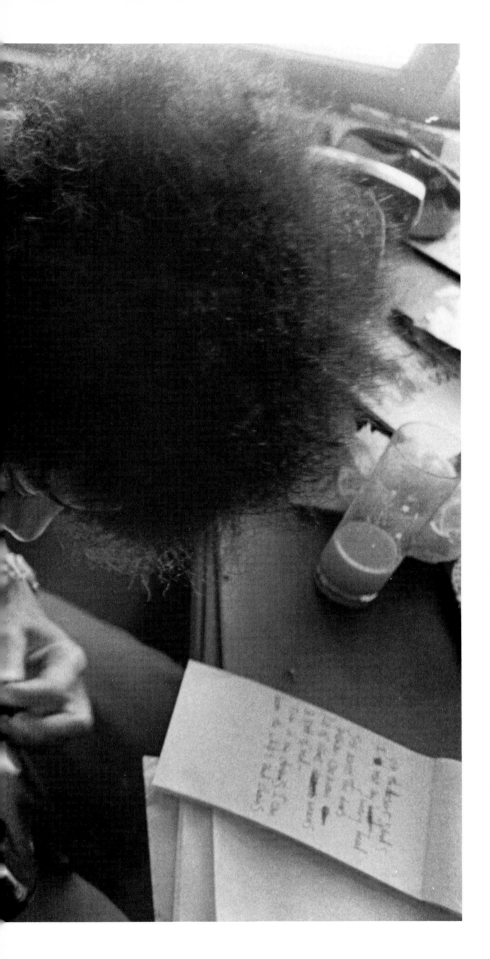

the band learn the song in the studio,
so I booked a rehearsal at the Averbach
House beforehand. Prior to that, we
had rehearsed in nightclubs. A good
mate of mine owned a string of clubs in
London, and the Animals used to be
pretty big spenders in them, so he
would let me bring the band into them
when I needed to."

In addition to governing Hendrix's
contributions with a firm hand, Chandler was especially helpful to Redding,
providing useful insights about the bass
guitar. "Chas would come out into the
studio to show me various bass techniques," recalls Redding. "The bass was
still new to me, and I was taking in everything I could. Chas told me about
little things like different scales and
what was classified as a 'walking bass'
line, which were simple but very
effective."

To create the master, Chandler essentially recorded the group live in the
studio, paced by Jimi's contagious
rhythm guitar. "It only took us an hour
to cut the track," admits Chandler.
Overdubs were simple, specifically
Mitchell's inventive percussion, as well
as harmony vocals from Hendrix, who
also played additional guitar. In addition to "Stone Free," the group routined
a rough demo of "Can You See Me," a
second Hendrix original. A final mix of
"Stone Free" was prepared before the

session concluded. Hendrix and Chandler also made a reel-to-reel tape copy of the "Can You See Me" demo for further review.

With his master tape in hand, Chandler ventured out to secure a recording contract for Hendrix. "There was no point in me going out marketing myself as an ex-Animal — at least, not in my mind," explains Chandler. "That was virtually confirmed when I couldn't even get EMI Records to *listen* to the finished master of 'Hey Joe.' Here I was, an EMI artist still signed to the label as a member of the Animals, and I couldn't even get into the A&R Department to play the bloody record. Nobody would even see me. Over at Decca Records, Dick Rowe was just as bad. He looked at me as if I was completely out of my mind."

A chance meeting with Kit Lambert — who, along with Chris Stamp, co-managed The Who and owned Track Records — resulted in Hendrix's joining the label. "I did the deal with Kit Lambert at the Scotch of St. James nightclub," recalls Chandler. "The VIPs were playing that night, and being friends of mine I brought Hendrix down to jam with them. Kit was there and nearly knocked over the tables trying to get across to me. He was such an outrageous guy: we wrote out the deal on a beer mat at the Scotch."

With a recording contract secured, Hendrix now worked closely with Chandler at the flat they shared. With his Stratocaster and a small Vox amplifier, Jimi began to develop the riffs and rhythm patterns for songs such as "Can You See Me" and "Remember." Living with Chandler also began to have a pronounced influence on Hendrix's lyrics and poetry, as Jimi was soon exposed to Chandler's penchant for science fiction. "I had dozens of science fiction books at home," says Chandler. "The

first one Jimi read was *Earth Abides*. It wasn't a Flash Gordon type — it's an end-of-the-world, new-beginning, disaster-type story. He started reading through them all. That's where 'Third Stone from the Sun' and 'Up from the Skies' came from."

■ *Tuesday, December 13, 1966*
London, CBS Studios. 4:00 P.M. to 7:00 P.M.
Producer: Chas Chandler. Engineer: Mike Ross.

Unhappy with DeLane Lea and wanting to upgrade sound quality without squandering their thin budget, Chandler took Kit Lambert's advice and booked time at CBS Studios on New Bond Street. Lambert had produced some sessions for The Who there and would later record "I Can See for Miles" at the facility as well. Located in a former ballroom, CBS Studios had originally been home to Oriole Records and Levy Sound Studios. Owned by two brothers, Jake and Morris Levy, the studio had produced, recorded, and pressed a number of small British pop acts on its Oriole label. The label's most notable success to date had come via the 1957 single "Freight Train" by the Charles McDevitt Skiffle Group, featuring Nancy Whiskey, which peaked at number 5 on U.K. pop charts. In 1962 and 1963, Oriole Records had enjoyed a run of minor hits by a Swedish instrumental group known as the Spotniks. By 1965, however, the entire operation was purchased by CBS Records. Not particularly interested in either the studio or the artists under contract to Oriole, CBS instead wanted Oriole's modern, efficient pressing plant. Looking to establish a distribution arm in the U.K., CBS eyed the pressing plant as a significant asset.

Under Levy stewardship, Levy Sound Studios made three-track recordings in both mono and stereo. Following the studio's purchase in 1965, CBS installed a new Studer four-track machine and upgraded the studio's technical capabilities.

Despite the investment by CBS, the studio's spartan staff consisted of just one technician, recording engineer Mike Ross. Before moving to Levy Sound, Ross had started his career at London's Olympic Studios in 1962. "I was the only engineer at CBS studios," remembers Ross with a laugh. "I used to open up the studio, take the bookings, and act as my own tape operator. It was just me. I had to do everything."

At CBS, pop sessions could only begin after 4:00 P.M., so that the noise level would not distract the offices below. An injunction won by another tenant within the building limited the studio to mixing during the day and full recording after 4:00 P.M.

"Foxey Lady," one of Hendrix's most provocative songs, would be the focus of the evening's session. "Mitch arrived well before everyone else and was setting up his drum kit," remembers Ross. "In those days, miking techniques for drums was not that advanced. You would put a microphone on the bass drum and a microphone on top, above the kit. As I was setting up, Mitch pulled me aside and informed me that he had done some sessions at Landsdowne Studios recently, where he had been able to persuade the engineer to mike all of the tom-toms individually. He said they had achieved a great sound and asked if I would be interested in trying it here. I had never done it, but I gave it a go. In fact, that session was the first time I had ever used more than two microphones to record drums."

When Hendrix, Redding, and

Chandler arrived, Ross was taken aback by the sight of Jimi's amplifiers. "Jimi came in with four Marshall cabinets, which I couldn't believe," admits Ross. "How was I to mike this? Jimi told me to stick a microphone eight feet away from the cabinets and it would sound great. He actually showed me where to place the microphone, and I put a U-67 valve mike where he had instructed me

to." After Ross had set up the microphones and established the desired sounds, Chandler was eager to begin. A number of rehearsals prefaced the cutting of basic tracks. "Jimi didn't record a live vocal," recalls Ross. "I recorded Jimi's lead vocal as an overdub, as well as backing vocals from Mitch, Noel, and Jimi. Jimi also recorded a second guitar as an overdub."

Chas Chandler's love for science fiction novels rubbed off on Jimi and influenced such early Hendrix songs as "Third Stone from the Sun" and "Up from the Skies."
(K & K/Star File)

"Chandler was very much in charge," recalls Ross. "Jimi was very shy and quiet and didn't have much to say. He seemed very much in awe of Chandler. What Chas said was law. There was another aspect that was very odd. I was used to the band being a team and having some input. My immediate reaction during the Hendrix session was, 'These two guys are being treated like shit.' It was very much like, 'Play, and do what you are told.' Chandler was very much in command of what was going on. He obviously had a sound in his head and knew what he wanted to hear from Jimi. A lot of producers tend to sit in the control room and produce the engineer. They very rarely go out onto the floor to do anything musical. Chas was a good producer — he would actually go out on the floor and direct. He would work individually with Jimi and Noel and show Mitch what to play and what drums to hit. Most of my communication was directly with Chas."

In addition to completing "Foxey Lady," the group also recorded versions of both "Can You See Me" and "Third Stone from the Sun." "We recorded a lot of takes of each song," Ross remembers. "We went through quite a lot of tape. Chas was keen to keep everything, because he felt he could always edit the good bits together."

■

Thursday, December 15, 1966
London, CBS Studios. Producer: Chas Chandler. Engineer: Mike Ross.

According to Noel Redding, Mitch Mitchell did not show for this session. In his absence, a rehearsal was staged, with Hendrix and Redding recording two unnamed instrumental demos. Rough mixes of "Foxey Lady," "Can You See Me," and "Third Stone from the Sun" were also completed.

Chandler, according to Ross, praised the studio highly, citing its clear advantage in sound quality over DeLane Lea. Despite his enthusiasm for the facility, the Experience would never record there again, due to a bitter squabble between Chandler and Jake Levy. "At that time, I don't think Chandler had the money to pay the studio," explains Ross. "When it came to the second day, he still hadn't paid any money. Jake came over to Chas and said, 'Look, if you want to book any more time, you've got to pay for what you have used up to now.' Chas clearly wanted to book more time, but he said, 'I can't, because we are making an album. As soon as the album is finished, you will be paid.' Jake, however, was very mistrustful of people, and he told them that while he was sorry, they would not be able to record unless their bill was paid in full. Chandler got quite upset, telling Jake that this was not the way he had done business in the past, this was not how he conducted business with Kingsway [DeLane Lea], and that *he* was sorry, as he would never work in this studio again. It ended on a sour note, which was a shame, as I was enjoying the sessions."

Furious, Chandler left the studio and vowed never to return. One major problem remained, however. "Because Chas had been unable to pay the studio bill, Jake would not release the tapes

they had recorded," remembers Ross. "Sometime after, Chas had booked time at DeLane Lea and wanted to record some overdubs on those songs. He fought very hard to get the tapes, but Levy wouldn't release them. In the end, he did finally pay the bill, because he was desperate to get the tapes. The tapes had been stored in a cupboard in the studio, and when Chas paid the bill, Jake phoned me up and said, 'Chandler has paid his bill and is coming over to pick up the tapes.' When Chas arrived, he told me he was sorry that he would not be able to continue recording at CBS, as he considered Jake's attitude intolerable. I gave him the tapes, we shook hands, and that was the last I ever saw of him."

■

"Hey Joe" / "Stone Free"
Polydor 56139. Single release. Friday, December 16, 1966.

As Track Records was not quite ready to begin full-scale operations, Polydor Records, their distributor, issued "Hey Joe." Buoyed by an appearance on the penultimate episode of *Ready Steady Go!*, the single entered the U.K. singles chart on January 5, 1967, and, after a long, steady climb, eventually peaked at number 6.

The Experience in London, shortly after the successful release of the debut single "Hey Joe."
(Pictorial Press/Star File)

■

Wednesday, January 11, 1967

London, DeLane Lea Studios. Producer: Chas Chandler. Engineer: Dave Siddle.

With "Hey Joe" climbing the U.K. singles charts, Hendrix's early success increasingly justified Chandler's grand experiment. This would become even more apparent when Chandler escorted the group back to DeLane Lea to record "Purple Haze," Hendrix's superb sophomore effort.

While Hendrix later spoke of composing pages and pages of lyrics for the song, it was the striking riff that immediately captured Chandler's attention. " 'Purple Haze' was written backstage at the Upper Cut Club on Boxing Day [December 26, 1966], the nightclub owned by the British boxer Billy Walker," explains Chandler. "But the riff had come to him about ten days before. I heard him playing it at the flat and was knocked out. I told him to keep working on that, saying, 'That's the next single!' That afternoon at the

Upper Cut, he started playing the riff in the dressing room. I said, 'Write the rest of that!,' so he did."

In the weeks prior to the session, Chandler worked closely with Hendrix to refine the lyrics for the song, a function Chandler routinely performed. His intent was clear; he wanted "Purple Haze" to serve as the follow-up to "Hey Joe," which required Hendrix to pare his lyrics down to fit a more conventional pop structure.

With John Mayall and Peter Green looking on as guests, "Purple Haze" proved to be the group's most complicated studio effort to date. " 'Purple Haze' took four hours to record, which, at that time, represented a *long* time in the studio," says Chandler. "Recording 'Hey Joe' had been very conventional, but with 'Purple Haze,' we began experimenting with different sounds and effects. With 'Hey Joe,' I didn't know how to run the place. I was just a dumb bass player trying to become a producer." Although the group managed to complete a basic rhythm track on this

day, Hendrix and Chandler repeatedly returned to the master in an effort to upgrade Jimi's performance. "With 'Purple Haze,' Hendrix and I were striving for a sound and just kept going back in, two hours at a time, trying to achieve it. It wasn't like we were in there for days on end. We recorded it, and then Hendrix and I would be sitting at home saying, 'Let's try that.' Then we would go in for an hour or two. That's how it was in those days. However long it took to record that one specific idea, that's how long we would book. We kept going in and out."

Another song Hendrix had been developing at the Montagu Square flat he shared with Chandler was "51st Anniversary." "We worked on that over the course of one evening," remembers Chandler. "That song is a good example of Jimi just sitting around the apartment singing and playing his guitar. I would sit across from him and say, 'That's good' or 'No, change that to something like this.' These were pre-studio edits, if you like. Then we would get together with the band and rehearse the song. We were still rehearsing quite a bit then, because we were still trying to refine the act. As it was, we didn't have that many numbers to play, and we were always trying to push new songs in all the time."

Where "Purple Haze" had been the subject of some modest studio experimentation, "51st Anniversary" was the first Experience song to feature overdubbing rather than retakes as a recording strategy. "We rehearsed the song with the band, then went into the studio to record. That was the first song where guitar overdubs played an important role. There was quite a bit of overdubbing on that track, and it was the first time where we consciously thought of approaching the production that way. There were five guitar overdubs all linking in together [picking up where one left off] to sound like one guitar."

"Third Stone from the Sun" was also attempted, with Chandler opting to abandon the December 13, 1966, recording made at CBS Studios in favor of a new version. The group focused on recording the song's basic track, making multiple attempts to capture a finished master. Though Hendrix had already designed the song's arrangement, the group was unable to complete a master that met their standards.

While Chandler and the group could recognize improvement with each trip into the recording studio, they received convincing public confirmation of their hard work in late January 1967. " 'Hey Joe' suddenly burst on the charts during the first week of January 1967 and continued to climb throughout the month," Chandler remembers. "Jimi and I were staying at my mother's house in Newcastle, as the band had been booked to play at the New Cellar Club in South Shields [February 1,

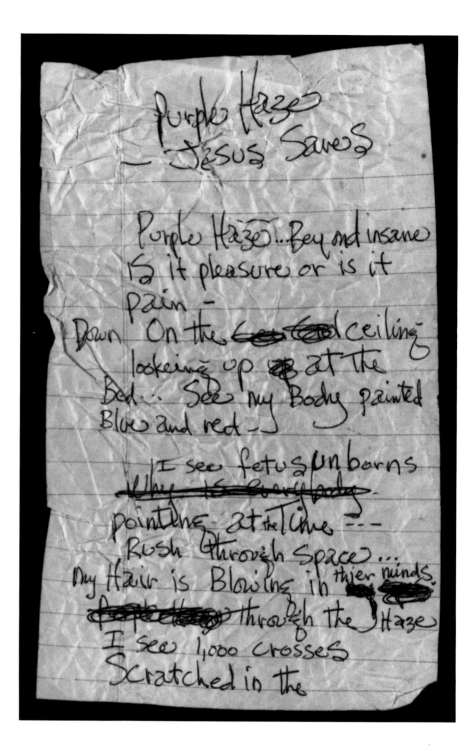

Alternate lyrics to "Purple Haze."
(James A. Hendrix)

1967]. As we were sitting there talking, I decided to walk down to the phone, because my mother had not put one in yet, to ring London and see how things were going. 'Hey Joe' had leapt to number seven in the charts, and I knew we were really on our way."

Friday, February 3, 1967
London, Olympic Studios. Producer: Chas Chandler. Engineer: Eddie Kramer.

Unhappy with the sound quality of the recordings made during the group's most recent session at DeLane Lea (January 11), Chandler had also tired of complaints lodged by DeLane Lea's neighbors regarding the volume of Hendrix's amplifier during recording sessions. "There was always trouble with the bank when you recorded at DeLane Lea," says Chandler. "There was a bank above the studio, and it was at the time when computers were just coming in. Every time we went in, we would play so loud that it would foul up the computers upstairs. As a result, we would always have trouble getting in there when we wanted."

The problems over volume and sound quality at DeLane Lea provoked Chandler into action. Brian Jones and Bill Wyman of the Rolling Stones had lobbied both Jimi and Chas to move to Olympic Studios, which was recognized as London's leading independent studio. With Jimi cultivating a growing backlog of new songs to record, Chandler's primary concern was cost. "We had been scratching money together to pay for sessions at DeLane Lea," Chas recalls. "With 'Hey Joe' a hit on the charts, I found myself dealing more with Polydor rather than Track. One day, I finally went storming into Polydor and had a row with them. I said, 'Look, we've got money piling up here. We are trying to put an album together, and I want to go to Olympic Studios. They won't fucking accept me because I have no credit history. They wouldn't even let me in without payment in advance!' So Polydor rang them up, opened an account in my name, and guaranteed that the bills would be

paid. For the first time, I wasn't worrying about how I was going to pay for sessions. Even though we now had carte blanche, we still recorded the same way, but at least we didn't have to worry about costs."

The move to Olympic was a clear sign that the group's standing had measurably improved. Olympic was the home of such top British acts as Traffic and the Rolling Stones. At the studio, Chandler and the group were introduced to Eddie Kramer, one of the studio's staff engineers. Kramer had been assigned the group by studio manager Anna Menzies, who described the Experience as a 'raggedy' group Chas Chandler would be bringing in. Born in South Africa in 1942, Kramer had come to Olympic in 1966 from Regent Studios. His career had begun at London's Advision Studios in 1963. As a 'tea boy,' Kramer learned the basic principles of sound engineering, disc cutting, and film dubbing. In 1964, he moved to Pye Studios, recording the likes of the Kinks and Sammy Davis, Jr. Kramer's encouraging success at Pye led him to establish KPS Studios, his own two-track demo facility, in 1965. As a result of his work with such artists as Zoot Money and John Mayall, his reputation and that of KPS began to spread. Regent Sound would buy out KPS in 1966 and enlist Kramer to supervise the construction of its new four-track studio. Later that year Kramer moved to Olympic, where, under the tutelage of Keith Grant and Glyn Johns, his ability and reputation blossomed.

One of Chandler's priorities was completing "Purple Haze" so that the track could be issued as the group's second single. The existing master from DeLane Lea (January 11) was pulled out, and overdubbing began. Chandler was intent on upgrading Jimi's performance, so his lead guitar and lead vocal

parts were replaced with new takes. Using the Octavia — a device designed by electronics specialist Roger Mayer that boosted the guitar's octaves to various levels — the sound of Jimi's lead guitar was dramatically altered. To enhance the song's ending, Kramer suggested an additional guitar overdub. "At the end of the song," he explains, "the high-speed guitar you hear was actually an Octavia guitar overdub we recorded first at a slower speed, then played back on a higher speed. The panning at the end was done to accentuate the effect you hear."

Other overdubs included the song's distinctive background vocals, supplied by Noel, as well as some unique background ambience. As Chandler describes it, "A lot of the background sound on 'Purple Haze' is actually a recording being fed back into the studio through the headphones held around a microphone, moving them in and out to create a weird echo."

With these new overdubs completed, a final mix of "Purple Haze" was prepared and readied for release before the session concluded.

February 1967
London, DeLane Lea Studios. Producer: Chas Chandler. Engineer: Dave Siddle.

Because of the group's crowded schedule of engagements, coupled with Olympic's popularity, Chandler was forced to return to DeLane Lea so that progress on the group's as-yet-untitled debut album could continue.

One of the more notable recordings from these sessions was an alternate version of "Red House," with Jimi holding close to the arrangement featured on the December 13, 1966, CBS Studios recording. Each of the takes re-

Chas Chandler and Michael Jefferey, Hendrix's managers, used television skillfully during the group's formative days in London. The band's interracial, intercontinental makeup was especially striking in 1967.

(Pictorial Press/Star File)

corded was cut live in the studio, with Jimi's lead vocal driving the dark, moody rhythm backing. Early takes clearly revealed the song's vast potential but were rendered unusable by the missed notes that plagued both Hendrix and Redding. Prior to another attempt, Jimi said, "Oh Lord! — see, one little thing throws me off," with a laugh to Chandler in the control room. Someone suggested that more of the studio's lights be turned off, which elicited an immediate response from Hendrix: "Oh yeah, those lights! That's what it was. Oh Lord!" When Jimi was told that no more lights could be extinguished because of fire laws, he laughed, remarking, "In other words, we're making all this smoke in here. In other words, we're cooking. Is that what you're trying to say?" Chas and Jimi shared a laugh before Noel counted off the intro for the basic track, which would later serve as the final master.

Both the December 1966 version of "Red House" and this DeLane Lea effort were later issued. The earlier recording was the first to be released, added to the May 1967 Track Records *Are You Experienced?* This DeLane Lea rendition would be finished at Olympic Studios in early April 1967 and added to the popular Reprise Records compilation *Smash Hits*, first released in 1969. "The [*Smash Hits*] 'Red House' was definitely done at DeLane Lea, not CBS," says Chandler. "The 'Red House' on the [*Are You Experienced?*] album came about during the last fifteen minutes of another session. Noel even played rhythm guitar on the track, playing the bass line. Jimi just winged through one take for reference, and we started rolling. Later, when we were scrambling to put the album together, we carted that out and gave it a listen. We remixed it at Olympic and added it to the album."

Eddie Kramer engineering *Are You Experienced?* at Olympic Studios.

(Valerie Wilmer)

Work on "Remember" was also initiated at DeLane Lea. Like "Red House," it, too, would be revamped at Olympic in April 1967 before it was added to the Track *Are You Experienced?* and, later, *Smash Hits* in July 1969. " 'Remember' was an end-of-the-session demo first recorded at DeLane Lea," explains Chandler. "It was strictly a demo at DeLane Lea. We made a quarter-inch, seven-and-a-half i.p.s. reel to listen to

and work on the song at home. This was something we did often. The DeLane Lea recording was much too raggedy. Jimi tightened it up later at Olympic Studios, before it became part of the album. In fact, I don't think we kept much of anything on the final record from that original DeLane Lea recording.

■

February 1967

London, DeLane Lea Studios. Producer: Chas Chandler. Engineer: Dave Siddle.

A tremendous session, yielding two of Hendrix's most popular songs, "Fire" and "The Wind Cries Mary."

Compared to the modest experimentation accorded "Purple Haze" and the multiple overdubs completed for "51st Anniversary," "Fire" was relatively easy for the group to record. They performed the song's basic track live in the studio, experimenting with the tempo during early takes before settling upon a desired groove. Jimi recorded two lead guitars double-tracked, one playing higher up the fretboard than the other. After the basic track had been recorded to Chandler's satisfaction, Jimi put on his lead vocal. As a finishing touch, Mitch and Noel contributed the song's background vocals.

With "Fire" completed, Jimi turned his attention to "The Wind Cries Mary," a beautiful new ballad. " 'The Wind Cries Mary' was written right after Jimi had had a big row with [his girlfriend] Kathy [Etchingham]," Chandler recalls. "That was recorded at the tail end of the session for 'Fire.' We had about twenty minutes or so left, because in them days, I would book two hours and that was it. There would be someone else waiting to get in. I suggested that we cut a demo of 'The Wind Cries Mary.' Mitch and Noel hadn't heard it, so they were going at it without a rehearsal. They played it through once, and I remember saying that I really liked the feel of the song. Jimi came in and said, 'I have a good idea for an overdub.' So he went back in and played 'between,' as he called it, the notes he had already recorded. He didn't even come back into the control room after he had put the second guitar

on. He said, 'I have another idea. Can I put it on?' I said, 'Yeah!' In all, he put on four or five more overdubs, but the whole thing was done in twenty minutes. That was our third single."

With the group's confidence bolstered by their recent success, Chandler found himself slowly but nonetheless increasingly at odds with Mitchell and Redding, who desired a greater voice in the sound and shape of the recordings. Chandler, however, did not share this view. "By the time of 'The Wind Cries Mary,' Mitch and Noel were sort of fighting the fact that they had no say during recording sessions," Chandler remembers. "They were starting to come up with suggestions, but Jimi and I had already done as much work as we could *before* we got together with them and went into the studio. Up to that point, the most studio time I had booked had been four hours, for 'Purple Haze.' Even then, I had to scrape money together to finish it off at Olympic. 'Hey Joe' might have been in the charts, but we weren't going to be paid for ages. 'Purple Haze' was in the can and soon to be released, and now we had 'The Wind Cries Mary' recorded. We just had to see some more money before we could do anything else." Finances, reasoned Chandler, dictated not only the length of sessions; they ultimately determined what role Redding and Mitchell would have in the final shape and sound of the songs. "Sessions were always scheduled one day at a time," explains Chandler. "I can't remember spending two days on one song. We would scrape enough money together and book time in DeLane Lea to record. If DeLane Lea wasn't available, as it hadn't been when I was doing vocal overdubs for 'Hey Joe,' we just went somewhere else. On those early overdub sessions that we did, we just didn't bring Mitch and

Noel in. It wasn't anything against them, it was just pragmatism. There was no point in bringing in anyone else if they weren't going to be doing anything. They would have just been in the way. We didn't say it as such, but we knew that's how it was. Jimi would play me an idea for an overdub, and if I thought it worked, it was, 'Let's go get this bloody thing done.' We didn't need to be arguing with Noel for ten minutes and Mitch for five. We *knew* what we wanted to do. We just couldn't afford the time."

■

February 1967

London, DeLane Lea Studios. Producer: Chas Chandler. Engineer: Dave Siddle.

The Experience's as-yet untitled debut album received a major boost on this evening, as work on "I Don't Live Today" was initiated.

Typical of Chandler's approach, the group focused initially on crafting an acceptable basic track. Once the arrangement and tempo had been decided, Jimi turned to refining his guitar parts. Especially notable was his use of a hand wah-wah unit, a sound device that many fans have come to identify as an important component of the Hendrix sound. While the device would soon be replaced by foot-controlled models, Hendrix manipulated the hand unit with skill, incorporating the distinctive tones onto the master tape.

Before the session concluded, Chandler had a working master. Further improvements, such as a new lead vocal from Jimi, were later overdubbed at Olympic. A final mix of the track would ultimately be prepared there by Jimi, Chandler, and Eddie Kramer and included on *Are You Experienced?*

Mitch Mitchell listening to playback during the April 1967 sessions for *Are You Experienced?* at Olympic Studios.

(Eddie Kramer)

March 1967

London, DeLane Lea Studios. Producer: Chas Chandler. Engineer: Dave Siddle.

Unable to reserve time at Olympic Studios, Chandler and the Experience returned to DeLane Lea. The focus of this evening's session was "Manic Depression," another superb new Hendrix original.

According to Chandler, Hendrix developed the song's distinctive riff quickly. The challenge was to unify the song's intricate rhythm pattern, as Jimi's driving guitar was buttressed by Mitch Mitchell's revolving drum part. Mitchell's performance on the song represented his finest studio effort to date, with his fondness for such jazz legends as Elvin Jones clearly apparent.

While Chandler would prepare a rough mix following the close of recording, the effort was later rejected. A final mix was created at Olympic Studios with Jimi and Eddie Kramer during the first week of April 1967.

Wednesday, March 1, 1967

London, DeLane Lea Studios. Producer: Chas Chandler. Engineer: Dave Siddle.

While "Like a Rolling Stone" had become part of the Experience's stage repertoire, on this evening the group was unable to complete an effective studio rendition.

According to Noel Redding's comprehensive diary, the group did rehearse on this day, and it is probable that "Like a Rolling Stone" was among the songs the group devoted time to. Despite this effort, the Experience, much to Chandler's disappointment, was unable to realize a finished master. "I always wanted to do a studio version of 'Like a

Rolling Stone,'" explains Chandler. "We did it a few times, but for some reason, Mitch could never keep the time right. It used to drive them nuts, because Mitch would either be winding up or slowing down. The thing that bugged me about that one was that the first time I saw Hendrix at the Cafe Wha? in Greenwich Village, the first thing he did was 'Hey Joe' and the second was 'Like a Rolling Stone,' and for the first time, hearing Jimi sing it, I understood what the lyrics were trying to say. I was a Dylan fan, but I started cooling on him at the time he wrote 'Like a Rolling Stone.' It was the first Dylan song I was struggling with. So we both wanted to record it, but we were never successful. I tried over and over to get it."

■

"Purple Haze" / "51st Anniversary"

Track Records 604 001. Single release. Friday, March 17, 1967.

With Track Records now in place, "Purple Haze" made an impressive chart showing, building on the success and momentum of "Hey Joe." "Purple Haze" entered the U.K. singles charts on Thursday, March 23, 1967, and rose to number 3, lasting a total of fourteen weeks.

■

Monday, April 3, 1967

London, Olympic Studios. Producer: Chas Chandler. Engineer: Eddie Kramer. Second engineer: George Chkiantz.

Returning to Olympic, the group made significant headway toward completing their debut album. They recorded a handful of new songs and added over-

dubs to some unfinished masters. "Are You Experienced?," the breathtaking title track for the Experience's forthcoming debut album, was built start-to-finish during this session. Eddie Kramer recalls the song's construction. "The structure of the song was recorded first, with Jimi's rhythm guitar, Mitch's drums, and Noel's bass recorded forward." The song's distinctive introduction, Kramer says, came from Jimi's penchant for discovering new sounds. "Jimi had practiced that riff at home, so he knew what it would sound like backwards," explains Kramer. "At Olympic, we experimented with the sounds and placements to see what would work best."

Hours of private studying had helped Hendrix master this difficult technique on his personal reel-to-reel tape machine. Fascinated with sounds, Jimi would listen to tapes backward just to study the possibilities of the technique.

Jimi's fascination with backward tapes caused some mild friction with Mitch Mitchell, who struggled to replicate these unique sounds on demand. "Mitch had started to get uptight, because Jimi would want him to play all of the different rhythms we had discovered by playing tapes backwards at the flat," says Chandler. "We'd play around with backwards tapes to hear the rhythm, which was actually the drums backwards. Jimi would want Mitch to play that rhythm."

With the basic structure having filled three of the four available tracks, track four was dedicated to a backward rhythm track, featuring backward guitar, bass, and percussion. This was first recorded forward. Then the tape was turned around and played backward on a second machine while another machine recorded the output on the last open track. A four-track-to-four-track

transfer was made, reducing the original four tracks to two, creating two open tracks to accommodate Jimi's lead vocal and additional guitar parts.

Despite all the experimentation, the group's approach to "Are You Experienced?" was concise, Chandler encouraging Hendrix's creativity within the boundaries he had established. "This was when Chas's firm hand was on top of the creative process," states Kramer. "The session was very organized."

In addition to the hypnotic effect created by the backward guitar parts, Jimi further embellished the final master via the addition of a piano overdub. "That's Jimi playing the octaves on the wonderful old out-of-tune upright piano at Olympic," says Kramer. "That piano sound, reminiscent of a bell tolling, was an essential part of the basic rhythm track."

The January 11, 1967, recording of "Third Stone from the Sun" was revisited during this session, with Chandler deciding to scrap nearly all the original recordings in favor of new overdubs. "We barely kept anything from the original session," Kramer remembers. Specific attention was devoted to the song's mixing, where Kramer repositioned Mitchell's percussion and Jimi's guitar to help foster the song's exotic atmosphere. "That song was like a watercolor painting," says Kramer. "To create a sense of movement within the overall sound, I pushed Mitch's cymbals forward in the mix and panned the four tracks of the finished master. Each track was composed of four fairly dense composite images. With four-track recording, you were restricted to panning these multiple layers of sound, whereas now, with twenty-four- and forty-eight-track recording, what you can pan is unlimited."

From the group's very first session with Eddie Kramer at Olympic, the engineer changed the way they had recorded at other London studios. The pre-Olympic recordings featured Redding's bass and Mitchell's drums recorded in stereo on two of the recording tape's four available tracks. Kramer's approach was to record Mitchell's drums in stereo on two tracks, reserving the two remaining tracks for bass and Jimi's rhythm guitar. As fellow Olympic engineer George Chkiantz explains, such a procedure was uncommon. "Kramer adopted a strategy with Hendrix of getting the original live sound down on four tracks — which, at the time, other engineers, including me, thought was crazy."

Kramer and Chandler would then take this tape to another four-track recorder, premixing the four tracks down to two and thereby creating an opening for two more tracks. These two open tracks could then accommodate Jimi's lead guitar, lead vocal, or any other overdub ideas.

Understanding Chandler's dislike of excessive retakes and Hendrix's penchant for perfection, Kramer's strategy accommodated both men, providing the security that the song's basic track had been recorded and premixed to their mutual satisfaction. On this foundation, Hendrix could focus his energies on recording as effective a lead vocal and lead guitar performance as possible. "Hendrix was a lot happier," says Chkiantz. "He felt that the track was never lost and that his stuff was always down on tape. He and Eddie could just sit there and listen."

The idea to approach Jimi's music in this fashion came partly as a result of Kramer's conversations with the guitarist. "Jimi had been exposed to eight-track recording in America," says Kramer. "He liked hearing the basic tracks across on four tracks. Hearing it this way, four-track recording did not

seem like the step backward it really was."

The gorgeous ballad "May This Be Love," another of Hendrix's impressive new compositions, was also completed. "For the solo, Jimi managed to create an effect which sounded backwards," recalls Kramer. "This multiple imaging was enhanced during the mixing process by simultaneously panning the rhythm and lead guitar." As detailed as some of this work was, sometimes mistakes were left in, because they added an unknown, intangible quality to the master. A close listen will reveal the sound of Jimi turning his lyric sheet over as he was recording his lead vocal.

Working with Kramer at Olympic Studios, Chandler mixed, banded, and mastered the album during the first week of April 1967. "When we finally finished the mixing and sequencing of the album, it was about three A.M.," recalls Chandler. "I'd promised Polydor Records that I would play it for them at eleven that morning. After we finished, I went home and caught a few hours' sleep, because I had a session booked at the cutting room to make a lacquer in the morning, as Polydor didn't want to hear a reel-to-reel tape copy. I took the lacquer to play for Horst Schmaltze, who was Polydor's head of A&R. As Horst started to put the needle on the record, I broke out in a cold sweat, thinking, 'Christ . . . when he hears this, he's going to order the men in white coats to take me away!' I was suddenly terrified that I had to play these recordings for someone outside the circle. Horst played the first side through and didn't say a word. Then he turned the disc over and played the other side. I started thinking about how I was going to talk my way out of this. At the end of the second side, he just sat there. Finally, he said, 'This is brilliant. This is the greatest thing I've ever

heard.' I let out a loud, 'Aaah!' Horst became a great supporter of the band from that point forward. Kit Lambert and Chris Stamp at Track were creative, but from that point on, we had a crusader for us within the Polydor establishment. He and Roland Rennie got behind the marketing and distribution of the album in a big way."

■

"Hey Joe" / "51st Anniversary"
Reprise Records 0572. Single release. Monday, May 1, 1967.

This was Hendrix's debut release for Reprise, his record label for North America. Reprise hoped to mirror the U.K. success "Hey Joe" had enjoyed. However, the single missed *Billboard's* singles chart entirely, as AM radio programmers deemed the recording too "hard" for their format, while black stations viewed the song as too rock-oriented for their tight playlists.

■

Thursday, May 4, 1967
London, Olympic Studios. Producer: Chas Chandler. Engineer: Eddie Kramer. Second engineer: George Chkiantz.

Noel Redding's "She's So Fine" was created at this session, providing the bassist with his Experience debut as a songwriter. " 'She's So Fine' was about hippies," explains Redding. "I had seen some bloke walking about with an alarm clock around his neck attached by a bit of string. He must have figured that it looked very avant-garde to walk around with an alarm clock hanging off of him. I wrote that while we were waiting to do the *Top of the Pops*. We went to the studio that night and put it down. I showed Hendrix the riff, and he liked

Jamming the blues backstage alone.

(Jim Marshall)

it because it was in A and there was an open G in it for him to play which he liked a lot. Hendrix said, 'Let's do it!' The session was great. Hendrix and Mitchell were doing those funny vocals in the background, and Chas thought it was wonderful. He also liked it because it was a pop-type record and it had been written by the bass player in his new band, which looked good from a PR point of view. Hendrix thought of the G solo in the middle, because I couldn't think of anything. I was overwhelmed that my song was being recorded."

Also recorded was "Taking Care of No Business," a song of Jimi's that dated back to his 1965–66 stint with Curtis Knight & the Squires. "I wasn't stoned," says Chandler with a laugh, "but the lads were a little high and were laughing and joking, wanting to record something. We began talking along the lines of doing a New Orleans walking band type of thing, and Jimi said he had something. It was meant to be a New Orleans party-styled thing."

Hendrix took another dip into his bag of older songs, reprising "Mr. Bad Luck," a staple of his sets with Jimmy James & the Blue Flames at the Cafe Wha? Although a finished master was completed, the recording was never released.

<hr>

■

Friday, May 5, 1967

London, Olympic Studios. Producer: Chas Chandler. Engineer: Terry Brown. Second engineer: Andy Johns.

With Kramer unable to attend this session, fellow Olympic engineer Terry Brown was recruited to serve in his place. "I was sort of dropped into the middle of it," remembers Brown. "It was Eddie's gig, and he knew everybody." On this evening, the Experience recorded "EXP," which would later serve as the opening track for *Axis: Bold as Love*, the group's second album. "The session was very intense, as the song was so abstract," explains Brown. "There were also quite a few people sitting around listening and watching. While the song was very experimental, Jimi was on top of what he was doing. We set up to get the sounds Jimi wanted and then worked for a long time trying to record these bizarre noises he wanted. The speaker system Jimi was using was pretty abstract. He had a small amplifier stack and this long, six-foot horn mounted on the side of one of his amplifiers. We dimmed the lights very low in the studio, and he worked on it until he was satisfied, which took a long period of time."

With the basic track down on tape, Mitch's and Jimi's "interview" was recorded next. The speed of Hendrix's

voice was manipulated by Brown, using a hand-cranked VSO (variable-speed oscillator). The "Paul Corusoe" character was based on Paul Caruso, a friend of Jimi's from Greenwich Village. "That was really nice of Jimi," admits Caruso. "I didn't know anything about it until I heard *Axis: Bold as Love* when it came out the following year. I couldn't believe he would do that."

<hr>

■

"The Wind Cries Mary" / "Highway Chile"

Track Records 604 004. Single release. Friday, May 5, 1967.

"The Wind Cries Mary," the group's third U.K. single, won wide praise from critics, who were impressed with Jimi's gentle touch with a ballad. One of his finest and most enduring works, "The Wind Cries Mary" entered the U.K. singles chart at number 27 and climbed steadily before cresting at number 6.

<hr>

■

Tuesday, May 9, 1967

London, Olympic Studios. Producer: Chas Chandler. Engineer: Eddie Kramer.

A demo of "If Six Was Nine" was recorded.

<hr>

■

Are You Experienced?

Track Records 612-001. U.K. album release. Friday, May 12, 1967.
Foxey Lady/Manic Depression/Red House/Can You See Me/Love or Confusion/I Don't Live Today/May This Be Love/Fire/Third Stone from the Sun/Remember/Are You Experienced?

Track followed the single release of "The Wind Cries Mary" with the

group's astonishing debut album. As was the custom in the U.K., a clear distinction existed between albums and singles. Unlike markets such as North America, for example, where Beatles albums issued prior to 1967's *Sgt. Pepper's Lonely Hearts Club Band* had been routinely reconfigured to include both singles and album tracks, "Hey Joe," "Purple Haze," and "The Wind Cries Mary" — as well as their respective B sides — were withheld from the album in favor of new material. "We never gave it a moment's thought," says Chandler simply. "The way Jimi and I looked at the situation was that the singles had paved the way for the album. It wouldn't have said much for him if half of *Are You Experienced?* was just those three singles."

Undoubtedly one of the finest debut albums in rock history, *Are You Experienced?* overwhelmed both critics and fans alike. The album entered the U.K. album chart (one week prior to the Beatles' *Sgt. Pepper's Lonely Hearts Club Band*) on May 27, 1967, and rose to number 2 during an impressive thirty-three-week stay.

<hr>

■

Monterey International Pop Festival

Monterey, California. Sunday, June 18, 1967. Remote engineer: Wally Heider.

On the recommendation of Paul McCartney, a member of the festival's board of directors, the Experience was booked to make its U.S. debut with a performance at the Monterey Pop Festival.

The group's dynamic performance at the festival ranks among their finest ever as they tore through nine songs: "Killing Floor," "Foxey Lady," "Like a Rolling Stone," "Rock Me Baby," "Hey Joe," "Can You See Me," "The Wind

Cries Mary," "Purple Haze," and "Wild Thing." Jimi was magnificent throughout, building momentum skillfully before concluding the group's performance by setting fire to his guitar and smashing it to pieces, an act of sheer destruction that left the Monterey audience stunned in disbelief.

In August 1970, less than a month before Hendrix's death, Reprise issued *Historic Performances Recorded at the*

Monterey International Pop Festival. This single disc, prepared by engineer Eric Weinbang, featured one side composed of four songs performed by the Experience ("Like a Rolling Stone," "Rock Me Baby," "Can You See Me," and "Wild Thing") backed with selections from Otis Redding's brilliant set the previous night.

In 1973, with footage of the group's devastating Monterey performance a central component of the Warner Films

Relaxing with Buddy Miles in San Francisco's Golden Gate Park.

(Jim Marshall)

SESSIONS

documentary *Film About Jimi Hendrix*, "Like a Rolling Stone," "Rock Me Baby," "Wild Thing" (which had been the sole Hendrix clip featured in the original *Monterey Pop* documentary) and the previously unreleased "Hey Joe" were remixed and issued as part of the film's accompanying soundtrack album.

The balance of the group's Monterey performance remained unreleased until 1984, when "Killing Floor" was added to the Reprise compilation *Kiss the Sky*. In 1986, the entire Monterey performance was finally issued as *Jimi Plays Monterey*, rendering the other releases obsolete.

■

June 28, 29, and 30, 1967
Los Angeles, Houston Studios. Producer: Chas Chandler.

Eager to continue recording, Chandler booked three days at Houston Studios, a small facility in Los Angeles. Despite the studio's poor sound quality, the group developed two new songs, "The Burning of the Midnight Lamp" and "The Stars That Play with Laughing Sam's Dice." Unfortunately, all the recordings made there were scrapped, as the technical quality did not meet Chandler's standards. "I had never recorded there myself," recalls Chandler. "I booked three days there because I had been told that it was a state-of-the-art studio. But it was dire. The place was like a rehearsal studio compared to Olympic. Los Angeles was so far behind at that time. I had spoken to Jimi about ideas for 'The Burning of the Midnight Lamp' up in San Francisco. One of the ideas we spoke about was using female vocals again. I even lined up three girls from L.A. who had been groupies of the Animals to sing." No such overdubs, however, were ever recorded, as the group simply used the time they had booked to hone the arrangements for both songs.

Where "The Stars That Play with Laughing Sam's Dice" came to life during these Los Angeles sessions, the first traces of "The Burning of the Midnight Lamp" had appeared during the May 1967 sessions at Olympic, when Hendrix toyed with the song's melody on the harpsichord stored in Studio A. A demo recording was made, and Hendrix took away a reel-to-reel copy for further

Hendrix onstage in New York's Central Park, July 5, 1967.
(Linda McCartney/Star File)

study. In Los Angeles, Redding took credit for inspiring the song's introduction, as he remembers being intrigued with the sounds he had made playing a twelve-string guitar hooked up to a wah-wah pedal. The balance of the song came to life under Chandler's watchful eye as he steered Jimi and the group toward completing an acceptable basic track. Despite this work, no masters were achieved. With the group destined to return to New York in early July, Chandler decided to schedule their next recording sessions there.

■

Thursday, July 6, 1967

New York, Mayfair Studios. 4:00 P.M. to 7:00 P.M. Producer: Chas Chandler. Engineer: Gary Kellgren.

Through Chandler's friendship with producer Tom Wilson, with whom Chandler had worked during the final stages of his tenure with the Animals, the Experience booked time at Mayfair Studios in New York. Mayfair was run by engineer Gary Kellgren, who came highly recommended by Wilson. Though smaller in size than Olympic's impressive Studio A, Mayfair's sound quality offered a distinct improvement over L.A.'s Houston Studios.

Listed on the tape box as "client: Jim Hendricks," the Experience toiled under Chandler's direction for six hours. Thirty takes and two reels of tape were required before "Burning of the Midnight Lamp" would be complete. " 'Burning of the Midnight Lamp' had actually begun as a demo at Olympic," Chandler recalls. We intended to record it there, but Jimi found the solution to the song in America, and we decided to just do it there." In addition to the Baldwin harpsichord played by Jimi, another distinctive touch was provided by the famed gospel vocalists the

Sweet Inspirations. Kellgren's wife, Marta, who also worked at Mayfair, knew the singers well, having hired them on many previous occasions for other studio clients. "We were still trying to make commercial singles, but we always tried to feature a shift in our sound," explains Chandler. "We had used female vocals before with 'Hey Joe,' and it seemed appropriate that we feature them again. The Sweet Inspirations were a natural fit."

■

Wednesday, July 19, 1967

New York, Mayfair Studios. 7:00 P.M. to 1:32 A.M. Producer: Chas Chandler. Engineer: Gary Kellgren.

Twenty-one new takes of "The Stars That Play with Laughing Sam's Dice" were recorded. Having abandoned the Los Angeles recordings of this track, the Experience recorded these new takes, with take 21 selected the master.

■

"Purple Haze" / "The Wind Cries Mary"

Reprise 0597. U.S. single release. Wednesday, August 16, 1967.

Prefacing their release of *Are You Experienced?* in North America, Reprise tried again to crack *Billboard's* elusive singles chart. "Purple Haze" fared slightly better than "Hey Joe," entering the chart at number 90 and climbing to a high of 65. Reprise would have far greater success with the *Are You Experienced?* album, as steady airplay of "Purple Haze" on underground FM radio stations in major markets like New York and San Francisco dramatically fueled sales of the album rather than either of the first two U.S. singles.

■

"The Burning of the Midnight Lamp" / "The Stars That Play with Laughing Sam's Dice"

Track 604 007. U.K. Single release. Friday, August 18, 1967.

Hendrix had invested a great deal in the writing and recording of "The Burning of the Midnight Lamp." He was stung by the lukewarm reaction accorded the song by U.K. music critics, who had been elated by the group's first three singles. Public response was also somewhat diminished, as "The Burning of the Midnight Lamp" lacked the chart impact of its predecessors. The single entered the chart on Wednesday, August 30, 1967, and peaked at number 18 during its nine-week stay. Hendrix was unfazed by the song's sales performance, his belief in "The Burning of the Midnight Lamp" never wavering. "I really don't care what our records do as far as chartwise," Jimi explained. "Everybody around here hated [that record], but to me that was the best one we ever made. Not as far as recording, because the recording technique was very bad. You couldn't hear the words so good. That's probably what [the problem] was."

■

Are You Experienced?

Reprise RS 6261. U.S. album release. Wednesday, August 23, 1967.
Purple Haze/Manic Depression/Hey Joe/Love or Confusion/May This Be Love/I Don't Live Today/The Wind Cries Mary/Fire/Third Stone from the Sun/Foxey Lady/Are You Experienced?

Where the two singles issued by Reprise had fared poorly in the U.S. charts, *Are You Experienced?* enjoyed tremendous success, spending a remarkable one hundred six weeks on

Billboard's album chart, including seventy-seven weeks in the Top 40. The album's incredible success firmly established Reprise as a rock label to be reckoned with. Following its birth as a boutique label for then owner Frank Sinatra, Reprise became the recording home for such Sinatra confidants as Dean Martin and Sammy Davis Jr. Label vice president Morris "Mo" Ostin, himself a former Sinatra employee, oversaw the label's transformation and subsequent embrace of rock n' roll. Hendrix quickly became the jewel of a label whose ranks soon included the Grateful Dead, the Kinks, and Van Morrison.

The popularity enjoyed by *Are You Experienced?* continued throughout Jimi's career. It was his most popular release at the time of his death in September 1970 and remained so for nearly twenty years, before it was finally surpassed by the Reprise compilation *Smash Hits.* It remains an invaluable introduction to the Hendrix legacy.

■
Tuesday, October 3, 1967
London, Olympic Studios. Producer: Chas Chandler. Engineer: Eddie Kramer. Second engineers: George Chkiantz, Andy Johns.

With Hendrix eager to mine a backlog of material he had accumulated over several months, Chandler brought the group back into Olympic Studios. Bursting with confidence, Hendrix seemed eager to assume a more prominent role in the recording process. Chandler accommodated this to a degree, allowing the group increased time to develop material in the studio. "Because the band was well established, Mitch and Noel could hear Jimi's new songs for the first time in the studio, rather than going over them in a sepa-

rate rehearsal," explains Chandler. "We found that there was less aggravation this way. Jimi would explain the chord sequences to Noel and the tempo he desired to Mitch."

The roles within the control room at Olympic were clearly defined, although Chandler granted Hendrix more latitude than in past sessions. "Eddie Kramer was the engineer on all of *Axis: Bold as Love,*" says Chandler. "I remember George Chkiantz dragging in Keith Grant to help him work some effects out, but it was Eddie who worked directly with us. Eddie and I would be at the desk [console] and George Chkiantz or Andy Johns would be in the corner near the tape machines. Roger Mayer built electronic devices for Jimi, and he was often in the control room with us as well."

Over the course of this long evening, progress was made on both "You Got Me Floatin' " and "One Rainy Wish." Redding made use of his Hagstrom eight-string bass with notable effect. In addition, Graham Nash of the Hollies and [The Move's] Trevor Burton and Roy Wood contributed back-up vocals.

Despite the session's jovial atmosphere, Chandler never quite warmed to "You Got Me Floatin.' " "That was one of the weak songs on the record for me," admits Chandler. "That's why I put it first on the album's second side. I just wanted to get it over with. I never felt that any of us had ever really been into the song. In fact, we added other people's harmonies to the track because we didn't have any other ideas. Trevor Burton and Roy Wood were mates of Noel's, and that's how they came in and sang on that. To me, it just wasn't one of his best works."

Conversely, Chandler was excited by the prospects for "One Rainy Wish," a superb new ballad. "I was very keen

on that song from the very first moment I heard him play it to me," explains Chandler. "Jimi recorded three guitars for that song — not counterplaying, as he had done with 'The Wind Cries Mary.' These guitar parts each picked up where the other one left off. We had some trouble recording it, as there were originally some gaps between the notes, which caused Noel to struggle a bit with the tempo, but it all came together nicely in the end."

The lyrical imagery of "One Rainy Wish" provided an insight to Hendrix's fascination with colors. Jimi had begun to describe his sound in colors, primarily when discussing subtle shadings of his sound. Hendrix would speak to Kramer of sounds playing in his head or sounds he had heard in a dream. These were the sounds he wanted to include on disc, these were sounds that frustrated him — he could hear them clearly, but he could not translate the ideas to the guitar. Colors, as Hendrix described, could also describe emotions. "Some feelings make you think of different colors. Jealousy is purple — I'm purple with rage or purple with anger — and green is envy. This is how you explain your different emotions in colors towards this certain girl who has all the colors in the world. In other words, you don't think you have to part [with these emotions] but you are willing to try."

Following a break to accommodate a string of engagements and media appearances in both Britain and France, additional sessions were booked at Olympic on October 25. With the lucrative Christmas season fast upon them, both Track and Reprise were pressuring the group to complete the album and capitalize on the dramatic success of *Are You Experienced?* On October 23, Chandler booked DeLane Lea Studios so that the group could rehearse in preparation for the forthcoming sessions at Olympic. On the following evening, the group headlined London's Marquee Club, supported by The Nice. Having heard Jimi jam with Keith Emerson, the group's keyboard wizard, Chandler briefly considered bringing Emerson to one of the Olympic sessions, just to see what might come from such a pairing. "Keith Emerson was a guy Jimi should have done some work with," says Chandler. "Jimi often sat in with The Nice, and Keith really played well with him. They could have really put something together, but I was under the gun to finish up the album and we couldn't spare the time."

■

Wednesday, October 25, 1967

London, Olympic Studios. Producer: Chas Chandler. Engineer: Eddie Kramer. Second engineers: George Chkiantz, Andy Johns.

Following a rehearsal at Regent Sound, Chandler and the Experience traveled to Olympic, where work was completed on "Wait Until Tomorrow" and "Little Wing." Hendrix, according to Chandler, had had "Wait Until Tomorrow" under wraps for some time, tinkering with the song over the months prior to these October sessions. "That was originally written as a put-on," explains Chandler. "When he was first experimenting with it, we saw it as a joke, as a comedy song almost." By the time of these October sessions, Hendrix had dropped whatever comedy intentions he may originally have considered.

Of all the tracks that found their way onto the final album, "Wait Until Tomorrow" proved to be one of the hardest for Hendrix to complete. "For no apparent reason, Jimi could not play the opening notes to his satisfaction,"

Jimi rehearses prior to the Experience's August 18, 1967, performance at the Hollywood Bowl.

(ChuckBoyd/Flower Children Ltd.)

recalls Kramer. A number of unsuccessful attempts were made to try and finish the song, but Chandler, not wanting the session to bog down, put the track aside for the time being and moved on.

"Little Wing," one of Hendrix's finest and most enduring compositions, came next. The original idea for the song, Hendrix told reporter Jules Freemond, had come from an idea he had originally developed while playing in Greenwich Village. "I dig writing slow songs, because I find it easier to get more blues and feeling into them," he said. "Most of the ballads come across in different ways. Sometimes you see things in different ways than other people see it. So then you write it in a song. It could represent anything. Some songs, I come up with the music first, then I put the words that fit. It all depends. There is no certain pattern that I go by because I don't consider myself a songwriter. Not yet anyway. I just keep music in my head. It doesn't even come out to the other guys until we go into the studio."

The group concentrated on capturing a basic track on which to build. Jimi's guitar was fed through a Leslie organ speaker. By the evening's end, the group had successfully established a working master onto which overdubs would follow.

■
Thursday, October 26, 1967
London, Olympic Studios. Producer: Chas Chandler. Engineer: Eddie Kramer. Second engineers: George Chkiantz, Andy Johns.

As he had done the night before, Chandler again booked Regent Sound to accommodate another pre-session rehearsal. After running through two songs, however, the Experience was tossed from the studio for being too

loud! Undaunted, they continued on to Olympic, where Hendrix mastered the troublesome opening notes to "Wait Until Tomorrow" and completed the song. Mitch and Noel contributed backing vocals, and, as Jimi put on his lead vocal, the tape caught him laughing as he listened to Mitchell and Redding finish their vocals.

"Ain't No Telling" was also completed on this evening. The song placed the spotlight squarely on Mitch Mitchell, whose superlative performance ranked among his finest work with the group. Mitchell challenged Hendrix throughout, doubling Jimi's rhythm guitar and incessantly pushing his solo. Chandler and Hendrix encouraged such participation from Mitchell, recognizing his emerging skills. Outside Mitchell's function of establishing the tempo or providing a particular accent, Hendrix granted him complete freedom to create different textures to fit each of his songs.

■
Friday, October 27, 1967
London, Olympic Studios. Producer: Chas Chandler. Engineer: Eddie Kramer. Second engineers: George Chkiantz, Andy Johns.

With Noel using a Hagstrom eight-string bass, the basic track for "Spanish Castle Magic" was completed. The group had tinkered with "Spanish Castle Magic" on a number of occasions during these October sessions before finally perfecting the arrangement.

With the basic track in hand, overdubbing began. Hendrix recorded his lead vocal and added his lead guitar parts. Using his own Hagstrom eight-string bass patched through an Octavia, Jimi also punched in some bass riffs, replacing portions of Redding's original track. When Jimi heard Kramer experi-

menting with the piano, he immediately recognized another element for the song. "I was fooling around with these chords on the piano," recalls Kramer. "I was playing some jazz chords when Jimi heard me and said, 'Man, what are those chords? Show me those chords!' I showed him what I had been playing, and he said, 'Man, I gotta put those in this song. You play it.' I said no, but I offered to show them to him, and those were the chords he played on the final record."

■
Saturday, October 28, 1967
London, Olympic Studios. Producer: Chas Chandler. Engineer: Eddie Kramer. Second engineers: George Chkiantz, Andy Johns.

A busy day for the Experience, as the group managed to squeeze in a productive session in addition to a performance at the California Ballroom in Dunstable.

Important work on two songs, "Spanish Castle Magic" and "Little Wing," was completed. "For 'Little Wing,' Jimi used the glockenspiel that was kept in Studio A," recalls George Chkiantz. New lead vocals were carefully recorded for each. *Axis: Bold as Love* was the first Hendrix release where the priority was stereo compatibility," Chkiantz remembers. "Some of the vocals were put on one side to 'enhance' the effect." After this work was completed, mixes of both "Spanish Castle Magic" and "Little Wing" were prepared.

Hollywood Bowl, August 18, 1967.
(Chuck Boyd/Flower Children Ltd.)

Sunday, October 29, 1967

London, Olympic Studios. Producer: Chas Chandler. Engineer: Eddie Kramer. Second engineers: George Chkiantz, Andy Johns.

A full evening of work helped the Experience realize three of *Axis: Bold as Love*'s finest songs: "Castles Made of Sand," "Up from the Skies," and "Bold as Love."

"Up from the Skies" began the evening and was especially noteworthy for Mitch Mitchell's superb jazz drumming. "Bold as Love" introduced stereo phasing as yet another component of Hendrix's sound.

When the Beatles had come to Olympic to record "Baby You're a Rich Man" (May 11, 1967) and "All You Need Is Love" (June 14, 1967), Kramer — who worked on both recordings — discussed phasing sound with George Martin, as well as a new technique EMI had been utilizing on Beatles recordings: artificial double tracking, or ADT for short. Martin had remarked that its secrets could be found in the handbook of the BBC Radiophonic workshop. Phasing sound had actually been discovered by accident when, in 1959, an American disc jockey tried to fatten the sound of "The Big Hurt," a recent single by Toni Fisher. To make the song's sound seem bigger, the DJ cued two dubs of the song to begin play simultaneously. Soon thereafter, phase cancellation ensued, and a new technique was born. Hendrix had been trying to describe an underwater sound that had come to him in a dream, in the hope that Kramer, as he had in the past, could dial up the effect on the recording console. This particular sound had proven more of a challenge to create.

To fellow Olympic engineer George Chkiantz, whose concentration had focused on the whole concept of tape loops and tape delay, ADT was close, but it was still not exactly what *he* wanted to hear. "I had been bugged for ages by the fact that tape loops and tape echo always gave an even number of beats," explains Chkiantz. "I was always trying to work a system that gave an odd number of beats."

Kramer and Andy Johns both recall Chkiantz's big breakthrough. "One night, while we were working on *Axis: Bold as Love*, George had taken a Small Faces tape ["Green Circles"] and locked himself in Studio B," Johns recalls. "He burst into Studio A with a mad expression and said, 'Come and listen to this!' So we all went in, Jimi too, and George had created sound from a stereo mix, depending on the dynamics of the song, coming from behind your head. It wasn't phasing, but it was the first big step."

Further refinements of Chkiantz's discovery were difficult, because he was using up every available machine at Olympic in an effort to capture the sound on tape. Chkiantz appealed separately to Kramer and Glyn Johns for assistance. Johns wanted to use this new sound, a combination of phasing and flanging — yet another EMI variation of ADT — as part of "Itchycoo Park," a new recording by the Small Faces. Via this breakthrough, the process, applied during the mono mixing, had made a debut of sorts, but Chkiantz still hadn't made the breakthrough in stereo.

Spurred by Chkiantz's progress, Kramer had been thinking about phasing and its possible applications for Hendrix. It was decided that they would try to utilize the process on "Bold as Love." Kramer asked Hendrix to listen to a sound he wanted to introduce. Upon hearing phasing, Hendrix exclaimed, "That's it! That's the sound I've been hearing in my dreams!" Kramer, Chkiantz, and Andy Johns then set

about organizing what was still a complicated process, and overdubs — complete with phasing — began. A careful listen to the finished master will indicate exactly where the process kicked in. At 2:46 into the song, Mitch's phased drums are audible, and just as his roll is rushing from left to right, Kramer pans the drum sound through the speakers, effectively canceling just a split second before Hendrix's guitar dramatically reappears, now awash in this new sound. For the first time, phasing had been recorded in stereo.

"The elements of that song were written quickly," recalls Chandler. "Then Eddie and George began experimenting with this sound and that sound until they found what they wanted. I do remember expressing some concern to Eddie that the phasing sound, initially, seemed a bit too pompous or overblown. I just wanted to make sure that the effect didn't overwhelm the entire track. The song, though, was so strong that the phasing only added to its greatness."

As for the nimble bass lines that frame the song's melody, they were overdubbed by Hendrix. Redding had cut the basic track, but during all of the experimentation, Hendrix had decided to rerecord portions of the bass line, especially during the song's phased outro. The master was further enhanced when Jimi spotted Kramer improvising on the studio's harpsichord, which was left from a previous session. Kramer demonstrated the appropriate chords and Hendrix played them, adding a finishing touch.

Phasing was also applied to the October 28 master of "Little Wing." Although the basic track had been completed, Kramer half-phased Hendrix's vocal and fed it through a revolving electronic Leslie speaker.

"Castles Made of Sand," another of Jimi's delicate ballads, was also com-

Mitch Mitchell.

(Michael Ochs Archives)

put down a basic guitar line, which we later erased during overdubs and replaced with the parts he wanted."

■

Monday, October 30, 1967
London, Olympic Studios. Producer: Chas Chandler. Engineer: Eddie Kramer. Second engineers: George Chkiantz, Andy Johns.

Finishing touches were applied to the May 4 master recording of Redding's "She's So Fine" so that the song could be added to the *Axis: Bold as Love* album. Hendrix and Mitchell contributed backing vocals. On September 27, Redding had apparently booked time on his own at Rye Muse Sound Studios to work on "She's So Fine." As neither Chandler nor Hendrix was present, what effect that session had upon the overdubbing done this evening is unknown.

■

Tuesday, October 31, 1967
London, Olympic Studios. Producer: Chas Chandler. Engineer: Eddie Kramer. Second engineer: George Chkiantz.

This was a marathon mixing session presided over by Chandler, Hendrix, and Kramer. Thirteen songs, including "EXP," would make up the new album. Somehow, after the lengthy session had concluded, Hendrix managed to lose the mixes for what was to become side one. Apparently he had intended to take the masters home. "He went off to a party and took the masters with him. Coming back, he left one of the boxes in a taxi. It was all scheduled for release! So we rang up Eddie and went into Olympic the next night and mixed the entire A side of the album again, all in one night."

"It was mixed beautifully," lamented

pleted this evening. "That track was almost like 'The Wind Cries Mary,' where, after Jimi had put down his rhythm guitar, there were big gaps to be filled by overdubs," recalls Chandler. "The main problem had been that Jimi had the guitar parts written out in his head. We had a hard time getting Mitch and Noel to play in time, because they just couldn't get a feel for the tempo. To help them get right smack on time, Jimi

Hendrix. "But we lost the original mix, so we had to redo it. Chas and I and the engineer, Eddie Kramer, all of us had to remix it the next morning within eleven hours, and it's very hard to do that."

"EXP," the album's opening track, proved difficult to reproduce, because the basic track for that recording had been engineered by Terry Brown. Many of his techniques, with regard to panning and level changes, had been done during the premixing process. A remix based on an acetate recording subsequently failed, leaving the three no option but to begin from scratch.

"The one we had the most trouble with was 'If Six Was Nine,'" Kramer remembers. "I could never get close to what we had already done in terms of quality with the previous rough mix. We were left scratching our heads. Chas asked if anybody had a tape of that rough mix. As it turned out, Noel did. Chas sent someone off to his flat in a cab, and they came back with this tiny, three-inch plastic reel that the tape was falling off of. Before we put it on the machine, I had to iron out all of the wrinkles. It was recorded at seven and a half i.p.s., and the tape was just a nightmare. That tape, though, was transferred to fifteen i.p.s., and that's the version that you hear."

"Considering what we had done to salvage the original, it sounded great," says Chandler. "Later on, we licensed the track to be used in the *Easy Rider* movie, and it sounded brilliant in the cinema. I still get compliments about it today!"

■

Axis: Bold as Love

Track Records 613 003. U.K. album release. Friday, December 1, 1967. Producer: Chas Chandler. Engineer: Eddie Kramer. Second engineers: Terry Brown, George Chkiantz, Andy Johns.
EXP/Up from the Skies/Spanish Castle Magic/Wait Until Tomorrow/Ain't No Telling/Little Wing/If Six Was Nine/You Got Me Floatin'/Castles Made of Sand/She's So Fine/One Rainy Wish/Little Miss Lover/Bold as Love.

Rush-released by Track in order to maximize sales during the lucrative Christmas season, *Axis: Bold as Love* enjoyed a warm reception from fans, peaking at the number 5 position during a sixteen-week stay on the U.K. album charts.

■

"Foxey Lady" / "Hey Joe"

Reprise 0641. U.S. single release. Wednesday, December 13, 1967.

Perhaps as a counter to Capitol Records' release of *Get That Feeling* — a collection of Hendrix's performances as a sideman to Curtis Knight — Reprise issued this single. While both tracks had become staples of underground FM radio outlets, this third Experience single peaked at number 67 during a brief four-week run on the *Billboard* chart.

■

Wednesday, December 20, 1967

London, Olympic Studios. Producer: Chas Chandler. Engineer: Eddie Kramer. Second engineer: George Chkiantz.

This session signaled the beginning of production for what would become *Electric Ladyland*, the group's third album. Hendrix began in fine style, re-

cording the marvelous "Crosstown Traffic." Kramer again declined Hendrix's invitation to play piano on the track. The chords Hendrix performed were similar to those he had incorporated into the final master of "Spanish Castle Magic." "The piano sound was very heavily compressed with a Pye limiter, and as it was going through that, it was also being EQ'd," explains Kramer. "I also varied the EQ to make it sound like a mini wah-wah. Jimi doubled up the melody line by singing what he's playing on the guitar. Then he put a kazoo on top of that!" Traffic's Dave Mason, observing the session, then joined Noel Redding to contribute background vocals.

"Dream" and "Touch You," two of Noel's new songs, were also recorded. "Dream," only Redding's second lead vocal performance with the Experience, was an unexpected surprise. The track, somewhat reminiscent of Hendrix's own "Love or Confusion," was particularly noteworthy, powered by Redding's lead guitar work and Hendrix's nimble bass playing. "Hendrix really liked that one," Redding remembers. "I played it to him on the guitar, and he picked up the bass. That one was never completed, but it was a good tune with a lot of validity."

As Redding had been given a slot on the *Axis: Bold as Love* album, Hendrix renewed his invitation to Mitch Mitchell to include a song on the new album. Mitchell had nothing prepared, but Redding offered "Dance," another of his new songs. A demo version of the song, with Mitchell handling lead vocals, was recorded. While a rough mix was prepared, Chandler deemed that more work was required before the track could be included. As Chandler explains, "Dance" soon evolved into "Cat Talking to You." "That's what it ended up being called," says Chandler. "Even though, in the end, Mitchell

Accepting flowers from a young fan.
(Jim Marshall)

never got a song onto the album, Hendrix and I sat at home and doctored Noel's lyrics to improve them." While "Cat Talking to You" never materialized, Hendrix lifted Redding's lead guitar line and would later develop the riff as "Ezy Ryder." "The riff to 'Dance' later came out as a tune ["Ezy Ryder"] credited to Hendrix," says Redding. "If I was doing one of my songs in the studio, I'd just pick up a guitar or turn Hendrix's guitar around backwards and go through the tune quickly. Hendrix heard me play the riff and he said, 'Yeah, I like that.'"

Neither "Dream," "Dance," or even "Cat Talking to You" ever progressed past the demo stage. In addition, the concept of developing a vocal vehicle for Mitchell quickly lost steam and was never reconsidered.

■
Thursday, December 21, 1967
London, Olympic Studios. Producer: Chas Chandler. Engineer: Eddie Kramer. Second engineer: George Chkiantz.

Final touches for "Crosstown Traffic" were recorded before a final mix was completed.

Hendrix had also, according to Chandler, already devised an opening for the new album: the sounds of a spaceship landing on earth. "It didn't go by that name at the time, but 'And the Gods Made Love' was an idea that definitely began at Olympic," Chandler recalls. "The spaceship landing was a sound he thought of there."

Another track that began in London was "Have You Ever Been (to Electric Ladyland)." "That was a very R&B–influenced track, which, when Jimi first played it, didn't sound like him at all," Kramer recalls. "The drum sound was very dark. Mitch's drums were actually recorded at a higher speed and then slowed down to make them sound heavier, which was a hangover from 'And the Gods Made Love.' The solo was done at the Record Plant, with Jimi using a wah-wah pedal. The bass part was also recorded there by Jimi as an overdub. Gary Kellgren recorded the three-part harmony vocal overdubs at the Record Plant."

■

Axis: Bold as Love

Reprise Records RS 6281. Wednesday, January 10, 1968. Producer: Chas Chandler. Engineer: Eddie Kramer. Second engineers: Terry Brown, George Chkiantz, Andy Johns. EXP/Up from the Skies/Spanish Castle Magic/Wait Until Tomorrow/Ain't No Telling/Little Wing/If Six Was Nine/You Got Me Floatin'/Castles Made of Sand/She's So Fine/One Rainy Wish/Little Miss Lover/Bold as Love

Track Records, Reprise's London counterpart, issued *Axis: Bold as Love* in December 1967, but Warner Bros. held up the release to avoid conflict with Capitol Records' December release of *Get That Feeling*, a tepid collection of recordings featuring Hendrix backing Knight as a member of the Squires. Even with the delayed release, U.S. sales of *Axis: Bold as Love* were hurt by the resulting confusion. Nonetheless, the Experience's skyrocketing popularity, fueled by the phenomenal success of *Are You Experienced?*, propelled the album to the number 5 position in

Billboard's Top 200 album chart in February 1968.

■

Sunday, January 21, 1968

London, Olympic Studios. Producer: Chas Chandler. Engineer: Eddie Kramer. Second engineers: Andy Johns, George Chkiantz.

Recording of *Electric Ladyland* resumed with Hendrix's definitive remake of Bob Dylan's "All Along the Watchtower." Jimi's admiration for Dylan expressed itself on many occasions, perhaps no more eloquently than by his stirring rendition of "Like a Rolling Stone" at the June 1967 Monterey Pop Festival. The Experience had previously tried to record an interpretation of the song, failing as recently as March 1, 1967, to realize an effective studio version. This was not the only Dylan composition in the Experience's repertoire, however. On October 17, 1967, the group had included a rendition of Dylan's "Can You Please Crawl Out

Your Window?" as part of their four-song set recorded for *Alexis Korner's Rhythm & Blues Show*, a radio program broadcast on the BBC's World Service.

When and how Jimi was inspired to record "All Along the Watchtower" is not entirely clear. Traffic's Dave Mason has suggested that a small party thrown by Viv Prince, where Mason, Jimi, Linda Keith, and Rolling Stones guitarist Brian Jones first heard Dylan's *John Wesley Harding* album, provided the impetus. Olympic engineer Andy Johns offers a second perspective. He clearly recalls Hendrix playing recordings of Dylan songs at the studio on more than one occasion. "That was the first time any of us had heard those reels," Johns recalls. "He came in with these Dylan reels, and we played them in the studio." Publicist Michael Goldstein, who also worked for Dylan's manager, Albert Grossman, provided Jimi with reels of new Dylan songs. This practice, openly encouraged by Michael Jeffery, was not an unusual one for Grossman. Placing Dylan's songs with artists interested in

Traffic's Dave Mason made a number of contributions to the Experience, guesting on such tracks as "Crosstown Traffic" and "All Along the Watchtower."
(Linda McCartney/Star File)

recording them was a lucrative practice. With the recent U.S. chart failure of "Up from the Skies," Jeffery hoped that a Dylan interpretation could help Hendrix crack what seemed to be impenetrable AM radio playlists.

Joining the Experience for the session was Mason, who, it was decided, would contribute acoustic guitar. "Dave hung out a lot with Jimi and was a regular in the studio," says Kramer. "Jimi was aware of his ability and knew that he could cover the part adequately." To maximize the effect, however, it was de-

cided that a twelve-string guitar was needed instead. With Mason in tow, Andy Johns volunteered to travel to his South London flat to pick up the instrument. "I had my brother Glyn's Harmony twelve-string at this dreadful dive that I was living in," explains Johns. "Mason drove me out there in his Jaguar, but as I was in the process of being evicted, I had to climb through the upstairs window to get the guitar."

Upon their return, Hendrix led the group through a series of rehearsals before proper takes ensued. Jimi, says

Kramer, had a firm understanding of just how the song was to be arranged and performed. Mason, playing guitar in the studio's vocal booth, earned the brunt of Hendrix's reprimands as he struggled to master the song's chord changes. Hendrix and Redding also clashed, and Noel, angered by Jimi's seemingly ceaseless quest for perfection, bolted from the studio midway through the session. Mason, who regularly assumed bass chores for Traffic's studio recordings, took over in Redding's absence, but Hendrix would later overdub the part himself, using a small, custom bass guitar that Bill Wyman had given to Andy Johns.

While no record was kept of the countless rehearsal takes, twenty-four takes of "All Along the Watchtower" were recorded before work stopped, and a four-track-to-four-track transfer was prepared. Two additional takes were then recorded onto that new master, and the basic track had been successfully achieved. A rough mix was also prepared.

■

Friday, January 26, 1968
London, Olympic Studios. Producer: Chas Chandler. Engineer: Eddie Kramer. Second engineer: Phil Brown.

Hendrix again focused on a song he had not composed, as the Experience recorded their interpretation of Bo Hansson's and Janne Karlsson's "Tax Free." The session began with five rehearsals of the song before formal attempts were made. A version marked "retake" was attempted before the actual recording of take 1, which assistant engineer Phil Brown marked "good." Takes 2 and 3 broke down, but the group rebounded with a solid fourth attempt. Hendrix pressed for another op-

portunity, and this version, take 5, realized the master. There was a slight breakdown at the song's close that Chandler felt could be improved. After four attempts to record "Edit Section," the fifth proved successful. "Tax Free," by Chandler's estimation, was now complete. Hendrix, on the other hand, was not quite sure. He would later re-record the number at the Record Plant in the months ahead — unable, even then, to decide whether or not he had recorded the song to his full satisfaction.

After the basic track had been completed, guitar overdubs followed. Mixes were then prepared for both "Tax Free" and "All Along the Watchtower."

■

Sunday, January 28, 1968
London, Olympic Studios. Producer: Chas Chandler. Engineer: Eddie Kramer.

Additional work was completed on the January 26 master recording of "Tax Free."

■

Saturday, February 24, 1968
New York, Mayfair Studios. Producer: Chas Chandler.

With the Experience in the midst of its extensive U.S. tour, Chas Chandler booked time at Mayfair to transfer a number of half-inch, four-track masters made at Olympic Studios to one-inch, eight-track tape. Unlike the four-track masters, these eight-track submasters could be played on a twelve-track machine, such as the new Scully at the Record Plant, the New York studio where Chandler and the Experience planned to resume production of the unfinished *Electric Ladyland* album.

Chandler transferred "Dream," "Crosstown Traffic," "Touch You," "Tax Free," and the Soft Machine's "Making Sun While the Hay Shines" for fellow producer Tom Wilson, so that additional work could be done on these new submasters if necessary.

■

"Up from the Skies" / "One Rainy Wish"
Reprise 0665. U.S. single release. Monday, February 26, 1968.

Overlooking such possible contenders as "Little Wing" and "If Six Was Nine," these two *Axis: Bold as Love* tracks were coupled for release as the lead single from that album. "Up from the Skies," however, was unable to improve on the performance of the two previous Experience singles, reaching only 82 before falling off the chart after a four-week run.

■

Wednesday, March 13, 1968
New York, Sound Center Studios. Producer: Jimi Hendrix.

With the Experience in New York enjoying a brief respite from their U.S. tour, an interesting session materialized, yielding "My Friend," which would be added posthumously to 1971's *Cry of Love*.

Joining Hendrix on this date was an interesting group of musicians that included Stephen Stills, drummer Jimmy Mayes, guitarist Ken Pine from the Fugs, and Paul Caruso on harmonica. Chas Chandler was not present, so Hendrix assumed the role of producer, organizing the talent he had assembled.

"He called me at home one afternoon, which really surprised me, as I

SESSIONS

Smashing his guitar at the Fillmore East, May 10, 1968.

(Ken Regan/Camera 5)

had not spoken to him for some time," remembers Ken Pine. "He asked if I would play twelve-string guitar on a session he wanted to do. He was looking to add a bluegrass, country-rock feel. He picked me up and we parked in a parking garage near the studio. He had the wide-brim hat with a feather in the band. The attendant looked at him as if he was from Mars. At the studio, he pulled out some papers and said, 'Check this out.' He had written out the lyrics to Bob Dylan's 'All Along the Watchtower' by hand and told me he had recorded the song in London. He

wanted to know what I thought of the song and did I think it was any good!"

"We cut two takes of 'My Friend,'" Paul Caruso recalls. "Kenny Pine was on twelve-string guitar, Jimi was on bass, Jimmy Mayes was on drums, and Stephen Stills, who, except for the piano in the introduction, didn't contribute anything else."

With his guitar parts recorded to Jimi's satisfaction and the basic track completed, Pine departed. Noel Redding arrived soon thereafter, leading the group through a formative instrumental workout of "Little Miss

Strange." Jimi also cut a demo of his own, recording a stark rendition of "1983 (A Merman I Should Turn to Be)" before the impromptu session concluded.

Problems that had surfaced during the sessions in December and January still had not been resolved. On more than one occasion, Jimi had chafed at Chandler's firm hand in the studio. Redding was even more frustrated, having bolted from the January 21 "All Along the Watchtower" session, miffed at Jimi's insensitivity. There would be little respite ahead, as the Experience

resumed their grueling U.S. tour in support of *Axis: Bold as Love*, ultimately performing sixty-six engagements in just sixty days. Work on the album would not resume until April.

Rather than return to London and Olympic, Chandler booked time at the Record Plant, the new twelve-track studio in New York built by engineer Gary Kellgren, Revlon executive Chris Stone, and producer Tom Wilson.

The Record Plant, which would be Hendrix's creative haven for almost two years, came about as the result of an unexpected friendship between

Kellgren and Chris Stone. "I was working for the Revlon Corporation in 1967," remembers Stone. "My wife had recently given birth to our first child, and our next-door neighbors knew this young woman about to have her first child who was scared to death. Her name was Marta Kellgren. So they arranged for my wife to get together with her. Gary, her husband, came along as well. While the two women talked about what it was like to have children, Gary and I sat in the living room staring at each other. We were forced into a social situation, and Gary, in those days,

was extremely shy. He just didn't talk. During our conversation, he invited me down to see Mayfair Studios, where he worked. At Mayfair, Kellgren was everything. He was the engineer, the janitor, and the equipment technician. I had always had an interest in recording studios, so I asked Gary if I could get into the bookkeeping office. He couldn't see a reason why not, and let me have a look at the books. I found out that they were billing five thousand dollars a week and paying Gary two hundred. I played this out and told him that what he needed was a manager. I basically didn't want to be his manager, but he was a nice guy, and our wives had become friends, so I offered to go see his boss with him. The next afternoon, we sat down with his boss, and Gary's salary was raised to one thousand dollars a week."

Kellgren was greatly impressed by Stone's tenacity and skill as a negotiator. In confidence, Kellgren informed Stone of his desire to own his own recording facility. "Kellgren came back to me about a month later," Stone remembers. "He wanted to have his own studio, but felt he didn't know how to put things together. He asked if I would be interested in working with him, and I was. I put the package together and got us some money to get started."

Still employed by Revlon, Stone's association with the cosmetic giant afforded him two crucial advantages: credibility and access to venture capital. "Originally we had asked [engineer] Wes Farrell to be a part of everything, but he didn't want to go along. Tom Wilson became a partner, Kellgren was a partner, I was a partner, and the money was a partner," explains Stone. "The money was Ankie Revson, the former wife of Charles Revson. Everyone thought that Revlon owned the Record Plant, because to get business or credit information they had to call me, and to call me you had to call Revlon. Creditors assumed Revlon owned the studio, and I never said they didn't, so we got credit from everybody."

Buttressed by Revson's financial support, work on Stone's, Kellgren's, and Wilson's daring gambit quickly accelerated. "Ankie Revson financed the entire cost of building and equipping the Record Plant," explains Stone. "That meant building and outfitting one studio and doing all the structural work for the second. We purchased a twelve-track, four-track, two-track, and a mono

Mitch Mitchell cuts loose during the October 1968 sessions at TTG Studios.
(Michael Ochs Archives)

tape machine. That line of machines cost us thirty-five thousand dollars. Finished and ready to open, our entire costs were eighty-two thousand dollars."

One of the facility's principal attractions was its Scully twelve-track tape machine, marketed to studios as a considerable upgrade over four- and eight-track recording. *Magical Mystery Tour*, the Beatles' most recent release, had been recorded on only four tracks — as had all of Hendrix's previous sessions at Olympic Studios. These new tape machines were extremely rare — so much so that when the Record Plant opened its doors, it owned one of only two units in circulation.

In addition to the technical advantages, Kellgren wanted to upgrade the creative atmosphere within the recording studio. Previously, artists contracted to such labels as Columbia were obliged to record at facilities owned and staffed by their labels. Unlike the producer, the engineering staff was strictly governed by union rules and regulations. Kellgren was sympathetic toward rock n' roll and more tolerant of its relaxed rules and open experimentation. He insisted on making subtle changes that would make his clients feel more comfortable. Chris Stone explains: "When we got into the business, recording studios were like hospitals — fluorescent lights, hardwood floors, and white walls. Kellgren turned the recording studio into a living room. The biggest compliment a client could pay us would be to look around and say, 'Wow! I'd like to live here.'"

Kellgren's growing reputation as an engineer, coupled with the respect Tom Wilson enjoyed throughout the industry, helped to soothe any concerns artists and A&R representatives might have voiced about working in a new, independent facility. The Record Plant took matters a step further by hiring engineer Eddie Kramer away from Olympic Studios in London. "We brought Eddie over because he was the star of Olympic," explains Stone. "Tom Wilson told us about him, and we hired him because we figured that's what we really needed." "Having an English engineer was a bit of a coup for them," says Kramer. "The major factor in bringing me over was my relationship with Jimi and the role I played in creating his sound. I had also worked with Traffic and the Rolling Stones, and they wanted to insure that those clients came to the Record Plant and stayed there." Luring the Experience there as clients firmly established the Record Plant as the leading independent recording studio for rock n' roll in Manhattan, if not the entire U.S.

Its plan in place, the Record Plant opened for business on Wednesday, March 13, 1968. Because of delays resulting from his immigration status, Kramer did not join the staff until April 17. The studio's first major clients were the Jimi Hendrix Experience, whose lengthy stint provided a tremendous assist to the facility's reputation. As a result, the fledgling Record Plant, which billed out at eighty-five dollars per hour, was booked solid for its first three months in operation. Kellgren's and Stone's gamble had become a phenomenal success story. "We had a very profitable business," admits Stone. "Look at the ratios. We opened for under one hundred thousand dollars and charged eighty-five dollars an hour. Today, it costs you almost two million to open and you charge one hundred seventy-five an hour, or two thousand dollars a day for a lockout rate. It doesn't compute anymore, but it certainly did in those days."

■

Thursday, April 18, 1968
New York, Record Plant. Producer: Chas Chandler. Engineer: Gary Kellgren.

This day's session at the new studio resulted in basic tracks for "Long Hot Summer Night," another of Hendrix's songs whose development traced back to the October 1967 sessions for *Axis: Bold as Love*.

Organist Al Kooper later overdubbed piano on the track. As a gift for his contribution, Hendrix gave Kooper one of his Stratocasters. "Jimi and I shared the same music publishers," remembers Kooper. "We had also jammed at the Generation Club together. At the session for 'Long Hot Summer Night,' I played piano rather than organ. Jimi saw me fooling around with one of his Stratocasters and he offered the guitar to me as a gift. I refused, but he later had the guitar shipped to my home."

■

Smash Hits
Friday, April 19, 1968. Track Records 613 004. U.K. album release. Producer: Chas Chandler. Engineer: Eddie Kramer, Dave Siddle. Second engineers: George Chkiantz, Andy Johns.
Purple Haze/Fire/The Wind Cries Mary/Can You See Me/51st Anniversary/Hey Joe/Stone Free/The Stars That Play with Laughing Sam's Dice/Manic Depression/Highway Chile/The Burning of the Midnight Lamp/Foxey Lady

To satisfy those fans who preferred albums to singles, Track compiled this extremely popular release, blending the group's first four singles with such *Are You Experienced?* favorites as "Fire" and "Manic Depression." *Smash Hits* enjoyed strong and steady sales, peaking at number 4 during a healthy twenty-five-week stay on the album chart.

Gary Kellgren, Record Plant impresario, pictured here in 1973. Soon after *Electric Ladyland* was completed in August 1968, Kellgren announced plans to open another Record Plant in Los Angeles.

(Herbert Worthington)

■
Saturday, April 20, 1968
New York, Record Plant. Producer: Chas Chandler. Engineers: Gary Kellgren, Eddie Kramer.

"Lilacs for Captain Curry's Coffin," also known as "Little Miss Strange Test Session," actually yielded the basic tracks for Redding's new song.

■
Sunday, April 21, 1968
New York, Record Plant. Producer: Chas Chandler. Engineer: Eddie Kramer.

More work completed on the April 20 "Little Miss Strange Test Session" master, now known as "Little Miss Strange."

Record Plant, April 18, 1968. Recording "Long Hot Summer Night." *Left to right:* publicist Michael Goldstein, Chas Chandler (head turned), and engineer Gary Kellgren. (Eddie Kramer)

■

Monday, April 22, 1968

New York, Record Plant. 7:00 P.M. to 5:30 A.M. Producer: Chas Chandler. Engineer: Eddie Kramer. Second engineer: Steve (surname unknown).

Five takes were made of the first section of Hendrix's extended sound painting "1983 (A Merman I Should Turn to Be)." Overdubs and rough mixes were also prepared for "Three Little Bears" and "Gypsy Eyes."

■

Wednesday, April 24, 1968

New York, Record Plant. Producer: Chas Chandler. Engineer: Eddie Kramer.

The complicated rhythm pattern of "Gypsy Eyes" required a great many takes, fraying nerves and testing Chandler's patience, as little progress was made.

■

Monday, April 29, 1968

New York, Record Plant. 5:15 P.M. to 7:30 P.M. Producer: Chas Chandler. Engineer: Eddie Kramer.

With only Hendrix and Mitchell present, forty-one takes of "Gypsy Eyes" were recorded, though none was identified as a master. "I remember trying to get as big a bass drum sound as possible," says Kramer.

At a separate session later that evening, Gary Kellgren, working with Redding, prepared a rough mix of "Little Miss Strange."

Tensions deepened between Hendrix and Chandler as Jimi continued to openly challenge Chas's decisions. The problems were compounded by the hordes of uninvited guests and hangers-on, whose presence served only to distract Jimi from his task. Chandler was concerned with Jimi's drug use, which had gradually begun to erode the honest, direct communication the two men

had previously shared. "It was slow going from the moment we started at the Record Plant," Chandler remembers. "I was sitting there listening to him play the same song over and over again, thinking to myself. What is going on? Jimi had wanted this to be a double album, and I distinctly recall being glad that I had done so much at Olympic, because at this pace, the album would never be finished."

■

Wednesday, May 1, 1968

New York, Record Plant. Producer: Chas Chandler. Engineer: Eddie Kramer.

Basic tracks for "House Burning Down" were recorded. "Gypsy Eyes" was revisited, with take 5 marked complete. The group also revived "Tax Free," recording two takes with Jimi playing guitar through a Leslie speaker. Take 2 was complete and marked "use."

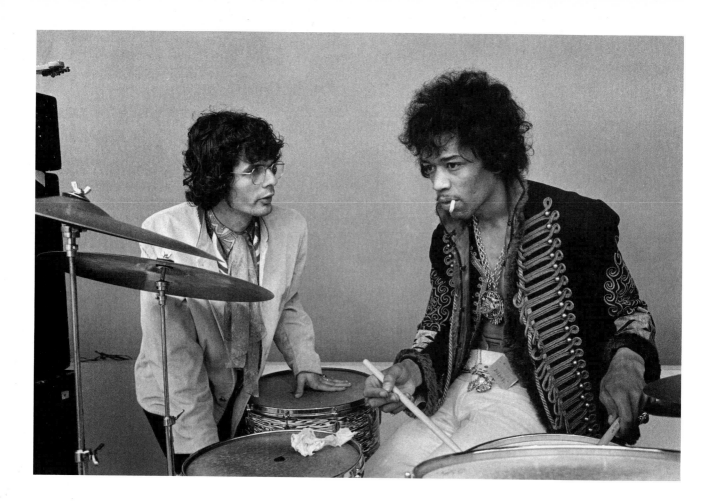

With Al Kooper.

(Jim Marshall)

Jimi pulls out the stops onstage at Singer Bowl, Queens, N.Y., August 23, 1968.

(Joe Sia)

■

Thursday, May 2, 1968

New York, Record Plant. Engineer: Eddie Kramer.

The group focused its attention on "Three Little Bears." During the cutting of the basic track, the Experience never stopped playing. "Three Little Bears" had by now evolved into a free-form jam session. Hendrix soon settled into the rhythm pattern that has become known as "South Saturn Delta." While no structured attempt at recording the song was made, the jam session boasted several noteworthy moments, especially a beautiful passage of slow, melancholy notes performed by Hendrix. At this time, Jimi titled the jam "Cherokee Mist."

During this session, a confrontation between Redding and Hendrix flared, causing Noel to unleash some of his pent-up frustration. "I took it out on Jimi, letting him know what I thought of the scene he was building around himself," said Redding in his autobiography, *Are You Experienced?* "There were tons of people in the studio — you couldn't even move. It was a party, not a session. He just said, 'Relax, man . . .' I'd been relaxing for months, so I relaxed my way right out of the place, not caring if I ever saw him again."

Redding's blowout with Hendrix soon blew over, but it apparently excluded him from a separate session staged early the following morning. After enjoying a long evening at the Scene Club, just around the corner from the Studio, Hendrix, Mitchell, Kramer, Steve Winwood, Jack Casady, and a host of friends traveled back to the Record Plant to jam. Beginning at

7:30 A.M., Kramer frantically set up microphones and made various sound and level adjustments, while Hendrix discussed "Voodoo Chile" with Mitchell, Winwood, and bassist Jack Casady from the Jefferson Airplane. Guitarist Larry Coryell was also among the invited guests, but he declined Hendrix's invitation to contribute. "Jimi asked me to play," remembers Coryell, "but for the first time in my life, I said, 'No. There is nothing I can add to this.' "

Three takes were recorded, although the first take served primarily as an introductory rehearsal. Kramer was ready by the time the musicians began a second take. That rendition was not completed, but the third take provided the master. It was this majestic performance that became one of the centerpieces of the magnificent *Electric Ladyland* album.

The task of capturing the dramatic session on tape fell to Kramer, who organized his strategy as quickly as possible. "The reason that sound was so open was that Jimi was in the room live, playing guitar at the same time his vocal microphone — one of my favorite Beyer M160s — was open. The bass tone wasn't exactly the best it could have been, but it doesn't really detract, because the vibe was so strong. Jimi was playing through a Fender Bassman top, and his amp sound was very warm. The track had such great atmosphere and tremendous dynamics, it went from nothing to full-blast. I loved the effect that Winwood created. At one point he created a very English, hornpipe-like dance which was very Traffic-like and just terrific. There was so much excitement when we were cutting that track, I remember being on the edge of my seat hoping that it was all going to work. We had been over at the Scene all night when Jimi said, 'Hey man, let's go over to the studio and do

Chas Chandler shares a private moment with Jimi.
(SKR/London Features)

this.' The idea was to make it sound as if it was a live gig. Even though there were some people watching in the studio, the applause was added as an overdub, so that the track would have a party feel. The tape delay effects were done by Jimi and I in the mix. All of the various background vocals and comments were tracked two or three times, as you can hear Jimi's voice coming from both sides."

While Hendrix wanted to feature the ambient crowd noise as part of the song's atmosphere, the noise level generated by those who had observed the session wasn't sufficient. To correct this, Hendrix improvised and overdubbed crowd sounds from 9:00 A.M. to 9:45 A.M.

In addition to "Voodoo Chile," a strange hybrid of the three takes recorded here was later included as part of 1994's *Jimi Hendrix: Blues*. That track, entitled "Voodoo Chile Blues," is actually a composite track, digitally assembled in 1993 by engineer Mark Linett. Linett fused portions of takes 1 and 2 and coupled them with a small

Eddie Kramer makes a point during a mixing session for *Electric Ladyland,* May 1968.
(Linda McCartney/Star File)

section of the previously released take 3 to create this new master.

■

Friday, May 3, 1968
New York, Record Plant. Producer: Chas Chandler. Engineer: Eddie Kramer.

Experience publicist Michael Goldstein had successfully arranged for ABC-TV to produce a short news feature based primarily on the Experience's triumphant success in America. Filming began on this day, with 16mm cameras capturing the recording of "Voodoo Child (Slight Return)," of one of Hendrix's signature songs. The cam-

eras, recalls Kramer, filmed the Experience recording and mixing the track. In addition, ABC filmed interviews with Kramer, Chandler, and Michael Jeffery. As the group worked in the studio, Nancy Reiner, Jeffery's girlfriend, made sketches of Jimi recording.

"We learned that song in the studio," Redding recalls. "They had the cameras rolling on us as we played it." "We did that about three times, because they wanted to film us in the studio," Jimi later explained. " 'Make it look like you're recording, boys' — one of those scenes, you know? So 'OK, let's play this in E, now a-one and a-two and a-three,' and we went into 'Voodoo Child (Slight Return).' "

It is not known whether ABC ever used any of the footage they shot this day. All the camera originals were stolen from ABC's archives sometime after Jimi's death. This included footage of the group performing at the Fillmore East (May 10) and the Miami Pop Festival (May 18).

■

Saturday, May 4, 1968
New York, Record Plant. 4:30 A.M. Engineers: Gary Kellgren, Eddie Kramer.

One complete take of Noel's "Little, Little Girl" was recorded, featuring harmonica and twelve-string guitar. Hendrix did not take any part in the recording. A rough mix of "Little, Little Girl" was also prepared. Redding enjoyed what he described as a "fantastic jam" with guitarist Larry Coryell.

Jimi completed work on his own as well, preparing rough mixes with Kramer of both "Voodoo Child (Slight Return)" and "House Burning Down."

■

Sunday, May 5, 1968
New York, Record Plant. Engineer: Eddie Kramer.

A rough mix of "House Burning Down" was prepared, but it was later marked "Don't Use" and discarded.

Overdubs, including Jimi's lead guitar part and a final mix of Noel's "Little Miss Strange," were completed, insuring the bassist a spot on the projected double album. "Jimi had a lot of fun putting the lead guitar on," recalls Kramer. "It was a DI [direct injection] with a wah-wah pedal, recorded on top of a ton of acoustic guitars Noel had already put on."

While the move from four-track recording at Olympic to twelve-track at the Record Plant seemed like a significant upgrade, the Record Plant's balky Scully twelve-track tape machine frustrated Kramer on more than one occasion and made the task of overdubbing more complicated. "That Scully twelve-track was a nonstandard machine and a technical nightmare," says Kramer. "Especially for overdubbing. The punch-

ins were full of clicks, bangs, and pops, and they generally sounded like shit."

■

Wednesday, May 8, 1968
New York, Record Plant. 12:00 midnight. Engineer: Eddie Kramer. Second engineer: Steve (surname unknown).

Rough mixes of "Voodoo Chile," "Three Little Bears," and "Long Hot Summer Night" were completed.

Hendrix also returned to "1983 (A Merman I Should Turn to Be)." The master reel from April 22 was pulled out, and new recordings made this evening were added as edit sections to create a single, unified master.

At a separate session, Redding, working with engineer Gary Kellgren, completed work on "How Can I Live," another solo effort drawn from his growing sack of new material.

Fed up with Hendrix's lack of compliance, Chandler elected to step down as the album's producer. "Looking back, I walked out very quickly at the Record Plant," admits Chandler. "I would go in there and wait for Jimi and he would show up with eight or nine hangers-on. When he finally did begin recording, Jimi would be playing for the benefit of his guests, not the machines." A further source of frustration for Chandler was Hendrix's inability to judge his own performances or allow Chandler to be the final arbiter, as he had done previously. "We'd be going over a number again and again and I would say over the talkback, 'That was it, we got it.' He would say, 'No, no, no' and would record another and another and another. Finally, I just threw my hands up and left."

The breakdown can be traced in part, Chandler reasons, to the schedule he and the Experience had maintained over the past eighteen months. "Both

the group and I were exhausted. I had spent three years with the Animals, and the next day I was working with Hendrix. I had put in as much time on the job as Hendrix, Mitchell, and Redding — plus my time with the Animals. The last thing I wanted to be doing was fighting with Jimi in the studio and then Jeffery in the office. I just walked away.

While the ramifications would not be felt for some time, Chandler's departure would be damaging. "Chandler had been there from the beginning," says Redding. "He was a guy you could talk to. He kept Hendrix in control — both in and out of the studio. Jeffery didn't care about Mitchell or I. To him, Jimi was *the* star. We couldn't have done it without Jimi, but Jimi couldn't have done it without us. We were working just as hard as he was. Chas understood that."

■

Friday, May 17, 1968
New York, Record Plant.

An overdub and mixdown session dedicated to "Gypsy Eyes" was completed.

■

Monday, June 10, 1968
New York, Record Plant. 4:00 P.M. to 4:30 A.M. Engineer: Eddie Kramer.

'Hendrix & Friends,' according to the tape box, banded together to record "Rainy Day, Dream Away." Joining Jimi were drummer Buddy Miles, Mike Finnigan on organ, percussionist Larry Faucette, and Freddy Smith on saxophone. "Tom Wilson had discovered and produced my little R&B band," explained Mike Finnigan. "He introduced us to Hendrix, and Jimi asked me, Larry

Faucette, and Freddie Smith to jam on this tune he had in mind. In the early 1960s, Jimmy Smith had made these great, obscure organ quintet albums, which featured organ, congas, guitar, tenor saxophone, and drums. Before we started the session, Hendrix reminded me of this and joked, 'We're going to do a slow shuffle in D. You be Jimmy Smith and I'll be Kenny Burrell.' Having heard Jimi's first two albums, I thought he'd be using stacks and stacks of amplifiers and electronic toys to get his sound," admits Finnigan. "To get

the right guitar tone for 'Rainy Day, Dream Away'/ 'Still Raining, Still Dreaming,' he was using this small, blond, thirty-watt Fender Showman amplifier. We couldn't believe it." These two tracks were recorded as one, then split by Hendrix and Kramer during a June 28 final mixing session.

In addition to "Rainy Day, Dream Away," some spirited jam sessions, described on the tape box as "Blow," were also recorded. Overdubs and mixes were also prepared for "Voodoo Chile," "House Burning Down," and "1983 (A

Jimi and Buddy Miles recording "Rainy Day, Dream Away," June 10, 1968.

(Eddie Kramer)

Merman I Should Turn to Be)."

Velvert Turner, a young black guitarist who was also present, and to whom Jimi served as a sort of mentor, remembers Jimi explaining his inspiration for "House Burning Down." "Jimi told me how much the riots in Los Angeles had affected him, and that this song had been inspired by what he felt there."

■
Tuesday, June 11, 1968
New York, Record Plant.

A session whose results are not known. No multitrack masters or tape copies are known to exist. Apart from the title "Inside Out" on the master list of tape boxes, no other documentation is available.

■
Monday, June 17, 1968
New York, Record Plant. Engineer: Eddie Kramer. Overdubs, 12:30 A.M. to 3:15 A.M. Remix, 3:15 A.M. to 10:30 A.M.

A long evening session dedicated to various overdubs and experiments for "Gypsy Eyes."

■
Friday, June 28, 1968
New York, Record Plant. Engineer: Eddie Kramer.

Final mixing completed for "Rainy Day, Dream Away." The idea to create two separate songs — "Rainy Day, Dream Away" and "Still Raining, Still Dreaming" — from this one recording stems from this mixing session. On the tape box Kramer noted, "2nd 1/2 edited out onto Side 2."

Jimi's handwritten notes to "1983 (A Merman I Should Turn to Be)."
(James A. Hendrix)

Virginia, 1968.
(Barry Gruber Archives)

■

Saturday, June 29, 1968

**New York, Record Plant. 8:00 P.M. to
11:00 P.M. Engineer: Eddie Kramer.**

Mixing session for "At Last . . . The Beginning," later known as "The Gods
Made Love." Hendrix would later describe this aural collage as "a ninety-
second sound painting of the heavens."

Eddie Kramer remembers that prior
to this mixing session, Jimi had already
worked out many of the sound effects
in advance. These thoughts were combined with the results of some inspired,
spontaneous creations designed specifically to replicate the sound of a
spacecraft landing. Kramer details how
the track came together. " 'And the
Gods Made Love' had loads of tape delay," he explains. "Jimi's voice was
slowed way below three and three-
quarters i.p.s. using a VFO, then sped
up again. We had tape loops running
and echo tape feeding back on itself. I
was panning one set with my right
hand, because there was a limit to how
much you could grab with one hand. I
rode the main levels on the console,
controlling the main feeds with my left
hand. Jimi would be using two hands to
pan other stuff. It was definitely a four-
handed mix that we edited together. In
the beginning, you can hear the tape
bias whistle changing in the background because it's down so low. Jimi's
voice comes in backwards, and Mitch's
tom-toms were slowed down ridicu-
lously. The track is phased, and we put
a lot of Mitch's cymbals in backwards
for the effect. The end was the flying
saucer effect which Jimi wanted."

■

Monday, July 1, 1968

New York, Record Plant.

Unfortunately, this recording of a lively
jam session with Graham Bond was
marred by technical difficulties. The
poor quality of the recording has rendered it useless.

■

Sunday, July 7, 1968

New York, Record Plant. 6:45 P.M. to 7:50 P.M.

A short session experimenting with the
crossfades that would eventually link
the first three songs of *Electric
Ladyland*'s first side.

■

Wednesday, July 24, 1968

New York, Record Plant.

A rough mix of "Gypsy Eyes" was prepared.

■

Friday, July 26, 1968

New York, Record Plant.

A rough mix of "House Burning Down"
was completed.

■

Monday, July 29, 1968

**New York, Record Plant. Engineer: Gary
Kellgren.**

A mix of "Long Hot Summer Night"
was completed.

■

Monday, August 12, 1968

**New York, Record Plant. Engineer: Gary
Kellgren.**

A fascinating, sparse demo of "Room
Full of Mirrors," with Hendrix's live vocal and guitar backed only by a harmonica, most likely performed by Paul
Caruso. With Hendrix sounding somewhat tired, three soulful takes were
attempted. The first two provide tantalizing sketches but fall incomplete. The
third was extremely good, but it too, unfortunately, came apart without a definitive conclusion. These three takes
are all of what was recorded this
evening.

■

Friday, August 23, 1968

**New York, Record Plant. Rough mix,
2:00 A.M. to 7:00 A.M. Overdubs, 7:30 A.M. to
8:00 A.M. Engineer: Eddie Kramer.**

Another track was now finished, as
Hendrix and Kramer labored with great
care to complete "House Burning
Down," one of *Electric Ladyland*'s strongest efforts. This lengthy, late-night session included a variety of mixes and
overdubs before Hendrix settled on a
final mix.

Having devoted hundreds of hours
to the making of *Electric Ladyland*, Jimi
was sensitive to suggestions that songs
such as "1983 (A Merman I Should
Turn to Be)" and "House Burning
Down" overrelied on gadgets or clever
studio wizardry. "On some records, you
hear all this clash and bang and
fanciness, but all we're doing is laying
down the guitar tracks," Hendrix stated.
"We [use] echo here and there, but
we're not adding false electronic things.
We use the same things everyone else
would, but we use it with imagination

and common sense. With 'House Burning Down,' we made the guitar sound like it was on fire. It's constantly changing dimensions, and up on top of that the lead guitar is cutting through everything."

■
Tuesday, August 27, 1968
New York, Record Plant. Rough mix, 7:00 P.M. to 12:00 midnight. Twelve-track overdub, 12:00 midnight to 1:00 A.M. Rough mix, 1:00 A.M. to 3:00 A.M. Recording, 4:00 A.M. to 8:00 A.M. Engineers: Gary Kellgren, Eddie Kramer.

Last minute work on the 'flange version' of "Gypsy Eyes." Flanging sound was a technique in which an engineer manually varied tape speeds during a recording by applying and releasing slight pressure to the reel flange with his thumb. This technique was used extensively by both Kellgren and Kramer. Kellgren flanged a guitar overdub from Jimi, creating a watery texture and tone that closed out the song.

With Hendrix and Kramer busy preparing the master copy of *Electric Ladyland*, Kellgren recorded "How Can I Live," a new Redding original, starting at 4:00 A.M. Twelve takes were attempted, with numbers 1, 3, 8, 9, 11, and 12 complete. Track 12, which featured Mitch Mitchell on drums, Redding on twelve-string guitar, and an unnamed harmonica player (possibly Paul Caruso), was considered a master, but not for *Electric Ladyland*. This track would be set aside for the debut album of Fat Mattress, Noel's solo outfit.

Needing one more song to complete the double album, the Experience, working on short notice, rallied to record an interpretation of Earl King's "Come On (Part 1)." Fourteen takes, in all, were attempted, with the last selected as the basic track. "That was

Rehearsing at the Hollywood Bowl, September 14, 1968.

(Chuck Boyd/Flower Children Ltd.)

done to fill out the album," admits Redding. "I was amazed, because it was just a jam in E. It was boring for the bass player. We just played it live, and they took it, thank you. We wouldn't have had a situation like that with Chandler, would we?"

At the end of this marathon session, copies of the album's sequenced, final masters were struck from the originals for Warner Bros. Records. Much to the relief of all parties involved, *Electric Ladyland* was now complete.

■
"All Along the Watchtower" / "The Burning of the Midnight Lamp"
Reprise 0767. U.S. single release. Wednesday, September 4, 1968.

Hendrix's compelling rendition of this Bob Dylan composition provided the Experience with the crossover single both Jeffery and Chandler, as well as Reprise, had long been hoping for in the U.S. market. "All Along the Watchtower" broke quickly from the box, entering the *Billboard* chart on September 21, 1968, at 66 and climbing steadily to number 20. Much to the delight of the Experience's record company, the success of "All Along the Watchtower" was so dramatic that the single ultimately shifted more units than the combined sales of the group's four previous Reprise singles.

Adjusting his wah-wah pedal between takes at the Record Plant, 1968.

(Eddie Kramer)

■
Electric Ladyland
Reprise 2RS 6307. U.S. album release. Wednesday, October 16, 1968. Producer: Jimi Hendrix. Additional production: Chas Chandler. Engineers: Gary Kellgren, Eddie Kramer. Second engineers: Tony Bongiovi, George Chkiantz, Andy Johns.
And the Gods Made Love/Have You Ever Been (to Electric Ladyland)/Crosstown Traffic/Voodoo Chile/Little Miss Strange/Long Hot Summer Night/Come On (Part 1)/Gypsy Eyes/The Burning of the Midnight Lamp/Rainy Day, Dream Away/1983 (A Merman I Should Turn to Be)/Moon, Turn the Tides . . . Gently, Gently Away/Still Raining, Still Dreaming/House Burning Down/All Along the Watchtower/Voodoo Child (Slight Return)

The Vanilla Fudge prepares to throw Mitch

into the pool at the Hollywood Bowl,

September 14, 1968.

(Chuck Boyd/Flower Children Ltd.)

Completed at a cost of roughly $70,000, *Electric Ladyland* had a significant chart impact, supplying the group with its first number-one disc.

Despite the album's popularity, Hendrix was disappointed with Reprise's decision to change its artwork, compromising his detailed, written instructions apparently without notification. Moreover, Jimi revealed that the album's final mix, the result of countless hours of intense preparation, had been adversely altered during the mastering and disc-cutting process completed by Warner Bros. "We were recording when we were touring, and it's very hard to concentrate on both," Hendrix complained. "Some of the mix came out muddy, with too much bass. We mixed it and produced it, but when it came time for them to press it, quite naturally they screwed it up, because they didn't know what we wanted. There is 3-D sound being used on there that you can't even appreciate because they didn't know how to cut it properly. They thought it was out of phase."

While both Gary Kellgren and Eddie Kramer were acknowledged on the album's inside jacket for their engineering contributions, the name of one prominent contributor — Chas Chandler — was conspicuously absent. Despite having produced a number of tracks on the double album, including "Crosstown Traffic," "Burning of the Midnight Lamp," and "All Along the Watchtower," Chandler received no credit for his role in the album's production. "When the album came out and I saw that it was 'produced and directed by Jimi Hendrix,' I was pissed off," admits Chandler. "I was especially surprised to see how much of what I had done was on there, because I know how much more time they spent at the Record Plant after I had walked off the project. In all truth, I had expected to

see a much different album. While I was pissed that I had received no credit, I put that down to being a maneuver by Michael Jeffery. I saw it as being his way of trying to wipe my name from the history book and nothing more. Quite honestly, I just put the whole thing behind me and moved on."

In the aftermath of its Herculean effort to finish *Electric Ladyland*, the Experience was left exhausted. The incredible pace, coupled with their staggering drug use, afforded them — and Hendrix in particular — virtually no opportunity for creative rejuvenation. Their seven-week U.S. tour came to a temporary close following the September 15 performance in Sacramento. The final two weeks of September were set aside for a much-needed vacation in Los Angeles.

■
October 1968
Los Angeles, TTG Studios.

Having accepted Michael Jeffery's invitation to produce Eire Apparent's debut disc for Buddah Records nearly six months before, Hendrix struggled to apportion adequate time for the project. Eire Apparent had been featured as an opening act for most of the Experience's concerts since mid-August, which afforded Hendrix some opportunity to formulate his strategy for the album. While his many commitments would not allow him to supervise the group's songs and arrangements as Chas Chandler had for his own debut disc, Hendrix was able to review Eire Apparent's live appearances and fill out the balance in the studio.

With the Experience now temporarily based in Los Angeles, the decision was made to resume recording at Hollywood's TTG Studios. Located at

1441 N. McCadden Street in Hollywood, TTG was owned and operated by engineer Ami Hadami, a tough, enigmatic veteran of the Israeli military. Opened in 1965 and named for one of Hadami's military regiments, TTG enjoyed a strong following in the burgeoning Los Angeles market, competing with Bill Putnam's Western United Studios and Wally Heider's renowned Heider Recording. For a mere fifty-five dollars an hour, clients could make use of the studio's recently installed Ampex sixteen-track tape machine, one of the first units to be placed in service in Southern California.

As the Animals had been clients of the studio, both Chas Chandler and Michael Jeffery had befriended Hadami. In October 1968, following the Experience's three-night stand at San Francisco's Winterland Ballroom (which celebrated the group's two-year anniversary), TTG's Studio B was block-booked to accommodate new recordings by both the Experience and Eire Apparent.

While *Sunrise* — as Eire Apparent's debut album would eventually be titled — would not be completed at TTG, Hendrix and the band made significant progress there. In addition to his role as producer, Hendrix stepped out from behind the console to lend guitar to a number of the group's original compositions, including "Captive in the Sun," "Morning Glory," "The Clown," "Let Me Stay," "Mr. Guy Fawkes," "Magic Carpet," "Someone Is Sure to (Want You)," and "Yes I Need Someone." Following the group's last documented session at the studio (October 31, 1968), all of the session tapes were shipped to the Record Plant, where work on the album would continue.

The encouraging advances made by Eire Apparent were not achieved with-

Hollywood Bowl, September 14, 1968. Fans overrun security and dive into the pool separating the band from the audience. (Chuck Boyd/Flower Children Ltd.)

out incident. Hendrix clashed with TTG staff engineer Jack Hunt, who had been assigned by Hadami to engineer the sessions. The problem, explains fellow TTG engineer Angel Balestier, was centered in Hunt's rigid adherence to structured sessions and standard engineering procedures. "Jack was an excellent engineer, but he ran sessions strictly by the numbers," says Balestier.

"If a session was booked until eight P.M., then at eight P.M. you were finished. That wasn't something Jimi was looking for. In those days, you were just waking up at eight!"

Another contentious issue had its roots in Hendrix's and Hunt's inability to compromise on recording techniques. "Eire Apparent was just too sterile," Balestier recalls. "Jimi was

the growing tension between Hendrix and Jack Hunt ultimately resulted in a confrontation. "I had just finished recording the Everly Brothers upstairs in Studio A," recalls Balestier. "Eire Apparent was recording in Studio B, and I walked into the control room to grab a long T-plug cord I needed for my next session. Hendrix was just sitting in the [producer's] chair staring up at the ceiling. When he saw me, he said, 'You're going to do my next album, aren't you?' That created a complete scene, because Jack was floored that Jimi hadn't asked him to do it — especially as he had been doing the Eire Apparent sessions. I had never met Jimi prior to that point, but I had seen him perform at Monterey and owned his albums. I told him, 'Sure, I'd love to.' I hadn't gone into the control room to solicit the work — I had only wanted to borrow that particular cable. I explained this to Jack and Ami later, but the issue was never fully resolved. Jack took it pretty hard. He never came in to any of the Hendrix sessions and for years remained pissed off at me."

Though Hendrix's primary responsibility at TTG had been on the Eire Apparent project, the Experience made an earnest effort to record tracks for their fourth studio album. With *Electric Ladyland* completed only six weeks before, any notion of formal preproduction for these sessions was immediately forsaken. Armed with only a handful of old songs and new ideas, the Experience struggled to focus their energies on the task at hand. Jamming, once Hendrix's principal creative respite, increasingly formed his entire approach to composing and recording new material.

While the Experience was still capable of channeling their tremendous talent in unison, the relationship between Hendrix and Redding had further deteriorated. Their return to the

studio, coming so quickly after the difficult *Electric Ladyland* sessions, did little to resolve the two men's differences toward recording. At TTG, Redding's frustration with what he perceived as Hendrix's inability to judge his own performances left him rankled. Redding's own diary notations detail his mounting dismay: "20 October. Recording (nothing done). 24 October. Recording (nothing done). 25 October. Recording (nothing done, again)."

Once a private concern known only to those closest to the group, the growing divide between Hendrix and Redding was immediately apparent to those who worked with the group during its stint at TTG. "The distance between Jimi and Noel was *very* apparent," recalls Angel Balestier. "It was sad. You could see it, it was so obvious. They kept two different crowds. They both would say hello to each other but would keep to their own corners. When people would come for Jimi, Noel would withdraw. The sessions were peaceful, however. I never witnessed any verbal or physical confrontations, but the vibe was always there. Once they got to playing, though, it still worked."

Despite Hendrix's clashes with Jack Hunt during the Eire Apparent sessions, the guitarist placed no restrictions on Balestier, asking only that the tape machine never stop recording. "Jimi told me that once we started recording, I was never to stop the tape or let the tape run out," Balestier explains. "As a result, we recorded every tune as it evolved, changing tape only when people stopped to breathe." Also unique to both Balestier and the staff at TTG was the Experience's penchant for performing at maximum volume. "When the Experience first began rehearsing, Ami Hadami came downstairs and wanted the monitors turned down, because the sound was coming right up

looking to give their sound the same edge he gave his own. Jack, though, was very structured in the studio. Each instrument was to be baffled and recorded on separate tracks. He also did not want to put that much recording level on the tape because of the possibility of distortion — but that was just the effect Jimi was looking for."

With their differences unresolved,

Hendrix's lens snares Janis Joplin backstage at Winterland, 1968.

(Jim Marshall)

through the studio upstairs. I pointed out through the control room window to the studio and said, 'Ami, that's not the monitors, that's the *band*.' He couldn't believe it."

While a cauldron of problems simmered beneath the surface, the popularity and standing of Hendrix and the Experience were unprecedented. The Experience's sessions at TTG confirmed their celebrity status in Hollywood, as a bevy of friends, invited guests, and groupies made their way to

the studio. Most were content simply to observe, while others sought a much-coveted invitation to play. In either instance, Hendrix, says Balestier, was always obliging. Though the studio had tried to maintain a low profile, the excitement created by the Experience's sessions was nearly impossible to contain. "The visitors that would come by were incredible," Balestier remembers. "With Hendrix, if someone walked into the room, it wasn't like, 'Get him out of here!' Jimi would say, 'Come on in,' or

Lost in the music, Noel Redding records at
TTG Studios, October 1968.

(Michael Ochs Archives)

he'd ask us to make room for people. He was extremely polite. He never said no to anybody and never threw anybody out."

With such a policy in effect, a steady stream of well-wishers descended upon the studio. "A lot of the guys from the Buffalo Springfield would come by, especially Dewey Martin and Stephen Stills," Balestier recalls. On one such occasion, Balestier recorded a spirited acoustic jam whose highlight was a furious guitar battle between Hendrix and Stills. "That was a great jam," states Balestier. "Those guys were playing their asses off." Sadly, tapes of this session have been either lost or stolen, as they are not to be found in the Hendrix tape library.

In addition to Buffalo Springfield, Buddy Miles was a frequent guest, joining a number of sessions, as did organist Lee Michaels. "Lee Michaels had been recording upstairs in Studio A when he found out Hendrix was going to be working downstairs," remembers Balestier. "I admitted that he was, but I told him that I was supposed to keep it quiet. Lee laughed and said he was going to come down anyway, so we moved his B-3 organ into Studio B."

In addition to jams with Stills, Michaels, and Buddy Miles, Mitch and Jimi jammed with bassist Carol Kaye. On another occasion Vic Briggs sat in with the Experience. Other notable guests who visited the group included Sonny Bono, Bill Cowsill of the Cowsills, Lou Reed, the Fraternity of Man, the Association, Jim Keltner, Jim Gordon, the Olympics, and even actor Tony Scotti, best known for his role in the film *Valley of the Dolls*.

A number of Jimi's old acquaintances from the chitlin' circuit also made welcome appearances, including Leon Heywood, Billy Preston, and Ike Turner. "Ike Turner came by, and, while

SESSIONS

Recording basic tracks at TTG, where the Experience's penchant for maximum volume often disrupted sessions upstairs in Studio A. (Michael Ochs Archives)

Balestier explains. "He said, 'I hear you have somebody I worked with downstairs.' Bumps came downstairs and walked into the control room behind Jimi with a plate of food and said, 'Hey Jimi, you want some chicken?' Jimi turned, and when he saw who it was, he started laughing. Bumps sat down and started telling old stories. Out of the blue, Jimi turned to me and said, 'I heard you had a spat with Little Richard.' I told him that *I* didn't have a problem with him, but Ami had wanted me to turn off the equipment because Richard owed the studio money. I went to shut the power off, but Bumps, who was producing, intervened. When I didn't do it, Ami did it himself, which sent Richard into a rage. He started screaming at Ami and told him that he was going to take off his sissy wig and whip his ass right there! By this point, Jimi and Bumps were laughing hysterically, as if they had lived through this one hundred times before. You could see that there was something between Jimi and Bumps. They were genuinely pleased to see each other."

While at the studio, Hendrix, in turn, took a sincere interest in some of Balestier's recent clients. "Ricky Nelson stopped by one of his sessions, and he and Jimi got on great. They talked about all kinds of music. On another night, Jimi asked to hear some of the Country and Western sessions I had done. I played him some recent things — Everly Brothers recordings I had engineered — and he thought it was real cool. Then he looked at me in a strange way and said, 'How does a Puerto Rican from Brooklyn learn how to do *that* stuff?' I laughed and told him that I was from way, way out in the West Indies, and he burst out laughing."

During Experience sessions at TTG, the atmosphere was electric. The

he didn't jam, Jimi was very pleased to see him," Balestier recalls. Another notable visitor was legendary Specialty Records producer Bumps Blackwell. "I ran into Bumps upstairs in the office,"

equally plentiful. "Somebody brought a hash cake to one session. We had Kool-Aid that was laced, marijuana cookies, and Thai cigarettes from Vietnam at others. You name it, it was there."

Fortunately, such behavior never prompted an official visit by officers from the nearby Wilcox police station. Jimi's guitar playing did, however, attract the attention of a beat cop making his neighborhood rounds. Balestier explains: "One night, I looked over and saw a cop looking in on the session through the studio door. In a panic, I got Tom Hidley, who was in Studio C, on the phone and told him there was a cop outside the door. He said that he would take a look. Tom escorted the cop into the control room, and he was digging it. He had heard Jimi playing while he was outside walking his beat. He was from the Wilcox Station, in full uniform, badge and all, bopping his head, really into it. I was freaked. I thought we were all going in!"

While a bootleg recording of Hendrix jamming with Cream's Jack Bruce, Buddy Miles, and Jim McCarty at TTG (probably October 16 or 17) has surfaced in recent years, the first documented session for which multitrack tapes remain was staged on Friday evening, October 18, 1968.

Recording at TTG Studios, October 1968.

(Chuck Boyd/Flower Children Ltd.)

■
Friday, October 18, 1968
Los Angeles, TTG Studios. Engineer: Angel Balestier. Second engineer: Mark Kauffman.

Similar in name only to the versions of "Izabella" recorded at the Hit Factory and the Record Plant in 1969, this instrumental effort sported an entirely different arrangement, reminiscent of "Midnight." Two initial takes marked "tests" were put down on tape before proper recording began. Seven new

smell of incense wafted throughout, and the group was fueled by a steady supply of food from Stan's Drive-In on Sunset Boulevard, whose burgers Jimi loved. Drugs, marvels Balestier, were

takes followed, with numbers 2, 3, and 7 complete. Of these, the seventh take was deemed best. Following a tape change, however, recording continued. A series of false starts and breakdowns ensued before takes 15, 16, and 18 each increasingly developed, were made. Take 18, listed as a master and timed at 4:32, was clearly the strongest effort thus far, but Hendrix remained unconvinced. The group listened to a playback of take 18 and returned to the studio for more recording. Following false starts on takes 19 and 20, take 21 was complete and warranted a playback. After closely comparing takes 18 and 21, it was decided that the latter was not as strong as the former. Take 18 was once again selected the master.

With "Izabella" complete, work began on "Messenger," another promising new original. Two takes were recorded on this reel, with the second listed as complete. The first was a medium-tempo instrumental effort whose stylings are faintly reminiscent of "Castles Made of Sand." This recording, however, seems more an exploratory jam than a structured attempt to capture a basic track. A second take of "Messenger" was completed, but its tempo and arrangement were entirely different. While this second take's spirited rendition was debuted here, Hendrix did occasionally invoke familiar passages from "Lover Man." Overdubs were also recorded, with Mitchell adding additional percussion elements and Jimi adding additional guitar. Despite this effort, "The Messenger," as Jimi announced the song to engineer Angel Balestier, was not finished at this time.

■
"All Along the Watchtower" / "Long Hot Summer Night"
Track Records 604 025. U.K. single release. Friday, October 18, 1968.

"All Along the Watchtower," the group's fifth U.K. single, enjoyed strong sales and, as a result, triumphantly returned the Experience to the top of the charts. The disc peaked at the number 5 position during its eleven-week run.

■
Sunday, October 20, 1968
Los Angeles, TTG Studios. Engineer: Angel Balestier. Second engineer: Mark Kauffman.

Work on "Messenger" resumed, with the Experience electing to discard all the takes recorded on October 18 and begin anew. Fifteen new attempts were put on tape. These takes reveal an intriguing new song for which Hendrix planned, but never recorded, lyrics. Of those fifteen, the first eight were incomplete. The ninth, however, showed promise and warranted a playback, but it was rejected. Take 12 was strong enough for the group to stop and listen to their efforts once more, but it was rejected, as was an incomplete take 13. Obvious progress could be heard on take 14, but it, too, was discarded after a playback. A robust take 15 yielded the master. Overdubs followed, with the highlight a unique piano part performed by Hendrix and recorded at 59 cycles per second, a slower speed, for effect.

■
Monday, October 21, 1968
Los Angeles, TTG Studios. Engineer: Angel Balestier. Second engineer: Mark Kauffman.

A notable session, which began with the Experience recording the raucous "Calling All the Devil's Children." What began as a tentative writing collaboration between Hendrix and Redding soon evolved into a boisterous studio party. Twenty-seven takes of the song's gritty, infectious basic track were recorded before the master was achieved. In the process, Hendrix was duly inspired to create a comedy track — or, as Redding described it, a parody of the legendary BBC *Goon Show* comedy program. What followed was, indeed, sheer lunacy, as the Experience, joined by roadie Eric Barrett and a gaggle of visitors, gathered around a microphone. Standing on a chair, Jimi led a hilarious impromptu comedy sketch, impersonating, among other characters, a Bible-thumping preacher. "Bold as *what?*" Jimi's "preacher" asked. Amid the screams and ongoing chatter of his "followers," human sirens announced that a "bust" was about to occur, which caused Noel to bellow, "Flush the toilet! Flush the toilet!" In all, "Calling All the Devil's Children" was a terrific slice of the group's twisted humor, similar in style to the Beatles' "You Know My Name (Look Up the Number)." While Redding may not have known of Hendrix's intentions for "Calling All the Devil's Children" — or, as he chose to title the work, "The Devil's Jam" — a request Hendrix made earlier that evening to Angel Balestier provided the first clue that the plan would be — at the very least — unusual. "Before we started to cut those voices, Jimi asked me if I could get thirteen chicks in the studio. I told him that I would make a few calls and see what I could do. Then

October 21, 1968. Flanked by Redding and Mitchell, Jimi records his lead vocal for "Calling All the Devil's Children."
(Michael Ochs Archives)

so many girls came down to the studio it was unreal. There were girls in the studio, in the vocal booth, and even outside the door to Studio B. When he started to put some guitar overdubs on, Jimi walked over to this beautiful girl and asked what her sign was. When she replied, 'Sagittarius,' Jimi said, 'Does that mean I can ball you?' It was incredible."

With "Calling All the Devil's Children" a prime example of the group's spontaneous creativity, Balestier quickly realized that normal session

procedures would not apply to the Experience. "During jams like this, I'd line up a pile of tape reels," recalls Balestier. "We only had one multitrack machine, so as soon as they would stop for conversation, I'd pull the reels off the machine and throw on two new ones without even rewinding the old ones. Terry Betts, one of my tape operators, was real fast at that. He and Bob Porter would each grab a reel and I would grab the middle of the tape and line it up through the guides on the machine. We'd slam it on, hit play/record, and go!

Jimi would ask from the studio, 'Did you get that on tape?' and I would say, 'I got every bit of it!' When he played a jam like that, or even just a song idea, Jimi got so charged up knowing that you had recorded the complete take for him. Knowing that he had his ideas down on tape was extremely important to him."

Little could have followed "Calling All the Devil's Children" save for some inspired jamming, which was precisely what took place next. Two separate jam sessions were recorded, including four takes of "Jam #1," with Lee Michaels on organ. Take 4, an up-tempo blues-rock effort, features several spirited moments before it begins to unravel shortly after the four-minute mark. The expanded group was then joined by an unnamed harmonica player for "Jam #2." One complete take was recorded, with Lee Michaels again the driving source.

Following a playback, the group recorded the spirited jam "Hear My Freedom Call Me," minus harmonica but with Michaels again at the organ. Buddy Miles joined the proceedings to offer additional percussion. Several exceptional moments were marbled throughout this lengthy jam, including a section with Hendrix's occasional lead vocal. Sadly, however, like most efforts of this sort, the jam ended without any definitive resolution.

This ensemble also recorded "Electric Church," a frenetic blues jam that boasted some superb, stinging lead guitar from Hendrix but little sustained structure. Miles can be heard playing a second set of drums, providing a unique double-drum tandem with Mitch Mitchell. Take 4, which immediately follows three short, incomplete takes of tune-ups and general instructions among the players, was highlighted as the master. This recording,

however, is not the "Electric Church — Red House" cited in *Hendrix: Setting the Record Straight* or other Hendrix-related efforts. The version mistakenly described there and included on *Jimi Hendrix: Blues* is actually a skillfully edited combination of the *introductions* that precede "Electric Church" and a version of "Red House" recorded on October 29. While Buddy Miles can certainly be heard on the master recordings of "Electric Church," he does not play any part in the October 29 session. Michaels, however, appears on both and is joined on the October 29 session by flautist Jim Horn, whose contributions were later mixed out of the recording used to create the "Electric Church — Red House" composite master.

■
Tuesday, October 22, 1968
Los Angeles, TTG Studios. Engineer: Angel Balestier. Second Engineer: Mark Kauffman.

The Experience made a determined effort over the course of this evening to perfect "Mr. Lost Soul," which had also been known as "Mr. Bad Luck."

Recording began with twelve takes of "Mr. Lost Soul" recorded on reel one. A spirited first take, timed at 2:53, was complete and worthy of a playback. While the results were encouraging, the master take was clearly not in hand. A series of false starts and incomplete takes followed, until a complete take 7, which warranted a playback. Still not satisfied, the group returned to the studio. Ensuing takes featured little change to the song's arrangement. Instead, Hendrix seemed intent on refining his rhythm guitar part. One interesting aspect of these developing takes is that portions of the chord structure would later be incorporated into

"Stepping Stone." Take 12, also timed at 2:53, was complete but lacked cohesion, and no playback was required to determine its fate. More recording ensued before the master take was achieved with take 17.

In addition to getting Hendrix's guitar sound on tape, another crucial task was capturing his lead vocal performance — a maneuver that required a particular degree of delicacy. "I tried a number of different techniques to make him feel more comfortable," explains Balestier. "I would hang a C12 microphone in the middle of the studio and let him hold onto his guitar. Occasionally, I would hear a little noise on tape from him holding the guitar, but that instrument was his lady. On other occasions, Jimi would sing in the *studio* and his guitar amp would be in the vocal booth. I'd stick his amp in there and feed him some of the basic track through the speakers out of phase, so he wouldn't have to wear headphones. What I would try would depend on Jimi's mood. Sometimes he would get so disgusted, he'd throw his guitar in a corner and walk out. Then he'd come back later and ask to try it again. He was very moody during vocals and wasn't comfortable having people around. If people were there, he'd never vent his frustration at them. Instead, he would smash his guitar on the floor and walk out. If nothing seemed to work, I would just leave him alone. I kept Studio C unlocked, and he would go in there and lock the door. When he came out, he might not want to record again, but I had given him my home number. I told Jimi to call me, no matter what time it was. I lived on Fountain, right by McCadden, and it was a short walk to the studio. There were times when he would call me at three A.M., saying, 'You know, I've got this thing I want to do.' I'd say, 'Sure, I'll be

over in a couple of minutes.' These sessions could take all night, a couple of hours, or just a half hour. I didn't mind at all."

Balestier prepared a rough mix immediately following the session. Take 17, retitled "Look Over Yonder," was remixed by Eddie Kramer, Mitch Mitchell, and John Jansen so that it could become part of 1971's *Rainbow Bridge*.

Wednesday, October 23, 1968
Los Angeles, TTG Studios. Engineer: Angel Balestier. Second engineer: Mark Kauffman.

A long, productive evening session that featured the recording of three new songs. The session kicked off with two takes of the instrumental "The New Rising Sun," both recorded without Redding's bass guitar. Vastly different both in sound and scope from the "Hey Baby (Land of the New Rising Sun)" later featured as part of *Rainbow Bridge*, take 2 was deemed the master. Despite the relatively few takes recorded — certainly by the Experience's recent standards — considerable work ensued. Hendrix added a backward guitar part as well as a second lead guitar. A slow-to-medium-tempo instrumental, "The New Rising Sun" does feature several high points. While Hendrix was never known to have revived this particular arrangement after leaving TTG, portions of this second take of "The New Rising Sun" were briefly considered for use as part of the *Rainbow Bridge* film soundtrack. Pulled from the tape library by Electric Lady Studios engineer John Jansen on February 22, 1971, "The New Rising Sun" was reviewed and rejected for both the film's soundtrack and its accompanying album.

Jansen did, however, find a use for the track, varying its speed and using a snippet as part of an experimental composite master he was creating. Later, in 1974, when Alan Douglas assumed control of the Hendrix tape library, Jansen's creation, which also featured pieces from recordings at the Hit Factory, Record Plant, and Electric Lady, would be the subject of new overdubs by drummer Alan Schwartzberg and percussionist Jimmy Maeulen. Rechristened "Captain Coconut," it was included as part of 1975's *Crash Landing*.

Three takes of "Introductions" followed, complete with organ, harmonica, and piano, with Redding now on bass. Each was different and bore no obvious connection to the others. The first 'take' was actually a spirited twelve-bar blues jam. This lengthy effort features some fine playing from Hendrix and Michaels before coming apart shortly before the six-minute mark. The second 'take' begins with a beautiful solo guitar part from Hendrix. This lasts nearly two minutes before the band joins in. The next recording, announced by engineer Balestier over the talkback as "Introductions, take three," is actually a melodic solo piano piece performed by Hendrix. At its conclusion, Hendrix remarks, "Let's leave it like that for now."

Eight takes of "Peace" were also recorded. However, without Redding's bass to center the song's melody, timing problems hampered the group's efforts. As a result, no basic track was achieved.

Thursday, October 24, 1968
Los Angeles, TTG Studios. Engineer: Angel Balestier. Second Engineer: Mark Kauffman.

This was a session largely devoted to recording the muscular instrumental "Peace." All of the previous day's work was scrapped and, in all, fifteen new takes were attempted. Take 2, timed at 4:41, was listed as 'complete' but not chosen as the final master. Twelve more takes would follow, with each new take only slightly different from the one before. Take 15, the first take recorded on reel two, was selected the master.

Balestier made a concerted effort to reproduce the searing guitar sound Hendrix desired and heard clearly in his head but had struggled to verbalize. "Jimi had said that he was looking for a certain sound," explains Balestier. "I stood listening in the studio during a rehearsal, then went back into the control room and heard the playback. To my surprise, I wasn't hearing what Hendrix was hearing out in the studio — and that's what his ears were aimed at. So I changed my microphone positions. I put one behind his amplifier and another about six feet away. I instructed Jimi to crank up his amplifier some more, which really disturbed Ami upstairs. What Jimi had been hearing was the sound bouncing off the glass separating the studio from the control room. I put up a microphone to capture that, which now gave me three positions to mix and put on tape. He came inside, listened, and said, 'I'd like to get a little more of *that* here.' That's how Hendrix was. He wasn't like a lot of guys today who would say, 'Give me 3K more and you've got it.' I went back out, put three Manhasset music stands in a corner to bounce more of his sound, changed my microphone positions slightly, and he said, 'Yeah. *That's* what I'm looking for.' "

Jimi behind the console at TTG Studios,

Los Angeles, October 1968.

(Michael Ochs Archives)

While "Peace in Mississippi" was neither finished nor issued during Hendrix's lifetime, Alan Douglas filled out take 15 with new overdubs recorded in 1974 by guitarist Jeff Mironov, bassist Bob Babbit, drummer Alan Schwartzberg, and percussionist Jimmy Maeulen. Despite this work, the posthumously created master paled in comparison to the Experience's charged demo recordings. The heavy-handed overdubs ordered by Douglas stripped the original recording of the raw vitality that had made it so attractive in the first place. Nonetheless, the revamped "Peace in Mississippi" was included as part of 1975's *Crash Landing*.

Precisely when Hendrix composed "Peace" is not known, although the inspiration to change the song's title from "Peace" to "Peace in Mississippi," says Balestier, came as a result of a visit by another of Hendrix's old friends — J. W. Alexander, Sam Cooke's respected manager and music publisher. "Alexander, Bumps Blackwell, and a number of Jimi's old friends from his days on the chitlin' circuit had stopped by. One

Yale University, November 17, 1968.

(Joe Sia)

had carried along a big bag of pumpkin seeds that a relative down South had sent him. This guy bragged that his relative grew the best pumpkins in the county. That started everybody talking about the South. Bumps told us about an album Little Richard had recorded in Clarksdale, Mississippi. Bumps had sent a young black kid out for sandwiches in a red convertible. Shortly after, a local sheriff brought him back, thinking that the kid had stolen the vehicle. When a white employee tried to explain that he had only been sent out for sandwiches, the sheriff looked at him and said, 'Oh, a nigger lover. Well, see that your niggers stay out of my town.' Hearing that changed our mood, and there was silence in the control room. Jimi picked up on it and said he was going to call this instrumental song he had been doing 'Peace in Mississippi.' That's how the title came about."

■
Friday, October 25, 1968
Los Angeles, TTG Studios. Engineer: Jack Hunt[?]

According to listings published with both *Plug Your Ears* and *Electric Gypsy*, Hendrix contributed a bass guitar part to a Robert Wyatt demo recording of "Slow Walking Talk." Wyatt, the drummer and leader of the Michael Jeffery–managed combo Soft Machine, would later retitle the song "But I'm Clean as a Whistle." Some years later, Wyatt rerecorded the track as "Soup Song." Save for Wyatt's acetate, no multitrack copies of this recording exist in the Hendrix tape library.

■
Electric Ladyland
Track Records 613 008/9. U.K. album release. Friday, October 25, 1968. Producer: Jimi Hendrix. Additional production: Chas Chandler. Engineers: Gary Kellgren, Eddie Kramer. Second engineers: Tony Bongiovi, George Chkiantz, Andy Johns.
And the Gods Made Love/Have You Ever Been (to Electric Ladyland)/Crosstown Traffic/Voodoo Chile/Little Miss Strange/Long Hot Summer Night/Come On (Part 1)/Gypsy Eyes/The Burning of the Midnight Lamp/Rainy Day, Dream Away/1983 (A Merman I Should Turn to Be)/Moon, Turn the Tides…Gently, Gently Away/Still Raining, Still Dreaming/House Burning Down/All Along the Watchtower/Voodoo Child (Slight Return)

Despite keeping the same running order as its Reprise counterpart, Track's version of *Electric Ladyland* was the subject of a firestorm of publicity upon its release, as the label had substituted a cover featuring a bevy of naked women. The nude concept, conceived by Track's Kit Lambert and Chris Stamp, had been devised largely as a publicity stunt. With the Experience no longer based in London, Track was eager to foster the group's outlaw image among the members of the Fleet Street press. That goal was certainly achieved: reaction to the cover resulted in howls of protest and condemnation. Hendrix, angered that the controversy had cheapened the album's contents, moved immediately to distance the group from the issue entirely. "People have been asking me about the English cover, and I don't know anything about it," he stated. "I didn't know it was going to be used. It's not my fault. I don't even know what the B side to 'All Along the Watchtower' is!"

The resulting furor over the cover may have temporarily enhanced the group's value to London's notorious tab-

loids, but sales were not significantly affected, as the two-disc set peaked at number 6 on the U.K. album charts before its twelve-week run concluded.

■
Sunday, October 27, 1968
Los Angeles, TTG Studios. Engineer: Angel Balestier. Second engineer: Mark Kauffman.

This was another session devoted largely to jamming. Six takes of "Jam Session" were recorded, with the sixth marked 'hold' — although it plainly remains more a jam than a finished basic track. Take 6 began with solo acoustic piano, soon joined by Hendrix's wah-wah guitar. As Redding and Mitchell became involved, the song's slow tempo began to increase. The jam that followed — lasting in excess of fifteen minutes — provides a splendid early example of Hendrix's firm grasp of the genre later popularized as fusion. Similar in style to *Electric Ladyland*'s extended sound painting "1983 (A Merman I Should Turn to Be)," "Jam Session" was an engaging blend of jazz, blues, and psychedelic rock. Like many similar efforts, however, "Jam Session" began to fall apart at the close, as Hendrix's fellow travelers were left to guess where Jimi was headed.

Impromptu jam sessions such as these were commonplace at TTG, Angel Balestier remembers. Another such effort, again marked simply "Jam Session," was also recorded on this evening, the group's sound bolstered by Lee Michaels's distinctive Hammond B-3 organ. Four takes were attempted, with only the first complete.

SESSIONS

Writing the lyrics for "Gypsy Eyes" in the Record Plant's control room.

(Eddie Kramer)

■

Tuesday, October 29, 1968

Los Angeles, TTG Studios. Engineer: Angel Balestier. Second engineer: Mark Kauffman.

Perhaps the finest — and certainly the most charged — Experience session at TTG was staged on this long evening. Six robust takes of "Here He Comes," later titled "Lover Man," were debuted, sounding very much like a vintage Experience stage performance. Following two incomplete efforts, takes 3 and 4, with Hendrix's and Redding's amplifiers jacked to maximum volume, were complete. Take 3 was hampered by timing problems, as Mitchell struggled, under-standably, to maintain a tempo steered by Jimi's split-second improvisation. As Hendrix alternated between foot pedals, his concentration shifted, which caused a promising guitar solo to break down. Nevertheless, Jimi rallied to a close with some vocal scatting and a brief flurry of notes. Take 4 showcased a slight refinement, with Redding's bass accompanying Hendrix's opening rhythm guitar notes. Though Jimi muffed the song's opening vocal line, his solo was superb, soaring above the arrangement. Hendrix concluded once more with some vocal scatting and a short burst of guitar notes before bringing the song to a close. Hendrix then asked Mitchell and Redding to "go a little faster" before Balestier called for take 5.

While nearly as energetic, takes 5 and 6 lacked the brutish ferocity of the two previous efforts, especially the frenetic take 4. And while no finished master would be achieved in this session, takes 3 and 4 remain pristine examples of the post–*Electric Ladyland* Experience.

Next would be the group's primal remake of Them's Van Morrison–led anthem, "Gloria." Like "Here He Comes," these takes of "Gloria" — especially the remarkable take 8, issued in 1978 as a bonus single with the *Essential Jimi Hendrix Volume Two* compilation — provide another example of the sheer intensity the three-man Experience was capable of generating. And like "Calling All the Devil's Children," "Gloria" provided another glimpse of Jimi's risqué humor.

With "Here He Comes" and "Gloria" having set the appropriate mood, the group's lineup now expanded to include Lee Michaels on organ and Jim Horn on flute. This ensemble recorded a remake of Hendrix's own "Red House." Takes 1 and 2 were lengthy and enthusiastic but incomplete. Takes 3 through 5 were false starts. Reel three contains the version later pared down and coupled with the introductions to the October 21 recording of "Electric Church." This hybrid master would later grace both *Red House: Variations on a Theme* and *Jimi Hendrix: Blues*.

While neither "Here He Comes" nor "Gloria" was ever seriously considered for any of the posthumous albums prepared by Eddie Kramer, both recordings were cut and removed from the original sixteen-track master by Alan Douglas on September 16, 1974, presumably for inclusion as part of either *Midnight Lightning* or *Multicolored*

Blues. Either track would have strengthened either compilation immeasurably, but neither was utilized.

Following the group's departure, Balestier's final task was to transfer selected two-inch, sixteen-track session tapes to one-inch, eight-track tape. While TTG's sixteen-track capability had been one of the studio's strongest attractions, its two-inch tapes were not compatible with the Record Plant's increasingly obsolete one-inch, twelve-track machines. Once completed, these TTG masters and their new submasters were then forwarded to the Record Plant in New York, where they would remain, largely untouched, until Hendrix's death in September 1970.

■

"Crosstown Traffic" / "Gypsy Eyes"

Reprise 0792. U.S. single release. Wednesday, October 30, 1968.

Reprise hoped to capitalize on the popularity of "All Along the Watchtower" with this second single from *Electric Ladyland*. Though "Crosstown Traffic" was, arguably, as strong an effort as its predecessor, it managed to reach only number 52 before its eight-week chart run concluded.

As October came to a close, the Experience's tumultuous Hollywood stay ended. The group was slated to perform two concerts, in Minneapolis on November 2 and at St. Louis's Keil Auditorium on November 3. With nearly two weeks before the Experience was to perform in Cincinnati, Hendrix agreed to produce another group from Michael Jeffery's growing stable of clients: Cat Mother & the All Night Newsboys. While time at the Record Plant had been set aside for the Experience, the group made no effort to

record there or to prepare an album or even a single from the many recordings made at TTG. With "All Along the Watchtower" nested comfortably in the U.K. top five and providing the group with its first U.S. top twenty single, the need to follow up on the tremendous success of *Electric Ladyland* passed with little discourse. As a result, neither Track nor Reprise received new material to release.

Because Cat Mother boasted two fine guitarists in Larry Packer and Charlie Chin, Hendrix approached the project differently than with Eire Apparent. Rather than feature his own playing, Jimi opted for a less prominent role. While Hendrix had a greater influence in the control room than the recording studio, he left the balance of the album's production chores to Record Plant staff engineers Gary Kellgren and Tony Bongiovi.

The multitrack tapes recorded for this album have seemingly disappeared, mysteriously absent from both the Hendrix and Polygram tape libraries, so actual session dates are not available. These tapes seem to have been lost or misplaced in the years following Jeffery's death in 1973.

■

Wednesday, November 6, 1968
New York, Record Plant. Producer: Jimi Hendrix. Engineer: Tony Bongiovi.

Of the many sessions staged for Cat Mother's *The Street Giveth . . . and The Street Taketh Away* in November, these two reels of tepid jamming, with Hendrix accompanied by an unknown second guitarist, remain the only multitrack tapes known to exist.

"I enjoy producing records by other groups," Hendrix recalled in a 1969 interview. "As long as I like what they are

**A rare shot of Jimi performing with a
Gibson SG guitar. Philharmonic Hall, Lincoln
Center, New York, November 28, 1968.**

(Tom Lucas/Star File)

playing. I liked doing the Eire Apparent record, but it was never really finished according to my standards. Then I produced Cat Mother. They are presentable enough, but not as good as I wanted them to be. It was the same as our last LP [*Electric Ladyland*] — it could have been so much better, but we were working all the time and couldn't spend the time we needed in the studio."

Where Eire Apparent's *Sunrise* missed *Billboard*'s Top 200 album chart entirely, sinking quickly into oblivion, Cat Mother proved to be a most pleasant surprise. "Good Old Rock 'N Roll," the group's high-energy medley of "Sweet Little Sixteen," "Long Tall Sally," "Chantilly Lace," "Whole Lotta Shakin' Goin On," "Blue Suede Shoes,"

and "Party Doll," reached number 21 on *Billboard*'s Top 100 chart in July 1969. Fueled by the success of their single, "Good Old Rock 'N Roll," *The Street Giveth…and The Street Taketh Away,* their album debut, peaked at number 55, a highly respectable showing.

■

January 2-7, 1969

**London, Polygram Studios. 6:00 P.M. to
9:00 A.M. Producer: Jimi Hendrix. Engineer:
Carlos Olms.**

Shortly after the New Year, the Experience gathered in London to begin a
short European tour. While no recordings were undertaken by the group during this time, Hendrix nipped into
London's Polygram Studios to add a
lead guitar overdub to Eire Apparent's
"Rock 'n Roll Band."

"Eire Apparent had come in around
six P.M.," Olms recalled in a radio interview. "We messed around trying to get
the right sound until ten or eleven before Jimi arrived in his very colorful
dress. He sat very quietly in a corner.
After he heard our work, he started to
convert everything to his taste. He
started with the drums, setting up each
microphone to get the right sound, then
the right equalization. The boys had a
hard time trying to please him with
their sound, but I was impressed with
his way of working."

After the microphone and sound
adjustments had been made, the group
attempted to record the song's basic
track. "We did about five or six complete versions," Olms remembered,
"but Jimi always found something
which he felt was not correct, and we
would do it again. It was three A.M. before he started to put his [guitar] parts
down on tape. He had to play the
middle eight part and the ending."

As he had done for the group, Hendrix had specific technical instructions
for Olms to follow. "He asked me for a
very insensitive microphone, because
he said, 'I will play quite loud,' Olms explained. "We turned the lights down so
low in the studio that I could just see
the shadow of his guitar and amplifiers.
Every time he played his part, we
thought it was fantastic. Only Jimi
didn't think so. He always raised his
hand and said, 'Again.' He was still
playing his part at five A.M., but was not
satisfied. At the end, he agreed [to stop]
only because it was so late. We started
mixing and stayed until nine A.M. That
was the longest session I had ever been

involved with at Polydor. Other employees came into the studio that morning
and were surprised to see that we were
still there."

■

Tuesday, January 7, 1969

**New York, Record Plant. Engineer: Jack
Adams.**

With Jimi in London, Michael Jeffery
designated Record Plant engineer Jack
Adams to cull the highlights of the recent TTG sessions, so that an evaluation could be made of what had been
recorded and how close the Experience
had come to finishing an album. Without any direct input from either Hendrix or the group, Adams, instead,
followed the legends on each of the
tape boxes. He compiled the following.
"Messenger" take 15, "Mr. Lost Soul"
take 17, "The New Rising Sun" take 2,
"Jam Session" take 6, "Peace in Mississippi" take 15, "Izabella" take 18, "Jam
#1" with Lee Michaels and Buddy
Miles, "Jam #2 with Lee Michaels

Jimi and Buddy Miles.

(Jim Marshall)

again," "Electric Church," "Calling All the Devil's Children," "Jam #4" with extra percussion. It is not known what Jeffery may have done with these tapes, if anything at all.

■

Tuesday, February 11, 1969

New York, Record Plant. Recording, 12:00 midnight to 4:00 A.M. Rough mix, 4:00 A.M. to 5:30 A.M. Engineer: Tony Bongiovi. Second engineer: Dave Ragno.

Without a firm plan for the fourth Experience album, Hendrix looked for new creative challenges. His friendship with Buddy Miles and the members of the Express had deepened during his extended stay in Los Angeles the previous fall. "Jimi just seemed to be looking for different things to do," recalls Express bassist Billy Rich. "He and Buddy had grown pretty close. At that time, Buddy was trying to get Jimi to do anything he possibly could with him."

Hendrix enjoyed Buddy's vibrant personality and had developed friendships with the individual members of the Express, including Bill and Herbie Rich and guitarist Jim McCarty. "Jimi was tired of having to do 'Purple Haze' on the road every night," recalls McCarty. "He wanted to make the transition from psychedelia to his own style of funk rock. He was talking to people like Miles Davis and Buddy Miles about doing different projects, but his drug use was wearing him down."

Despite Hendrix's deteriorating relationship with Noel Redding, he still made no overt move to replace him, opting instead to try and develop a stable of players who might be used for recordings outside the Experience. "We did do a bunch of recording," explains Billy Rich. "We'd play all night, putting some little things down on tape and just having a ball." Despite Rich's budding friendship with Jimi, an invitation to replace Noel Redding as the bassist for the Experience never materialized. "Jimi never asked me to join the Experience, but he hinted that he wanted to get together with me at some point. It wouldn't have been with the Experience, because they were a solid thing. He was hoping to also do something else."

In addition to jamming at the Scene or hanging at such haunts as the Tin Angel, Hendrix enjoyed sharing his impressive record collection. "He and Buddy Miles would listen to Moms Mabley and Pigmeat Markham albums all the time," recalls Velvert Turner. "They had this whole shuck-and-jive routine they would do, which would make them laugh for hours. It was wild, especially when Tootie, Buddy's sister,

would make chitlins, sweet potato pie, and all kinds of soul food. Jimi loved that. He used to love to turn us on to the blues records from his collection. He played us Blind Lemon Jefferson, Robert Johnson, and especially Albert King. We would listen to those records for hours."

Having already contributed liner notes to *Expressway to Your Skull*, the Express's debut album, Hendrix agreed to produce *Electric Church*, the forthcoming Buddy Miles Express album. Anne Tansey, a mutual friend and Mercury Records staff producer, was assigned to work with Jimi and oversee the project for the label. While Hendrix's schedule would ultimately limit him to producing only four tracks, Tansey, a pioneering female rock producer, was a constant presence in the studio. "Though Jimi only ended up producing a few of the tracks, Anne Tansey would be at those sessions," explains Billy Rich. For those tracks supervised by Hendrix, Tansey would retreat, allowing Hendrix to shape the sound and arrangements as he desired. Without Hendrix present, Tansey took charge of recording the remaining tracks required to deliver the album to Mercury.

While the majority of sessions for *Electric Church* were staged at Mercury Studios, additional dates were held at the Record Plant. Sadly, nearly all the multitrack master tapes from the sessions at Mercury Studios have been either lost, stolen, or destroyed. All that remains is the quarter-inch, 15 i.p.s. album master. Any outtakes and/or alternate takes remain unknown. One superb jam session has survived, however. A spirited blues workout known as "Crying Blue Rain" or "Blue Window" has made the rounds of the bootleg circuit in recent years.

On this evening, Hendrix presided

over the production of "I Can See," which would later be retitled "Destructive Love." This recording sported the same arrangement as the released master, but in a higher key.

Eager to play, Hendrix stepped out from behind the console to jam, assuming the bass guitar while Buddy Miles moved from drums to guitar. Though Miles was a capable guitarist, the long, shambling jam session that ensued was largely uneventful. Following this, Jimi switched back to guitar as Miles returned to his drumkit and kicked off another jam. With this lineup, Hendrix led the group through two impromptu originals, "World Traveler" and "It's Too Bad." Though only one take of each was recorded, both were quite good. The up-tempo "World Traveler" was centered on a guitar-and-organ duel between Hendrix and Larry Young. "It's Too Bad," which was even better, was a deeply personal original blues composition based largely on Hendrix's relationship with his troubled stepbrother, Leon.

While Hendrix thoroughly enjoyed producing and recording with the Express, his pending commitments to the Experience loomed, beginning with a major concert scheduled for February 18 at London's Royal Albert Hall. Of the four tracks Hendrix would ultimately produce for *Electric Church*, his deepest involvement, says Billy Rich, came with the recording of "69 Freedom Special." The song's title was coined by Hendrix and inspired by Tansey's efforts to shorten Rich's recent military commitments. "A lot of energy was put into that session," Rich explains. "It was so much fun that it was like a dream. I'm just sorry that it was edited down before it was put on the album, because there are a few more great solos recorded on that track. I was out of the service and just starting to get a lot of shit off my brain for the first time in two years. The name I had picked out for the song was something like 'The Clap,' which wasn't too cool. In the studio, I was telling Jimi about my whole service thing, and he said, 'Well, why don't you call this thing the "69 Freedom Special"?' I agreed," Rich adds with a laugh, "because some of that shit I'm playing on bass I actually stole from him anyway!"

■

February 14, 15, and 16, 1969
London, Olympic Studios. Engineer: George Chkiantz. Second engineer: Ron (surname unknown).

In London to prepare for their upcoming engagements at the Royal Albert Hall on February 18 and 24, the Experience returned to Olympic Studios for the first time in more than a year. Unfortunately, the January European tour had only further exposed the growing disharmony within the group, especially between Hendrix and Redding, whose relationship had further deteriorated. At Olympic, with Chandler no longer at the helm, the Experience was unable to summon the energy and unity necessary to reverse their sagging spirits.

In the wake of the difficult January European tour, Noel Redding's scathing diary notations detail his mounting frustration. "On the first day, as I nearly expected, there was nothing doing," noted Redding. "On the second, it was no show at all. I went to the pub for three hours, came back, and it was still ages before Jimi ambled in. Then we argued. There seemed no way to get working. Either there was no one there or I'd show up to find the studio so crowded I had trouble squeezing in. Next day, Mitch was late. I suppose it was partly because we didn't want to

get it together. The pressure from the public to create something even more brilliant each time, while basically expecting us to stay the same, was crushing. On the last day, I just watched it happen for a while and then went back to my flat."

"We did those sessions in Studio B, and I thought they were terrible," says engineer George Chkiantz. "Hendrix was in a bad mood, but he wanted to come in and do *something*. Studio B was the wrong place for Hendrix to record anyway, because there wasn't room for his sound to properly expand. It was incredibly difficult to record him there. Hendrix's response was to double his amplifiers, which made it nearly impossible to hear anything in the control room. We stuck a couple of layers of screens between the studio window and the control room, but it ended up making zero difference. It was just stupid. He really seemed lost, and the whole thing was very sad."

■

Wednesday, February 26, 1969
London, Olympic Studios. Engineer: George Chkiantz.

This final Olympic session yielded only a rambling rendition of "Gypsy Blood" among littered jams and outtakes.

In all, the Experience realized little from these disjointed February Olympic sessions. Apart from an energetic reworking of Cream's "Sunshine of Your Love," which had been a highlight of the recent European tour, Hendrix made scant progress on the few songs he had been developing. Formative attempts at "Room Full of Mirrors" — arguably the strongest of these new works — held promise, but Jimi seemed to lack the concentration and desire required to complete the task.

■

Tuesday, March 18, 1969
New York, Record Plant. 4:00 A.M. to 9:00 A.M. Engineer: Gary Kellgren. Second engineer: Dave Ragno.

Hendrix's first known sixteen-track recording session came as a result of the Record Plant's recent installation of a new Ampex unit.

Perhaps inspired by the occasion, Hendrix crafted a unique rendition of "The Star-Spangled Banner." No bass or drum parts were recorded, and there is no evidence to suggest that either Mitchell or Redding was present at the session. The recording represented an approach quite unlike Hendrix's stage versions, including the definitive version performed at Woodstock.

While Hendrix never revisited this particular recording before his death, Eddie Kramer later remixed the track and posthumously added it to 1971's *Rainbow Bridge*. "I thought it was a pretty unique rendition of the song," explains Kramer. "I was intrigued by the fact that Jimi was able to make the guitar sound like an early synthesizer, predating the guitar synthesizers which came in later. It just showed another aspect of his playing. His variety of tone colors were limitless."

After "Star Spangled Banner" was completed, Jimi was joined by Buddy Miles and an unnamed organist. Two new songs, "Hey Gypsy Boy," with organ, and "Jimi I," with organ and voice, were recorded. "Hey Gypsy Boy" was actually an embryonic version of what would later evolve as "Hey Baby (Land of the New Rising Sun)." During early takes, Jimi can be heard instructing Miles about the drum pattern he desired. These few takes were nothing more than simple sketches. None represented anything close to a finished master.

Additional jamming followed, with

Jimi and Buddy now accompanied by organ, conga, and saxophone. The contents of this second reel featured one take of "Jam I" and three blues-influenced takes of "Jam II" performed by the same lineup. The third and final take was highlighted for Jimi's future consideration.

After Jimi's death, Alan Douglas chose take 8 of "Hey Gypsy Boy" for the extensive posthumous overdubbing sessions he supervised for 1975's *Midnight Lightning*. By the time this "new" master was complete, Douglas and co-producer Tony Bongiovi had almost en-

tirely recreated the track as a result of the various edits and looping of Jimi's lead vocal part.

■

Tuesday, March 25, 1969
New York, Record Plant. Engineer: Gary Kellgren. Second engineer: Llylliane Davis.

A busy evening that saw Hendrix record two separate jam sessions, the first with guitarist Jim McCarty of the Buddy Miles Express and the second with jazz guitarist John McLaughlin.

Jimi makes a point to Noel Redding during a break between takes.
(Michael Ochs Archives)

Madison Square Garden, March 18, 1969.

(Walter Iooss/Globe Photos)

Joined by Miles on drums and fellow Express bassist Roland Robinson, Hendrix and McCarty traded riffs. McCarty was unhappy that his impromptu exploratory effort was later edited and released as part of the 1980 *Nine to the Universe* compilation. "None of that stuff was ever intended to be released," complains McCarty. "To me it was embarrassing. I'm sure that Jimi would have said, 'You're out of your fucking mind!' and never let it happen. It was all about people trying to make a buck off of Jimi Hendrix. . . ."

Though the markings on the tape box incorrectly list "Jimi-Mitch-Dave," this is the fabled Hendrix-McLaughlin jam session, with the two guitarists joined by Buddy Miles and premier jazz bassist Dave Holland. While not without its flaws, this recording remains one of the most exciting unreleased performances in the Hendrix library.

"I'd received a phone call in the afternoon," Dave Holland remembers, "asking if I would like to come down and play. I'm not quite sure why I was called, but I was real happy to do it. It was a lot of fun and very informal. Nothing was really planned — Buddy Miles was on drums, and Jimi just organized a few jam lines for us to play on. We started and stopped and then started again. It was real loose, and Jimi seemed as if he was putting it together as he went. He put together a couple of riffs and we would play on that for a while, then Buddy Miles did a few things on the organ, and we would play on that."

"Alan Douglas came down to the Village Vanguard to see me," John McLaughlin explained in 1982. "He said that he was going to be recording tonight and why don't I come down. Jimi was there, but I didn't see it in the terms people see it. I wasn't even interested in that side of things. I walked

into the studio and the thing that knocked me out was Buddy Miles. I didn't know who this guy was, but he was playing some fatback boogaloo on the drums which just made me want to play. Basically, it was Jimi's session and Jimi's music. There was a lot of partying going on, and we had a loosely organized jam. We played from two to eight in the morning. I was playing acoustic guitar with a pickup and Jimi was playing electric."

While a faulty connection intermittently caused McLaughlin's signal to distort or drop out entirely, he still managed to fire off a series of his trademark runs and bends on top of Hendrix's roaring rhythm support. Jimi was more than equal to the task, with his ferocious blues-playing challenging McLaughlin at every turn. Though the jam reportedly lasted for hours, all that remains of this special summit is one thirty-minute reel of recording tape.

Despite the many scintillating moments it contained, McLaughlin remains unconvinced. "The music wasn't all that great, I'm sorry to say. I love Jimi, but the music wasn't that great. We played some good things. Just because it was my name and Jimi Hendrix's name is no excuse. Only since Mahavishnu came out and I began to receive some recognition was this event transformed into something other."

It is because of McLaughlin's reticence that this jam session remains unreleased. McLaughlin has not sanctioned its release, nor is he likely to do so.

■
Tuesday, April 1, 1969
New York, Olmstead Recording Studios.
Engineer: Eddie Kramer.

Though all their efforts to complete a fourth studio album had fallen apart, the Experience again attempted to extricate themselves from their creative doldrums. In an effort to improve the creative atmosphere and limit the number of distractions Jimi faced at the Record Plant, the Experience moved to Olmstead Recording Studios, a new facility.

Despite their new surroundings, the old problems immediately rose to the surface. Lacking the firm hand of Chandler, the group desperately needed a strong voice to moderate their disputes and channel Jimi's energies into productive recording. Chandler had always served that role in the past, but with Jimi now handling the dual responsibility of artist and producer, those duties were compromised. "I went over to Olmstead only to help Jimi out," Kramer remembers. "I wasn't being paid, but I hadn't worked with Jimi for some time and wanted to hear what he was doing. Olmstead was located at the top of a building on 54th Street in Manhattan. It was like a penthouse, all painted in white. Though it was a small studio, a lot of jazz sessions had been done there. I remember that the sessions didn't go very well, as things were pretty crazy. There was a *lot* of partying going on."

The group's initial session at Olmstead yielded no finished masters. Instead, the evening was dedicated largely to the recording of "Peoples, Peoples," an early, up-tempo rendition of "Bleeding Heart." While the general mood was encouragingly upbeat, these instrumental efforts revealed the group's inability to focus their efforts on

Mitch and Jimi leave the stage.

(Walter Iooss/Globe Photos)

the task at hand. "Midnight," which would be edited and posthumously issued as part of 1972's *War Heroes*, was among these instrumentals. One tape reel was appropriately labeled "Ramblin," while another was marked "Outtakes."

■

Wednesday, April 2, 1969

New York, Olmstead Recording Studios.
Engineer: Eddie Kramer.

This was an evening dedicated to the blues, as Jimi focused on "The Train," better known as "Hear My Train A Comin'," and "Midnight Lightning." Though structured takes were attempted for both numbers, the recordings made here were largely of jams.

■

Thursday, April 3, 1969

New York, Olmstead Recording Studios.
Engineer: Eddie Kramer.

Another difficult session, with the Experience again struggling to complete a suitable basic track for "Midnight Lightning." The group's best effort was probably take 5, which rambled for nearly eight minutes and was listed on the tape box as "Crying Blue Rain." Some of the passages from the jam sessions in between takes revisited "Peace in Mississippi." The instrumental had evolved from its debut at TTG Studios a half year earlier. The version recorded here was actually closer in sound and style to "Trash Man," which would appear on 1975's *Midnight Lightning*.

Friday, April 4, 1969

New York, Olmstead Recording Studios.

The evening's output consisted of three reels filled with jams based largely on the "Trash Man" jam. Portions of one such jam would later be fleshed out with new overdubs and included as part of *Midnight Lightning*.

■

"Crosstown Traffic" / "Gypsy Eyes"

Track Records 604 029. U.K. single release.
Friday, April 4, 1969.

With no other product scheduled for delivery, Track delved into *Electric Ladyland* to try to generate some sales action. This single release simply wilted, as the Experience, busy recording in New York, was unable to generate any momentum behind it. Lacking this effort, the disc managed to reach number 37 during its brief three-week chart stay.

■

Sunday, April 6, 1969

New York, Record Plant. 9:30 P.M to 8:30 A.M.
Engineers: Sandy (surname unknown), Lee
Brown.

The Olmstead experiment was dropped, and the Experience returned to the Record Plant, hoping to make progress here.

The tape box for this session was appropriately marked "Tape of False Takes." Apart from the jams recorded, some work was completed on "Lullaby for the Summer," the early working title for what would later evolve as "Earth Blues."

■

Monday, April 7, 1969

**New York, Record Plant. Engineer: Sandy
(surname unknown).**

Another attempt was made to complete
a finished master of "Hear My Train A
Comin'." Inexplicably, Jimi also attempted a remake of "Stone Free."
While the group's original rendition of
"Stone Free" had yet to be released in
the U.S., Jimi's decision to revisit his
very first Experience composition
rather than concentrate on new material spoke volumes about the creative
deterioration the Experience had suffered in recent months.

A take of "Stone Free" from this session was pulled by Alan Douglas on August 7, 1974, saddled with new
overdubs, and issued posthumously as
"Stone Free Again" on *Crash Landing.*

■

Wednesday, April 9, 1969

**New York, Record Plant. "Stone Free,"
1:00 A.M. to 1:30 A.M. "Get My Arse Back
Together," 1:30 A.M. to 4:00 A.M. Playbacks,
4:00 A.M. to 4:30 A.M. Overdubs, 4:30 A.M. to
6:00 A.M. Engineers: Sandy (surname
unknown), Lee Brown.**

This session began with Hendrix adding a guitar overdub to the April 7
"Stone Free" master. New takes of
"Hear My Train A Comin'," marked on
the tape box as "Get My Arse Back Together," were recorded, with Jimi also
adding a lead guitar overdub. No mixing of either track was attempted, as
Jimi no doubt decided that more work
was still required.

■

Monday, April 14, 1969

**New York, Record Plant. 3:00 A.M. to
7:00 A.M. Engineer: Gary Kellgren. Second
engineer: Lee Brown.**

Backed by an unknown group of musicians, whose ranks included a trumpet
player, bassist, and drummer, Jimi recorded a number of takes of "Ships
Passing in the Night," a promising,
moody original steeped in the Delta
blues tradition of John Lee Hooker.
These takes resembled little more than
engaging demos, as Jimi had only begun
to develop the song's arrangement. No
finished master was achieved.

■

Thursday, April 17, 1969

**New York, Record Plant. Engineer: Sandy
(surname unknown), Lee Brown.**

The tape box from this session is labeled "Jam with Harmonica. Chorus
left/Chorus right." Leading a group of
friends whose ranks included Jimi's girlfriend Devon Wilson, Paul Caruso on
harmonica, and an unnamed percussionist, Hendrix recorded a particularly
raw and raucous rendition of "Keep On
Groovin'," which was clearly the highlight from this wild, undisciplined jam.
Incredibly, Hendrix went to the trouble
of adding overdubs to this take. A rough
mix was prepared, but no finished master was achieved.

When Jimi was touring with the Experience in Memphis (April 18), he
reached out to his old army buddy Billy
Cox. Unable to locate Cox directly,
Hendrix phoned Wright's TV Shop and
gave Wright the assignment of tracking
him down. "Mr. Wright's shop was right
near my old place," recalls Cox. "Mr.
Wright's wife had passed away, and he
lived in the house above the shop. He

Madison Square Garden, March 18, 1969.

(Walter Iooss/Globe Photos)

Seeking to make a change, Jimi reached back to an old friend, bassist Billy Cox.

(Jim Cummins/Star File)

repaired televisions. Jimi knew that telephone number was intact and asked Mr. Wright to find me. It was a small community, and he found out where I had moved to and told me Jimi had been looking for me. I went to the concert at the Coliseum, and it was great to see him. He looked good, but he had changed since I had last seen him. He wasn't the tall, chubby guy I knew. It looked as if he had dropped about twenty-five pounds. We sat down in his dressing room and talked and talked. He asked for my help, and that was all he had to say. I told him I would do whatever I could to help him." Sensing Jimi's concerns as genuine, Cox agreed to come up to New York as soon as he could put his affairs in order. He left a few weeks later to record with Jimi.

■

Monday, April 21, 1969
New York, Record Plant.

Hendrix revisited "Room Full of Mirrors," but his progress stalled and he was unable to complete an acceptable basic track.

■

Tuesday, April 22, 1969
New York, Record Plant. Engineer: Gary Kellgren.

Shifting gears once more, Jimi teamed with Buddy Miles and Billy Cox to record four reels of "Mannish Boy," an up-tempo blues original of considerable promise. Many of the early takes were devoted to developing the song's infectious groove. Jimi offered direction throughout, suggesting changes to both Miles and Rich whenever he felt them necessary. Despite the many takes recorded, Jimi was again unable to complete a basic track to his satisfaction. As a result, "Mannish Boy" joined his growing pile of unrealized multitrack masters stored in the Record Plant's tape vault.

For 1994's *Jimi Hendrix: Blues*, engineer Mark Linett revived "Mannish Boy" by creating a composite master of the song. Linett digitally edited different takes to create a master.

■

Thursday, April 24, 1969

New York, Record Plant. 8:00 P.M. to 9:00 A.M. Engineer: Gary Kellgren. Second engineer: Bob Hughes.

Working again without either Mitchell or Redding, Jimi's unnamed backing musicians included a bassist, organist, and drummer. Recorded on this night were "Crash Landing Jam," an up-tempo rocker whose lyrics at this stage were openly inspired by Jimi's relationship with his girlfriend, Devon Wilson. Two blues-based jams, "Bleeding Heart" and "Hey Country Boy," were also recorded, although no finished masters were completed. "Night Messenger," the final track attempted here, showcased the continuing development of the "Ships Passing through the Night"/"Nightbird Flying" demo.

■

May 1969

[Tape box gives month only.] New York, Record Plant. 4:00 A.M. to 7:00 A.M. Reel two session time, 7:00 A.M. to 8:00 A.M. Engineer: Gary Kellgren. Second engineer: Jack Adams.

Jimi's focus for the session was recording overdubs for the April 7 master of "Stone Free Again." "Insert #1" required nine takes, while "Insert #2" required seven. Despite these overdubs, no finals were achieved, although take 11 was marked 'keep.'

■

Tuesday, May 6, 1969

New York, Record Plant. Playback, 6:30 P.M. to 7:00 P.M. Rough mix, 7:00 P.M. to 12:30 A.M. Then they switched studios, moving to Studio B for a mixdown session lasting from 1:00 A.M. to 2:30 A.M. Engineers: Lee Brown, Tony Bongiovi.

An overdub and mixing session was scheduled to accommodate the arrival of bassist Billy Cox, Jimi's old army buddy. Looking to reset his musical compass, Jimi hoped his old friend could help him through a difficult time in his life and career. When Cox arrived, he realized that Jimi's problems were not entirely musical. Cox explains: "Jimi had told me all of these fabulous stories about how a limousine would pick me up at the airport, and I believed all this, of course. Nobody from the office, however, was there to pick me up. That's when I started to realize that *Jimi* wanted me here, but the office didn't seem so sure. At that point, I knew it was going to be a battle from there on."

However unceremonious Cox's arrival, Jimi's stark admission that he feared his creativity had forsaken him left Cox stunned. "When I arrived in New York, Jimi sat me down and admitted that his creativity had drawn dry," he admits. "He just felt that he couldn't think of anything new."

By reaching back to Cox, Hendrix may have been trying to find someone who might allow him — privately — to examine just where and how he had veered off track. There was simply no one but Cox whom he could trust with such a sensitive issue. "With me, Jimi knew that I had a direct link to him musically," recalls Cox. "He knew that I was familiar with his style, sound, and creativity. I hadn't played with him in a long while, but when I first heard 'Foxey Lady,' I knew that to be an old

song of his we used to call 'Stomp Driver' in Nashville. Jimi's creativity had been stifled, and I guess he thought of me, because even in the early days we had always been able to make up stuff. We enjoyed doing that, but we could never use any of it, because our living depended upon playing cover tunes or behind an artist who had already recorded his own songs. Jimi must have felt that I could help him pull all of the pieces of ideas that he had together into something as good as those three albums he had released.

"The first session I did was at the Record Plant," Cox continues. "Jimi was basically trying to see how well we played together. After we started, I looked up and saw the smile on his face, and I was smiling too. We just fell right into it, and we jammed for two or three hours. His playing was just as I remembered, but now there was much more freedom. Finally, we went into the patterns for 'Hello My Friend' [which would later be developed as "Straight Ahead"] and 'Earth Blues.'

"We played better with each other — not necessarily note for note, but pattern for pattern. We remembered patterns, not notes. A lot of times we would come up with a pattern that was four bars long, eight bars, or sixteen bars — all even. Other times, Jimi would come up with patterns which were seven bars, nine bars, or thirteen bars, which was weird. On top of that, we did not tune to standard tuning. In order for him to sing, we tuned down a half step, which made playing and singing easier. When he asked me to tune down the half step, I wondered why. He told me that it made his singing much easier. 'Plus, there is nobody else onstage but me and you tuning guitars, so we could go down a full step if we wanted and nobody would know the difference.' "

Cox and Jimi spent a great deal of

private time together, getting reacquainted, defining Jimi's direction, and simply having some fun. "I was then called 'Jimi's bass player.' He and I would get a little amp, wherever he was or I was, and we would practice. We enjoyed this. We didn't bowl or play golf — music was our life. We loved every note we made."

Hendrix warned Cox not to spend time down at Michael Jeffery's East 37th Street office. "Jimi told me not to hang down there," Cox remembers. "Honestly, I didn't want to get into any of the politics. I had enough pressure on my mind just trying to play and remember all of this new music. I wasn't doing any gigs. We would do some jamming at the Scene and a few other clubs, but that was it. I owned a Panasonic cassette player and would take tapes home from the studio. I would listen and practice to those tapes all day so that I would be ready for the recording sessions."

As Jimi and Noel saw increasingly less of each other, Cox and Redding avoided the possibility of any embarrassing moments in the studio from their bumping into each other. "The Experience were just finishing up their last committed dates," recalls Cox. "That's all they were doing. I did meet Noel once, in the lobby of the Penn Garden Hotel, and it was very cordial."

Working in either Jimi's apartment or Cox's hotel room at the Penn Garden, Hendrix began mining Cox's extensive R&B and blues background in an effort to create new music. Even simple bass lines from Cox could spark new ideas. "Jimi needed the bass to work off of. He would take something I played and improve on it. We were always trying to top each other, and by the time I gave up — because he was just too good — he had created a song. It was nothing more than good-natured

competition. He would play through his little practice amp, and I had created a way with my General Electric tape recorder whereby I could plug my bass guitar in and get a helluva bass tone with just one or two watts. Jimi would oftentimes play on his acoustic, because it gave him a bit more presence than the electric. We made tape after tape of these informal sessions and would listen to them for ideas. Jimi would take the patterns that we played and create songs from them."

■

Wednesday, May 7, 1969
New York, Record Plant. Engineer: Lee Brown.

"Jam Part II," also known as Guitar Slim's "Things I Used to Do," was recorded during this wild session. After spending the early part of the evening at the Scene Club, Hendrix returned to jam at the Record Plant, where he, Cox, and Buddy Miles were joined by guitarists Steve Stills and Johnny Winter.

The tape began with a high-flying jam led by Stills, with Hendrix and Winter in close pursuit. As Stills's lead guitar soared above the music, Jimi continued to build a furious, high-speed foundation underneath. Unfortunately, the only drawback was that Jimi's guitar was heavily distorted. After "Jam #1" drew to a close, Jimi initiated "Jam #2," a heavy-handed, three-guitar stab at "Earth Blues." As Jimi had only provided the players with the song's riff, the players struggled to maintain cohesion. Nonetheless, spirits remained, with Stills, Hendrix, and Winter all trading licks. Later, Jimi yelled for them to bring the tempo down and make it more bluesy. When they did so, Jimi offered another rendition of "Ships Pass-

ing in the Night." Johnny Winter now began to add slide fills. When this particular take broke down, Jimi asked engineer Lee Brown if he had been recording all these various jams. Brown's reply was affirmative. Jimi then kicked the band off in the same tempo. This rendition of "Ships Passing in the Night" broke down, but Jimi changed gears, this time singing Guitar Slim's "Things That I Used to Do." Unfortunately, the recording of this jam was marred by technical difficulties, principally excess distortion on Jimi's guitar and tape dropout on track 2, his vocal track. Johnny Winter played well, his slide fills an obvious highlight. Jimi's performance, however, was nothing exceptional. No overdubs were attempted, Jimi correctly viewing the evening's recorded efforts as a welcome creative diversion and little more.

■

Tuesday, May 13, 1969
New York, Record Plant. 4:30 A.M. to 8:00 A.M. Engineer: Bob Hughes.

Resembling an audition more than an actual recording session, this session produced three reels of unfulfilled jamming without yielding a final master. Hendrix and Billy Cox were joined by organist Sharon Lane and percussionist Juma Sultan. "Jimi wanted to try and take his music in a number of different directions," recalls Cox. "He asked if I knew of any organ players. I told him that I knew a pretty nice one in Nashville. He said, 'Get him up here.' I said, 'Hey, it's a girl.' He shot me a look but told me to bring her up here anyway. She was playing at that time in a group called King James & The Scepters."

Her debut session, however, was a disaster. "She did two nights in the studio, but it didn't work out too well," ad-

As an unnamed trumpet player looks on, Billy and Jimi work out their respective parts.

(Willis Hogans, Jr./Bill Nitopi Collection)

Jimi returns home to Seattle once more. Seattle Center Arena, May 23, 1969.
(Barry Gruber Archives)

mits Cox. "She was so taken with being in a recording studio with, as she put it, *the* Jimi Hendrix, that it made her uptight."

■

Wednesday, May 14, 1969
New York, Record Plant.

"Blues Jam," better known as "Jam 292" of *Loose Ends* and *Jimi Hendrix: Blues* fame, was recorded on this night. This fun, rollicking jam was actually more structured than similar jams of this period. Both released versions were edited out of the longer, original master take.

■

Thursday, May 15, 1969
New York, Record Plant. 6:30 P.M. to 9:30 A.M. Engineer: Bob Hughes.

Spurred by Cox's enthusiasm, another marathon jam session was recorded. "Jimi wanted to experiment with having three or four horns," Billy Cox remembers. "The horn players from the Buddy Miles Express had said that they would help. I thought the move would have brought his music too far back to R&B — the style we had played long before the Experience — where he had been successful doing pop music. He scratched his head, obviously thinking the plan over, and decided to give it a shot."

"With the Power of God," later known as "Power of Soul," was recorded on this night, with Jimi augmented by drums, horn, piano, tambourine, and second guitar. Take 9 was marked "complete." " 'Power of Soul', explains Cox, "came together when Jimi heard me playing a riff from 'Mary Ann,' an old song Ray Charles used to do. I hadn't meant anything by

playing it — I was just goofing around. But that was all he needed to get started."

Because of their shared love for blues, rock, and R&B, a simple riff or rhythm pattern from Cox often ignited Hendrix's creativity. Inherently curious, Hendrix couldn't help but pick up on what he heard Cox play and add his own original twist. Cox explains: "With Jimi, the idea was always first. Then, when he figured he had played the idea long enough, it went from there to a groove. Ninety-nine percent of the time he wouldn't have any lyrics. He would have to go home and write the words out. Jimi was a stickler for getting a reel-to-reel copy made, taking it home, and writing lyrics to that, or making changes to what he had recorded."

"Ships Passing in the Night" was also recorded, but, like so many similar efforts, Jimi did not devise an appropriate ending, so the track fell apart. The final reel contained seven takes of "Jam w/piano." The seventh and final take was listed as complete. One false take of "Stone Free" was recorded before Jimi chose to abandon the effort. One take of "Blues Shuffle" came apart fairly early, and Jimi returned to "With the Power of God."

■

Wednesday, May 21, 1969
New York, Record Plant. 3:30 A.M. to 7:30 A.M. Engineer: Dave Ragno.

Another wild night of jamming, with little to show at the end of the session. "The party atmosphere seemed to be a deterrent to what Jimi was trying to accomplish," says engineer Dave Ragno. "If Devon wasn't trying to drive him crazy, then someone else would come into the control room chugging a bottle of tequila and portioning out cocaine to

anybody who wanted it. The session was just a big party. Some of the things we laid down on tape were nice, but they weren't serious. They weren't the things he really wanted to do. I didn't care to be on the sessions, because I didn't approve of some of the attitudes that people around him had."

Hendrix, Billy Cox, Buddy Miles, and an unnamed conga player attempted loose renditions of "Earth Blues," incorrectly marked on the tape box as "Lullaby for the Summer," but none was cohesive. A particularly uninspired jam followed, as Buddy Miles assumed lead guitar, supported by an occasional harmonica blast by an unnamed participant. Buddy returned to his drumkit for the next jam, which drew Jimi's participation once more, but the yield was minor — the group sounded as if they were simply having some spirited fun.

Following a tape change, another unsuccessful attempt was made to record the basic tracks for "Earth Blues." The effort was stalled by tuning and tempo problems. His interest in the track faltering, Jimi only occasionally provided a lead vocal. The evening's highlight was "Bleeding Heart," labeled "Peoples, Peoples" on the tape box. Comfortable with the blues arrangement Jimi desired, the group's performance was their most cohesive of the evening. While no finished masters were achieved, one take of "Bleeding Heart" was later edited and issued as part of 1994's *Jimi Hendrix: Blues*.

Before the session concluded, a ferocious rendition of "Hear My Train A Comin' " was also cut. In direct contrast to most of the evening's efforts, Jimi's tone was superb, and he sang and played with great spirit. This raw recording stands as one of the unreleased gems in the Hendrix tape library. Jimi also attempted a disjointed "Villanova

Junction Blues" and one final stab at "Earth Blues" before calling the session to a close.

■

Thursday, May 22, 1969

New York, Record Plant. 4:30 A.M. to 7:30 A.M. Engineer: Dave Ragno. Second engineer: Llyllianne Davis.

Joined once again by Billy Cox and Buddy Miles, Hendrix recorded "Message from Nine to the Universe," an engaging early hybrid of what would later develop as "Message to Love" and "Earth Blues." Partway through this extended take, Jimi coaxed his girlfriend, Devon Wilson, onto the studio floor to contribute lead vocals. While hardly a polished vocalist, Wilson accepted Jimi's invitation and proceeded to trade portions of the song's lyrics with him. Soon after their impromptu call-and-response vocals had concluded, Jimi brought the song to a close with a thunderous flourish.

A heavily edited version of this take was later issued as part of 1980's *Nine to the Universe* compilation. For that album, all of Devon's lively warblings were left on the cutting-room floor.

■

Sports Arena, San Diego, California

Saturday, May 24, 1969. Engineers: Wally Heider, Abe Jacob.

A vibrant performance by the Experience that included "Fire," "Hey Joe," "Spanish Castle Magic," "Red House," "I Don't Live Today," "Star Spangled Banner," "Foxey Lady," "Purple Haze," and "Voodoo Child (Slight Return)." One of the group's more memorable performances, this San Diego concert

Jimi ignites the crowd by playing with his teeth, May 25, 1969, Santa Clara, California.

(Chuck Boyd/Flower Children Ltd.)

is perhaps best known for the magnificent rendition of "Red House" that graced 1972's *Hendrix: In the West*.

"I Don't Live Today" was later included as part of 1982's *Jimi Hendrix Concerts*. When Reprise reissued that compilation on compact disc in 1987, "Foxey Lady" was remixed by Mark Linett and added as a bonus track. Finally, in 1991, Hendrix's entire performance was issued as part of *Stages*. Unfortunately, not every performance was worthy of release, particularly "Hey Joe," where Jimi was clearly struggling with his tuning.

■
Sunday, June 8, 1969
Hollywood, Wally Heider Recording, Studio 3. Engineer: Eddie Kramer.

On the heels of Wally Heider's location recordings of the Experience in concert (April 26, 1969, at the Los Angeles Forum and May 24, 1969, at the San Diego Sports Arena), engineer Eddie Kramer was dispatched to Los Angeles to review both recent Heider recordings, as well as a magnificent February 24, 1969, Royal Albert Hall concert that had also been recorded. Drawn from these three sources, a live album was prepared for Michael Jeffery's consideration. Jeffery had hoped that a live album could be quickly prepared as a possible release for Reprise or even Capitol Records, to whom Jimi still owed one album as per the settlement in his lengthy legal battle with producer Ed Chalpin and PPX Industries.

On this day, Kramer completed mixes and edits for "Star Spangled Banner" (San Diego), "Purple Haze" (San Diego), and "Little Wing" (Royal Albert Hall).

■
Tuesday, June 10, 1969
Hollywood, Wally Heider Recording, Studio 3. Engineer: Eddie Kramer.

While no tape boxes exist, Kramer did work on Monday, June 9, reviewing and preparing rough mixes of some of the tracks that figured to contend for a slot on the live disc. On June 10, mixes of "I Don't Live Today" (L.A. Forum) and "Getting My Heart Back Together" (Royal Albert Hall) were prepared.

At the end of Kramer's three days at Wally Heider Recording, an album of live performances was assembled and copies given to Michael Jeffery. Jeffery appeared to take no action, as by June 15, 1969, the tape boxes containing the mixes Kramer had prepared were marked "outtakes" and the project scrapped indefinitely. Though Reprise did not ultimately dismiss the concept of issuing a live album until early September 1969, the decision was made to compile a U.S. version of Track Records' successful *Smash Hits* album. With permission from Michael Jeffery, Reprise organized the details and scheduled a July release.

In the days after the Experience's June 29 performance at the Denver Pop Festival, Noel Redding elected to leave the group and focus his energies on performing and recording with Fat Mattress, his solo vehicle. With Redding's departure, Hendrix, despite Michael Jeffery's objections, was determined to try to realize a new concept he had in mind: a group whose extra percussion and second guitar would enhance and diversify his sound.

In this time of crisis, Hendrix had turned to his tiny band of close friends. The recent arrival of Billy Cox had helped provide a spark, so now Jimi looked to reunite with another old comrade, guitarist Larry Lee.

That Jimi chose the unsung Larry Lee, rather than a more notable rock contemporary, surprised many in Hendrix's camp — save for Cox, who understood Lee's unique link to Hendrix. "Jimi had played both the rhythm and the lead with the Experience," explains Billy Cox. "He thought it might free him up to concentrate on his lead playing if he had someone else playing rhythm. Larry Lee was the first and only guy considered, and Jimi gave me the assignment of finding him. In Nashville, Larry had been a sort of master to Jimi, teaching him some *very* important things that he would need on this journey. Larry had taken Jimi by the hand and taught him a lot of things about the blues that you couldn't find in a book. That instruction helped Jimi put everything in perspective. Jimi respected Larry, and he knew that Larry knew as much about his own music as he did. He said, 'If I get anybody in here to help, I want Larry, because he will know where to go.' "

Despite Cox's and Hendrix's unflinching admiration for Lee's ability, Lee had not quite grasped their new direction, a notion perhaps best exemplified by his decision to play the Gibson 335 guitar preferred by blues master Freddie King rather than the Fender Stratocaster, which Hendrix had long identified as his guitar of choice. "I preached to Larry about getting a different guitar, but he preferred to play that 335, which was not compatible with where we were at musically," admits Cox. "Consequently, it did not blend properly. I would tell him that he needed a Stratocaster, but he just didn't listen."

With a second guitarist in tow, Hendrix looked to bolster and diversify the role of percussion in his music. Percussionist Jerry Velez had met Jimi prior to the breakup of the Experience. "I met

Jimi at Steve Paul's Scene," remembers Velez. "I had just finished jamming with the McCoys, and when I walked over to my table, Jimi and his entourage were sitting behind me. A little later, I joined the band onstage again for a few more tunes. When I came back to sit down, he leaned over and said, 'Listen, I'm recording this jam over at the studio tonight. We'll be starting around four, after this thing ends tonight. Do you want to come down and jam?' I said sure. I went over that night and jammed with Jimi and Buddy Miles, and we seemed to hit it off."

Joining Velez was Juma Sultan. Sultan was well known within the Woodstock artistic community, a respected percussionist actively involved with the Aboriginal Music Society, which presented a broad mosaic of musical influences in semiconcert form on Sunday evenings at the Tinker Street Cinema. Sultan lived on a farm in Woodstock and accepted an invitation to jam with Hendrix during Jimi's Woodstock stay. The exchange went well, and Jimi extended an offer to play with his band.

"Jimi had broken up the Experience and wanted to do more ethnic music," Velez explains. "He wanted to try African and Afro-Cuban music with a bigger band." While Jimi enjoyed jamming with Velez, Michael Jeffery was suspicious of Velez's ability. "Jeffery said, 'Who the fuck is this kid Jerry Velez? I've never even heard of him.' Jimi explained that he liked playing with me and wanted me in the band. Then Jimi decided to have two percussionists, with Juma and I providing both an African and Latin flavor."

Because Jimi had not fully determined what his new musical direction would be, he struggled to verbalize his concept to each of the musicians he assembled. His ambiguity soon created

Larry Lee during a break at the Hit Factory, August 1969.

(Jim Cummins/Star File)

Mitch Mitchell records a basic track at the Hit Factory, August 1969.

(Jim Cummins/Star File)

friction among his supporting cast, since roles and responsibilities were never definitively outlined. The most pressing problem arose among the trio of percussionists, as Mitch struggled to mesh with Velez and Sultan. "There was a *lot* of percussion," admits Velez. "I was a novice, and both Juma and I overplayed. Mitch's style involved a lot

of playing as it was, with a lot of offbeat time signatures." The time issue frustrated Mitchell, who questioned the validity of Jimi's concept, feeling that three percussionists hopelessly cluttered the group's sound. "There was a problem with keeping time," Cox recalls. "Mitch was a great player who always stayed right on the edge of keeping in time. There were many times when Jimi and I would sneak each other looks, thinking, 'Uh-oh,' Mitch ain't gonna make it,' but then *bang*, Mitch would be right there. Jimi's intentions were good, but it just didn't work when you had congas and timbals competing with what Mitch was trying to play."

Jimi's base of operations was a large house on Tavor Hollow Road in the Woodstock village of Shokan. The concept behind the rental of this stately, eight-bedroom luxury home was to provide Jimi with a comfortable base away from the pressures of Manhattan. Here, it was thought, Hendrix could rest, refocus, and work on new material. The reality, however, was that his troubles simply followed him upstate, as financial pressures, the ongoing studio project, the recent breakup of the Experience, and his impending trial for heroin possession in Toronto weighed heavily on his mind. The demands persisted. "The telephone never stopped ringing," Cox remembers. "It was always 'Hurry up and do this. Get this done, get that going.' They never let him have any peace."

Hendrix seemed to be a magnet for trouble and, as a result, was besieged by hustlers and drug dealers hoping to win his favor. "Jimi wasn't a drug fiend by any means. He dabbled like all the rest of us, but on the coffee table downstairs, there would be every drug imaginable available," remembers Velez. "Every major drug dealer would come up to Jimi and say, 'Hey man, I just got this great stuff from Nepal,' or 'I just brought this from Marseilles.' These people all kept coming, wanting to get in with him."

Groupies and hustlers streamed to the house, hoping to win an audience with their idol. Most were turned away, but many succeeded, often disrupting

whatever modicum of privacy Hendrix had been able to establish.

Most in Jimi's management never seriously considered the expanded band a legitimate exercise, pointing to Hendrix's uneven Woodstock performance as proof. Billy Cox thinks otherwise, citing the progress Jimi made with his songwriting. "The time Jimi spent up at the house was very productive. He had broken away from the Experience and was able to place his focus on creating new ideas like 'Jam Back at the House' or tightening up 'Izabella' with small, intricate things which no one else would know except for those of us who had to play them. We weren't just jamming. Those patterns we created are what made the songs. Jimi would take pattern 1, add parts of pattern 9, and finish it off with a piece from pattern 3. That's how the songs would come together."

Perhaps the finest example of this approach was "Dolly Dagger," which began as a simple bass riff by Cox. "Early one morning at the Woodstock house, I was sitting outside on the patio. Someone had set up the amplifiers the day before, and we had let them stay outside all night. I don't know why, but I was thinking of Big Ben in England, so I grabbed my bass and started playing, *da do da do, da do da do.* Jimi came to the window in his shorts and started hollering, 'Hey man, keep playing that! Don't stop!' He came running down, grabbed his guitar, and said, 'How about this?' He had the first line almost together. Then I came up with some different notes to act as a close. 'Dolly Dagger' was born in that instant. That was how we complemented each other."

Writing sessions at the Shokan house were, as a rule, informal. "We would set up a circle in the round and play a lot," remembers Velez. "Upstairs,

across from these two bedrooms, was a large living room, where we did a lot of acoustic jamming. Then, downstairs, we had all of our heavy gear in a big room." "The roadies took care of us in fine style," recalls Billy Cox. "Mitch's drum kit would be set up for us, and we would sit and play."

To maximize the creative potential of these spontaneous jam sessions, Hendrix and Cox began recording these free-form efforts. "Jimi knew I was a recording buff," explains Cox. "At first we set up a Scully two-track machine, but it was just too difficult to operate and haul around. So we went to the office and got enough money to buy a Sony, which had sound-on-sound recording capabilities. I mastered that machine!"

■

Smash Hits

Reprise MS 2025. U.S. album release. Wednesday, July 30, 1969. Producer: Chas Chandler, Jimi Hendrix. Engineer: Eddie Kramer, Dave Siddle.
Purple Haze/Fire/The Wind Cries Mary/Can You See Me/Hey Joe/All Along the Watchtower/Stone Free/Crosstown Traffic/Manic Depression/Remember/Red House/Foxey Lady

With the group's fans eagerly anticipating a sequel to *Electric Ladyland*, *Smash Hits* filled the void nicely. It was an extremely popular and durable primer built around "Stone Free," "Remember," "Red House," and "Can You See Me" — the four tracks Reprise had withheld when it compiled its own version of *Are You Experienced?* in 1967. These four recordings, each new to the U.S. market, were presented along with standouts from *Are You Experienced?* and *Electric Ladyland*, oddly bypassing selections from *Axis: Bold as Love*. Sales were significant, as *Smash Hits* rose to number 6 on the *Billboard* album chart.

After Hendrix's death, the compilation became Hendrix's top seller, outperforming all his other Reprise albums.

August 16, 1969: Jimi and Billy relax with friends on the patio of Hendrix's rented vacation house in upstate New York.
(Willis Hogans, Jr./Bill Nitopi Collection)

■
Monday, August 18, 1969
Woodstock Music & Arts Festival. Engineer: Eddie Kramer. Second engineer: Lee Osbourne.

Despite their many jam sessions at Jimi's Shokan retreat, the expanded Gypsy Sun & Rainbows ensemble was not fully prepared for their debut. Some highlights were scattered throughout Jimi's unusually long, one-hundred-forty-minute performance, but the group distinctly lacked cohesion, often struggling to balance their contributions in such Experience favorites as "Fire" and "Foxey Lady."

■
Thursday, August 28, 1969
New York, Hit Factory. Engineer: Eddie Kramer. Second engineer: Joey Zagarino.

With new material ready to record, Hendrix bypassed the Record Plant, opting for the Hit Factory, a smaller studio owned by songwriter Jerry Ragavoy. Hendrix asked Eddie Kramer to return and supervise these sessions. Kramer had some knowledge of the expanded group, having made a few trips to the Shokan house during Hendrix's stay — installing a tape machine on one occasion — and later recording their Woodstock performance. At the Hit Factory, while Kramer's name was not listed on each of the tape boxes used there, it was he, much more often than staff engineer Joey Zagarino, who can be heard offering instructions over the talkback microphone.

These Hit Factory dates repre-

Jimi in full flight on the 1969 American tour.

(John Gardiner)

sented Hendrix's first formal return to the recording studio after having spent much of the previous two months writing and relaxing in upstate New York. Joining Jimi was the full contingent of Gypsy Sun & Rainbows, the aggregation he had led just nine days before at the Woodstock festival in Bethel.

The evening began with an attempt at "Message to the Universe," an early, slower-paced rendition of what would become "Message to Love." "Jimi had the opening guitar riff on a little tape he had made at home," remembers Cox. "When he played it to me, I suggested some changes to the riff he was playing, and that made one complete pattern. The next pattern was repeated twice before the melody came back to the top. That's all it was. It was nothing but two separate patterns linked together. The intro was really the same as the ending. We just went up the fretboard until we could go no further."

With Hendrix singing passionately to the enthusiastic backing of his band, "Message to the Universe" had obvious promise. While they recorded thirty-six takes without capturing the desired basic track, many fine moments appeared throughout, most notably the infectious interplay between Cox and Hendrix. Interspersed between takes was a sloppy, impromptu "Lover Man," offered without vocals. Some loose attempts at "Izabella" with vocals from Jimi can also be heard, although they seemed to represent more a creative diversion than any kind of structured effort. Additional takes of "Message to the Universe" followed before Larry Lee led the ensemble through an untitled blues original, of which his lengthy lead guitar work was the song's most prominent feature.

After a short break to accommodate a tape change, "Message to the Universe" was revisited before Hendrix

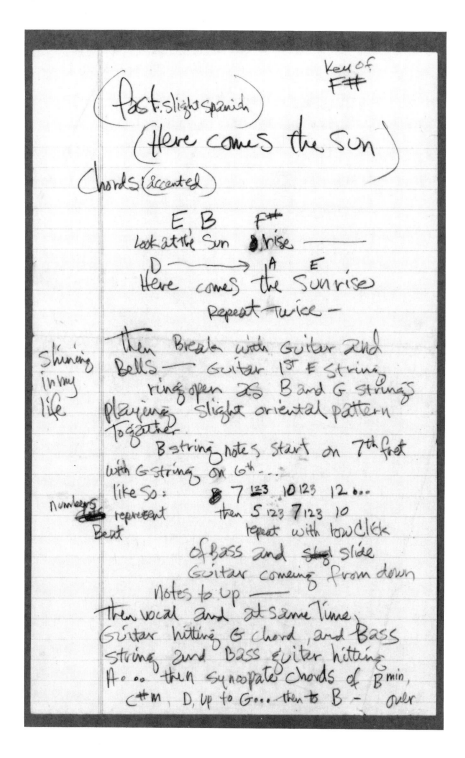

"Here Comes the Sun" highlights Hendrix's amazing, completely self-taught approach to composing, elaborately detailing frets, chord changes, and accompaniment.

(James A. Hendrix)

construction. This led to a spontaneous jam based on the tune, but Lee's solo broke down, causing the effort to end. Mitchell, who sat out the previous jam, rejoined the group as it began "Easy Blues," a marvelous, jazz-influenced instrumental jam. Years later, a heavily edited portion of this recording would be included as part of 1980's *Nine to the Universe*.

Recording continued with the group attempting six additional takes of "Izabella." An inspired workout of "Jam Back at the House" brought the session to a close. While none of these recordings would be designated finished masters, "Izabella" and "Message to Love" were exceptional new originals.

In addition to "Easy Blues," selected portions from this session were released after Jimi's death. Two sections of Jimi's vocal track for "Message to the Universe" were edited into a composite master created for "Message to Love," the opening track of 1975's *Crash Landing*.

On May 21, 1975, Alan Douglas edited "Jam Back at the House" out of this session's master reel, selecting this performance for *Midnight Lightning*. For that album, all the original recordings, save for Hendrix's voice and guitar parts, were scrapped in favor of new overdubs from guitarist Jeff Miranov, bassist Bob Babbit, drummer Alan Schwartzberg, and percussionist Jimmy Maeulin. The track was also retitled "Beginnings," a title used for a different recording of the same song issued on 1972's *War Heroes*.

shifted, with only moderate success, to "Izabella." Their momentum stalled, the band took a break to review what they had recorded. When recording resumed, Jimi could be heard explaining the guitar parts of "Burning Desire" to Lee. To elaborate his instructions, Hendrix performed the chord changes and made general comments on the song's

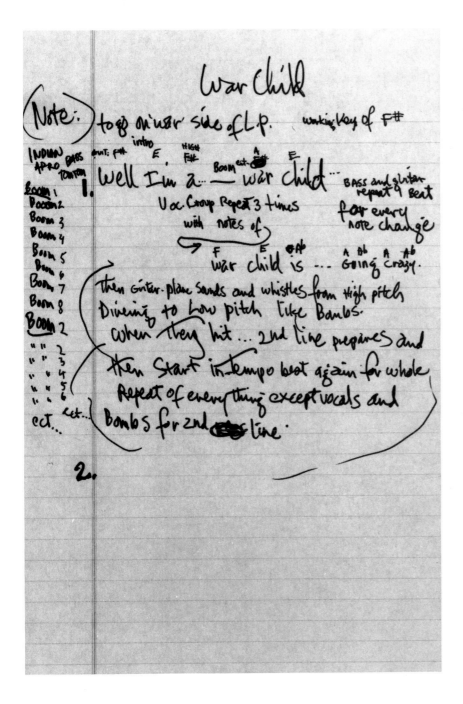

Unable to read music, Hendrix often crafted intricate instructions not just for his own guitar parts, but — as in this unreleased composition — for Mitch Mitchell and Billy Cox as well.

(James A. Hendrix)

■

Friday, August 29, 1969
New York, Hit Factory. Engineer: Eddie Kramer. Second engineer: Joey Zagarino.

Hendrix and company returned to "Izabella," struggling diligently to capture a suitable basic track. Despite the session's length (eight reels of tape were recorded — an unofficial record), no lack of desire is apparent on Hendrix's part, as his lead vocal and

guitar work were spirited throughout. The evening began with the band running the song down, adding refinements outlined by Jimi as he tried to establish the desired arrangement. Significant progress had been made by the beginning of reel four, which featured three strong takes. Take 3 from this reel was marked "hold." Later that evening, overdubs were recorded onto this version, with Hendrix replacing his lead vocal and recording two separate, additional guitar tracks. A variety of percussion instruments were also overdubbed, including a shaker, cowbell, and congas. Hendrix also provided a hilarious moment, prefacing his vocal overdub by licking his lips and making a huge chomping sound.

Though Hendrix would ultimately select take 3 from reel four as his working master, a number of takes from reel five were equally worthy. A robust take 2 was listed as "good," but take 8, timed at 4:45, was especially noteworthy. This rendition, arguably tighter and more polished than any previous effort — including the live version performed at Woodstock — provided a tantalizing glimpse into Jimi's new direction. While he did not specifically record a lead vocal for this track, he can occasionally be heard singing live, his voice acting, in this instance, as his own metronome.

Satisfied with the group's hold on "Izabella," Hendrix revived "Message to the Universe." Three long, loose attempts filled reel six. These versions represented little more than extended jams, the group experimenting with the song's main rhythm pattern.

By reel seven, the spotlight had once again focused on "Izabella." A flurry of false starts prefaced a complete take of "Izabella," which then evolved into a formative rendition of "Machine Gun." Despite the song's obvious promise, this effort gradually lost steam, fast digressing into a frenetic jam that was both out of tune and musical time.

Additional takes of "Izabella" and "Message to the Universe," as well as some ragged jamming, filled out the eighth and final reel of multitrack tape recorded on this evening. Before the session concluded, overdubs for "Izabella" followed, as did a mixing session, where Hendrix and Kramer reviewed the evening's highlights and prepared a rough mix of "Izabella."

While none of the recordings made on this evening would be issued during Hendrix's lifetime, the skeletal rendition of "Machine Gun" was later overhauled with overdubs recorded in 1974 and added to the posthumous compilation *Midnight Lightning*. Both the original demo and the overhauled master posthumously prepared by Alan Douglas and Tony Bongiovi paled in comparison to the Fillmore East performance that formed the centerpiece of the *Band of Gypsys* album.

■

Saturday, August 30, 1969
New York, Hit Factory. Engineer: Eddie Kramer. Second engineer: Joey Zagarino.

This evening was dedicated largely to the recording of Hendrix's "Sky Blues Today" and Larry Lee's "Mastermind." Nine takes of "Mastermind" were recorded, with Lee lending vocals to takes 1, 2, and 4. While the song's arrangement was nearly identical to the version performed at Woodstock, only take 4 was marked "good," and no finals were achieved.

"Sky Blues Today" was also recorded, although these versions were hardly polished. Marbled among the many takes were jams, but they sound

cluttered, with Mitchell struggling to keep time amid the competing percussion accents provided by Velez and Sultan. An uneventful spontaneous effort entitled "Jimi's Jam" closed out the third and final reel.

■

"Stone Free" / "If Six Was Nine"
Reprise 0853. U.S. single release. Wednesday, September 3, 1969.

Lifting "Stone Free" from the bestselling *Smash Hits* compilation, Reprise again tried, albeit unsuccessfully, to crack *Billboard*'s elusive Top 40 listing. For the first time since Reprise's May 1967 launch of "Hey Joe," a Jimi Hendrix Experience single missed the charts entirely.

■

Thursday, September 4, 1969
New York, Hit Factory. Engineer: Joey Zagarino.

Perhaps eager to establish the proper mood, Hendrix kicked off this session with a robust workout of "Jam Back at the House." Punctuated by Hendrix's blistering lead work, this rendition jumped off to a rousing start before becoming unglued, as, unfortunately, an effective ending had yet to be devised. The take collapsed abruptly during Jimi's final, frenetic climb up the fretboard of his guitar.

The balance of the session was dedicated to new takes of "Mastermind," with Larry Lee again supplying lead vocals. Steeped in R&B, "Mastermind" provided Cox, Lee, and Hendrix with a welcome opportunity to pay homage to Curtis Mayfield, one of their primary influences. Lee's modest vocal

effectively delivered the song's gentle plea, while Hendrix offered tasteful rhythm and lead guitar work in support. Eighteen takes in all were recorded, with take 4 the first to be highlighted, though that effort was described as only "fair." Take 9 was complete, as was 11, but, lacking both cohesion and spirit, neither could accurately be described as a master. Recording continued until a complete take 18 ultimately yielded the finished master.

■

Friday, September 5, 1969
New York, Hit Factory. Engineer: Joey Zagarino.

Hours after the group's scintillating performance at the United Block Association Benefit show on 139th Street in Harlem, Hendrix and company returned to the studio to tackle "Burning Desire," another promising new original.

Twenty-seven takes of "Burning Desire" were recorded, but none truly came close to realizing a finished master. While Hendrix and Cox maintained a firm grasp on the song's melody, the multiple takes attempted were hampered by a steady series of missed notes and timing problems. Hendrix added an additional guitar part and a conga overdub from Juma Sultan to take 27, but neither had a substantial impact. Despite many splendid moments throughout, a finished master would elude them on this occasion. In its present form, "Burning Desire" would require significant restructuring to warrant additional recording.

While the band had been unable to realize Jimi's vision for the song, Hendrix was undeterred. On this night, he remained at the studio alone, recording a unique working demo, which provides

Mitchell's drum kit. Six takes were put down on tape, but Hendrix still seemed unsatisfied. While Zagarino was effusive in his praise, Jimi remained unconvinced, instructing him to hold the tape aside for further consideration.

■
Saturday, September 6, 1969
New York, Hit Factory. Engineer: Joey Zagarino.

Despite the promise at which "Burning Desire" had hinted the previous evening, Hendrix chose to record "Valleys of Neptune," another fine work-in-progress. Recording began with three meandering, incomplete takes, each without vocals. Hendrix's enthusiasm seemed lukewarm, as the expanded band struggled to master the song's arrangement. Complicating his task further was that "Valleys of Neptune," despite its potential, was no more developed than either "Burning Desire" or "Sky Blues Today." The session's mood lightened when Hendrix and Lee kicked off "Blues for Me and You," a spontaneous, original blues workout.

One of the more recognized (and widely bootlegged) of Hendrix's many unreleased jam sessions, "Blues for Me and You" was originally slated by Alan Douglas to be featured as part of *Multicolored Blues*, an unreleased compilation of blues jams originally scheduled for release sometime in 1976. When that album was scrapped, "Blues for Me and You" was also left off *Nine to the Universe*, a collection of edited studio jams aimed at showcasing Hendrix's jazz leanings. Ironically, this jam was even excluded from the 1994 MCA compilation *Jimi Hendrix: Blues*. Though such decisions with regard to unreleased Hendrix recordings are never permanent, "Blues for Me and

August 1969. Returning to his studio with Billy Cox and his new band, Gypsy Sun & Rainbows.

(Jim Cummins/Star File)

a fascinating insight into his approach to composing. Working solely with engineer Joey Zagarino and the studio's eight-track tape machine, Hendrix recorded vocals, guitar, and a nimble bass line. To establish the tempo he desired, Jimi even climbed behind Mitch

Jimi jams at the Tinker Street Cinema in Woodstock, July 20, 1969.

(Willis Hogans, Jr./Bill Nitopi Collection)

You" appears destined to remain unreleased.

Five additional attempts at "Valleys of Neptune" followed, each with occasional vocals from Jimi and disorganized support from his group. After take 5 collapsed, Hendrix, desperate to ignite his rhythm section, tore into "Lover Man," hoping to establish the groove he desired. As "Lover Man"

came apart, Larry Lee moved to the fore, striking off an original blues jam, during which he assumed lead guitar chores. A few shining moments ensued, but little more.

Undaunted, Hendrix returned to "Valleys of Neptune," unsuccessfully directing the group through a host of unslated takes. Jimi's passionate live vocals rose infrequently above the din created by the rhythm section. Sultan and Velez sounded hopelessly cluttered, struggling to stay in time with Mitchell. Long jams founded on the "Valleys of Neptune" theme ensued, including one noteworthy effort where an occasional snatch of "Angel" could be detected in Jimi's playing. As with so many of Hendrix's sessions from this period, several shining moments were captured on tape, but they were simply moments and nothing more.

As he had done the previous evening, after the session had ended, Hendrix remained behind at the studio, creating another solo demo. Working again with the facility's eight-track tape machine, Jimi recorded five takes of "Trying to Be," later titled "Stepping Stone." Two separate complete takes were also recorded and marked "Different."

Unable to round his expanded group into shape, Hendrix wanted time to refocus before scrapping the experiment entirely. The ramifications of his lengthy legal battle with Ed Chalpin, coupled with cost overruns generated by the ongoing construction of Electric Lady Studios, had drained Jimi's cash reserves. Michael Jeffery organized a short U.S. tour to try to restore their depleted finances. At the last minute, Jimi balked, causing the cancellation of the entire tour. Hendrix argued that the band was not ready for touring. Furious at his troubled star, Jeffrey then demanded that Jimi — in addition to completing the album owed Capitol Records as per Hendrix's settlement with Ed Chalpin's PPX Industries — audition new musicians to back him. Much to Jimi's frustration, such an audition was actually staged at the Salvation Club.

"Jimi called me to ask if I had received my ticket," explains former Buddy Miles Express bassist Roland Robinson. "I said, 'What?' He told me to come on up and try things with the band. When I got up there it was really screwed up, because I had quit the Express on bad terms. Billy Cox was there, and he was really quiet. So I'm there feeling weird, and it occurred to me that Jimi hadn't told these guys that they weren't in the band anymore. We had two bands there. You had two bass players, two drummers, and a lot of real hostility in the air. Jimi's management was there, freaking out over all the people he was trying. Jimi started yelling, 'Just leave me the fuck alone! Let me play with the people I want to play with and I'll make you all the goddamn money you want!' We then got into this one jam, and Billy Cox was sitting in front of me with his arms folded, and Buddy was playing half-assed and scowling at me from behind the drums. Afterwards, Buddy started to get pissed off, and he told Jimi that if I was in the band, I'd be trying to take it over. So that set me off, and I'm shouting at Buddy that I'm going to kill him. It all got really funky, and I just said forget it. It just wasn't going to fly. We ended up going to the Salvation Club, and Jimi was embarrassed at what had happened. I got a week's pay and his apologies."

While no changes were made as a result of these auditions, they served only to widen the distance between Hendrix and his manager. "Jimi was wiped out," admits Velvert Turner. "He grabbed me at the Salvation and whispered, 'Don't you ever fuck up your life like I have.' He seemed tortured."

■ *Monday, September 15, 1969*
New York, Record Plant. 4:00 P.M. to 6:00 P.M. Engineer: Jack Adams. Second engineer: Tom Flye.

Leaving the Hit Factory behind, Hendrix returned to the Record Plant for this bizarre session, where the group's entire effort sounded oddly disjointed. Worse still, Hendrix's vocal microphone was incorrectly patched, rendering the tape's contents largely unusable.

Recording began with a rehearsal of "Sky Blues Today," followed by three formal takes. Take 1 was complete and, by a wide margin, the best of the lot. These initial takes were recorded without bass. Hendrix and Lee, however, can be heard working out the song's structure between takes. Following a tape change, Cox joined the group for two lengthy additional rehearsal takes, where sketches of "Villanova Junction Blues" and "Burning Desire" can be heard. Their rehearsals completed, six shambling takes of "Sky Blues Today" followed. The sixth and final take of the evening was complete and featured a vocal, but the tape box was marked "redo."

Nothing recorded on this evening came even close to resembling a finished master. Hendrix's condition sounded dubious, and the session was entirely unproductive.

With the pressures mounting around him, Hendrix seemed increasingly powerless to reverse the tide. Unable to realize the sound and direction he had hoped the expanded band would provide, Hendrix's brief tenure with Gypsy Sun & Rainbows was fast unraveling. Shortly after the disastrous September 15 session, Larry Lee threw in the towel and quietly returned to Memphis. "Larry just said, 'I think I'm probably in the way,' and took it upon

Michael Jeffery, Hendrix's manager.

(Jim Marshall)

himself to leave on good terms," remembers Billy Cox. "There was just too much bullshit around him to handle. He just decided that he had had enough."

■

Tuesday, September 23, 1969
New York, Record Plant. 3:00 A.M. Engineer: Jack Adams. Second engineer: Tom Flye.

With Larry Lee having returned to Memphis, Jerry Velez was the next to withdraw, leaving the group to pursue other opportunities. In their absence, a scaled down Gypsy Sun & Rainbows gamely attempted to finish "Valleys of Neptune," "Message of Love," and "Jam Back at the House," arguably the most promising of Hendrix's recent compositions.

Three takes of "Valleys of Neptune" set the session in motion, but none of these efforts was cohesive. "Drinking Wine," a modest, impromptu blues original, came next and provided the evening's sole highlight. Hendrix then returned to "Valleys of Neptune," recording seven instrumental takes. Take 7 was complete, but it hardly resembled a finished master. Individual takes of both "Message of Love" and "Jam Back at the House" were equally dispirited, and the session ground to a halt.

The mounting pressure and Jimi's deteriorating condition had soured Cox's outlook as well. In late September, he, too, decided to leave, checking out of the Penn Garden Hotel and quietly returning to Nashville. "The whole problem started as soon as we got to the house in Woodstock," admits Cox. "There were people who just did not want this band to succeed. It was one thing after another. There was the shootout down at the front gate of the Shokan house, the infiltration of people into the house, drugs being put into people's food — just a lot of unnecessary, underhanded things being done for no reason. I didn't have time to try and figure out who was behind all this and why were they doing so. When you get down to people fighting with guns out in front of the house, there is something *seriously* wrong. All I knew was that I was going to do the Woodstock gig, help out my buddy, and carry my ass back to Nashville. That was my focus. After Woodstock, I hung around as long as I could, but there was just too much bullshit going down all around him."

Hendrix's nerves were equally frayed. "Jimi had gone down into this well," recalls Cox. "He said, 'Man, I just can't get it together. I've gotta rest my head.' He told me that if he could, he was thinking of going off to Africa with [girlfriend] Colette [Mimram]. I wished him Godspeed and told him I was glad I had been able to help him. That was it. I didn't think I was ever going to be involved with him again."

■
Wednesday, September 24, 1969
New York, Record Plant. Engineer: Jack Adams. Second engineer: Tom Flye.

Working without a bassist, nineteen takes of "Jimi's Tune" — actually a rough-hewn attempt at "Power of Soul" — were recorded, with the last marked 'hold.' Seven takes of "I'm a Man," later known as "Stepping Stone," were also recorded, as was a lengthy jam with Juma Sultan.

Take 17 of "Jimi's Tune" was an early contender for 1975's posthumous *Crash Landing*. It was replaced, however, by a more structured rendition recorded by the Band of Gypsys on January 21, 1970.

■
Thursday, September 25, 1969
New York, Record Plant. 12:00 midnight. Engineer: Jack Adams. Second engineer: Dave Ragno.

Exhausted and frustrated by the lack of progress made by the expanded band, Mitch Mitchell returned to England. Unsure of Hendrix's immediate plans, Mitch set no timetable for his return. His departure sounded the death knell for Gypsy Sun & Rainbows, leaving Juma Sultan the sole remaining member.

Filling Mitchell's chair on this session was Buddy Miles. Eight takes of "Sky Blues Today" were attempted, with Hendrix and Miles joined by Juma Sultan. With little or no rehearsal, Miles did his best to learn the song on the fly, making adjustments dictated by Hendrix. Despite Miles's enthusiasm, Jimi was forced to devote crucial studio time to instructing Miles rather than focusing on improving his own performance. The eighth and final take would be held over, marked as the best effort of the evening. "Room Full of Mirrors" was also recorded, but it, too, sounded unrehearsed.

Exhausted and deeply depressed, Jimi shut everything down, retreating to his apartment and sinking beneath a wave of anxiety and self-doubt. As he had done once before, Hendrix appealed to Billy Cox to return and help him regain his focus. "When I agreed to come back, Jimi sat me down in his apartment and explained what was going on," recalls Cox. "My thought was to just give [PPX and Capitol Records] them something. Over the next couple of days, he came up with the concept that we would try something outside of the Experience. I asked whether he had talked to Mitch, but he only mumbled something I couldn't hear and wouldn't go any further with it. Buddy Miles called me, and I told him of the situation. He said, 'Well, I'll get help. Let's get him out and jam.' "

"The fall of 1969 was a real strange time for Jimi Hendrix," states Buddy Miles. "He wasn't doing anything. We were jamming constantly, but I wasn't getting paid for any of those sessions. I'm not the most subtle guy in the world, so I said, 'I have an idea. Let's put a band together.' We talked about different things, like having Stevie Winwood, who we both wanted, join the band, but in the end it came down to just the three of us."

Deep within the blues, Jimi performs at the San Jose Pop Festival, one of the last performances by the original Jimi Hendrix Experience.
(Nancy Carter/Flower Children Ltd.)

"We basically put together the Band of Gypsys group," states former Douglas Records executive Stefan Bright. "This was going to be the first time that Jimi was going to play with Buddy on a regular basis. The old group was gone, and Buddy was in because he gave Jimi a little more funk."

"The Band of Gypsys were put together in Douglas's office," admits Miles. "Between Alan and Bill Graham, who gave us the dates at the Fillmore East. Jimi and I had gone to him to ask if we could do it, and he couldn't believe it."

"Originally, the bass player was going to be Billy Rich," explains Bright. "Rich had played on the John McLaughlin album that we had done. We tried to bring Billy in to play with Buddy, but eventually, Jimi brought in Billy Cox, and that became the group."

Miles, Rich, Douglas, and Stefan Bright had worked before, when Miles and bassist Billy Rich had joined organist Larry Young to serve as the backing unit for John McLaughlin's Douglas Records debut. Rich had been the consensus choice for the new group, but Hendrix opted instead for Cox, whose steady presence and trusted friendship he valued above all else.

"Not playing with the Band of Gypsys and not being part of that live album is one of my real regrets," admits Billy Rich. "I had moved to Denver and begun working on a project in San Francisco for Columbia Records when Alan Douglas called, asking if I wanted to do this album with Jimi Hendrix. At that time, I just couldn't get away to do it."

■
October 1969

New York, Juggy Sound Studios. Engineer: Steve Katz. Second engineer: Richie Cicero.

Alan Douglas and Stefan Bright organized some sessions at Juggy Sound for the group, but Cox and Bright clashed almost immediately. The roots of their ill feelings centered over Bright's preference for bassist Billy Rich over Cox. Cox, states Bright, was not his or Alan Douglas's first choice to handle the bassist chores in the new group. This issue caused considerable tension between the two men, leading to one control-room incident that nearly resulted in a fistfight. "We were just goofing around during those sessions at Juggy," remembers Cox. "It was a lousy deal with a lot of bad vibes around. There was a spiritual side to the music we were creating, and the atmosphere at Juggy didn't allow Jimi to create. He sensed it, and nothing we ever did there worked out. I had words with Alan's partner, Stefan Bright. You couldn't create music under those circumstances. Those guys distracted my focus away from making music, and I couldn't get it together. People forgot what the recording studio is all about. The studio was for creative ventures, not social gatherings. We weren't the type of musicians who had music on a music stand in front of us. We played by ear, feel, and spirit. If there is anything negative surrounding that effort, it stopped any creativity from occurring. There were times when Jimi would just shoot me a look and I would know what to do. I don't know if you would call that being telepathic, but those cues would come from him without words, and you had to be looking at him and concentrating on what you were playing — not on what was going on in the control room."

Another point of contention was that Cox placed little faith in the production skills of either Bright or Douglas. The two, he reasoned, were entirely unnecessary to the recording of Jimi's music. As a result, whatever relationship Cox had had with Bright and Douglas quickly deteriorated. "Bright and Douglas knew that I didn't think they were necessary," remembers Cox. "I wasn't in their corner because I didn't think they were on Jimi's level. They weren't needed for the production of the music. Jimi was well equipped to do that. These songs were his creations, and he was entitled to produce his own stuff. He didn't need any outside person to produce music for him. But because of that, Bright would do things like tell Jimi and Buddy that they didn't need me. But Jimi was determined to have me play with him. Irregardless of whatever Alan or Stefan wanted, I played on most of those sessions anyway."

■
Friday, November 7, 1969

New York, Record Plant. Engineer: Jack Adams. Second engineer: Dave Ragno.

Although Alan Douglas's voice cannot be heard over the talkback microphone, he was most likely present, as "Douglas Records," his recording label, was written on the tape box as the "client" being serviced this evening. Billy Cox did not take part in the session.

Without a bass player, Hendrix and Buddy Miles ran through a number of energetic takes of both "Izabella" and "Room Full of Mirrors." Rather than perfecting structured takes, the efforts recorded here were geared more toward developing both songs and sharpening the polyrhythmic interplay between Hendrix and Miles.

Shortly after reel two began, technical problems slowed the pair's progress. Hendrix, in particular, was bothered by the volume and general quality of the recording being supplied to his headphones. Adams and Ragno feverishly attempted to remedy the situation, but when recording resumed, Jimi's amplifier started to malfunction, causing his guitar sound to drop out intermittently. This again caused a scramble in the control room. To help salvage the session, engineer Tony Bongiovi was sent for, and, though he was not listed on the tape box, his distinctive voice can be plainly heard from this point forward. When recording resumed, a series of unslated takes of "Room Full of Mirrors" was attempted. Both Hendrix's and Miles's performances were inspired, with Jimi singing live, straying from one take to an impromptu rendition of "Shame, Shame, Shame," a blues original whose lyrics seemingly detail Jimi's tenuous relationship with his stepbrother, Leon Hendrix. Another take included a raw, rough stab at "Ezy Ryder" before Hendrix returned to "Room Full of Mirrors" with a flourish.

No masters were achieved on this session, and the tape box was marked 'Outtakes.'

To the engineering staff at the Record Plant, the active participation of Douglas and Bright had come as a surprise. "Douglas and Bright just sort of came in and took over," explains Tom Erdelyi, who worked as second engineer on some of the sessions. "They were running the show. I was surprised, because I was a fan of the Jimi Hendrix Experience, and no one seemed to understand what Jimi was trying to accomplish. Jimi was such a perfectionist. It seemed as if he was just taking his time, because no tracks were being completed. We just thought that Douglas was being patient."

The specific roles of Bright and

Douglas on the relatively few multi-track tapes recorded under their supervision were unclear. Of the two, Douglas was the more vocal, although only slightly. "I don't know whether they had specific titles or not, but Stefan Bright was supposed to be the producer and Alan Douglas the executive producer," remembers Erdelyi. "There were times when just Stefan Bright was there, but Jimi just played what he wanted, and those guys made comments from the control room."

■

"Fire" / "The Burning of the Midnight Lamp"
Track Records 604 033. U.K. single release. Friday, November 14, 1969.

With no new product forthcoming, Track tried the singles market again with "Fire," a favorite from *Are You Experienced?* Interest in the disc proved minimal, however, as "Fire" missed the U.K. chart entirely.

■

Monday, November 17, 1969
New York, Record Plant. Engineer: Tony Bongiovi. Second engineer: Tom Erdelyi.

With Billy Cox back in the fold, "Room Full of Mirrors," "Ezy Ryder," and "Stepping Stone" were recorded. "Jimi had definitely come into the studio with a plan," says Bright. "Because 'Izabella' and 'Room Full of Mirrors' were planned songs which took very little time to do. 'Machine Gun' was something he had been working on for quite some time. He jammed on songs like 'Dolly Dagger,' but the basic tracks for 'Izabella,' 'Stepping Stone,' 'Message to Love,' and 'Room Full of Mirrors' were already arranged and were re-

corded in a very short time period."

The evening's focus was "Room Full of Mirrors." "Jimi was a perfectionist," Tom Erdelyi remembers. "He would record many different lead guitar solos, with each just as good as the other, but none to his satisfaction. It seemed to me that Jimi was looking for a sound that was in his head, and he was doing all kinds of things to try and capture that. He would do weird things like line a wall with stacks of Marshalls and crank them up to get this huge sustain. On 'Room Full of Mirrors,' he was trying to get a particular slide sound. He tried all kinds of slides — glass slides, metal slides, steel pedal slides — but none of them sounded like what he was hearing in his head." According to Alan Douglas, the solution to the problem came when Hendrix, still lacking the appropriate tool for his finger, slipped off his ring and used its stone to create the desired effect.

Hendrix did record a lead vocal track for "Room Full of Mirrors," although not without incident. "Jimi hated his voice," says Bright. "I guess the other people who had worked with him knew this, but we didn't. When it came time to record his vocals, he instructed the engineer and the assistant engineer to set up baffles around him and turn all of the lights in the studio out. I said, 'What the fuck are you talking about your voice for? Your voice is unique, and it's a part of your whole sound.' He said, 'I don't care what you say. This is the way I feel, and this is what we are going to do.' "

In addition to recording a lead vocal for the track, Hendrix recruited Albert and Arthur Allen, his longtime friends from Harlem, to provide backing vocals. The pair, known professionally as the Ghetto Fighters, were escorted to the studio by Hendrix, who instructed them on their parts. After this was com-

At the Record Plant, 1969.

(Warner Bros.)

pleted, Hendrix and the twin brothers visited Studio B, where Mountain was mixing their album. "Leslie West was recording 'Mississippi Queen' in Studio B, and Hendrix was so knocked out by the riff that he invited him over for a jam," remembers Arthur Allen.

West was thrilled by the chance meeting. "I first saw Jimi play at Woodstock," recalls West. "I missed meeting him there, but when we were recording *Mountain Climbing* at the Record Plant, he heard the riff to 'Mississippi Queen' and just walked into the control room. He sat down next to [Mountain bassist and producer] Felix Pappalardi and I, and we played him the mix to "Never in My Life." He was the first guy outside of the band to ever hear it. When he heard the lick I was playing, he just turned and looked at me. For some reason, the riff sounded like a horn line, and it got a rise out of him. Seeing him react like that made me think, 'Wow! He must think I have a little something in me!' In fact, he even came to see us play at the Fillmore East. He was sitting in one of those opera seats next to [Mountain drummer] Corky Laing's mother. She didn't know who the hell he was, but when we saw him there watching *us* play, that was a big deal."

■

Thursday, November 20, 1969
New York, Record Plant. 5:00 P.M. Engineer: Bob Hughes. Second engineer: Dave Ragno.

Six solid, but not spectacular, takes of "Them Changes," Buddy Miles's signature song. Takes 5 and 6 were complete, though neither was considered a master. Twelve subpar instrumental takes of "Burning Desire" followed, presented with barely a trace of enthusiasm. None was complete, and few even

The Electric Lady Studio A control room under construction, fall 1969.

(Eddie Kramer)

came close to the mark. Hendrix seemed unsettled about his guitar tone — varying it between takes, with little success.

Reel two began with two uninspired attempts at "Lover Man," described here as "Here Comes Your Lover Man." Three halfhearted takes of "Hear My Train A Comin'" followed, paced by a live vocal from Jimi. "That was a song Jimi had done with the original Experience," remembered Cox. "It was a simple blues song in the key of B, but he felt comfortable doing it, because it was Jimi's kind of blues. I think the lyrics he had for the song, about coming back to buy the town and put it all in his shoe, was his way of talking back to the establishment. That was Jimi's way of singing the blues. People weren't going to be able to push him out of the way, because he was going to get rich and buy the town out from under them."

A return to "Burning Desire" met with similar disinterest, as did a brief reprise of "Them Changes." The session collapsed at this point, the group sounding thoroughly disinterested. Though it would be difficult to detail what exactly had soured Hendrix's mood on this occasion, what is known is that this surely ranks among Jimi's most unproductive experiences in the recording studio.

Jimi onstage at the Boston Garden.

(Willis Hogans, Jr. /Bill Nitopi Collection)

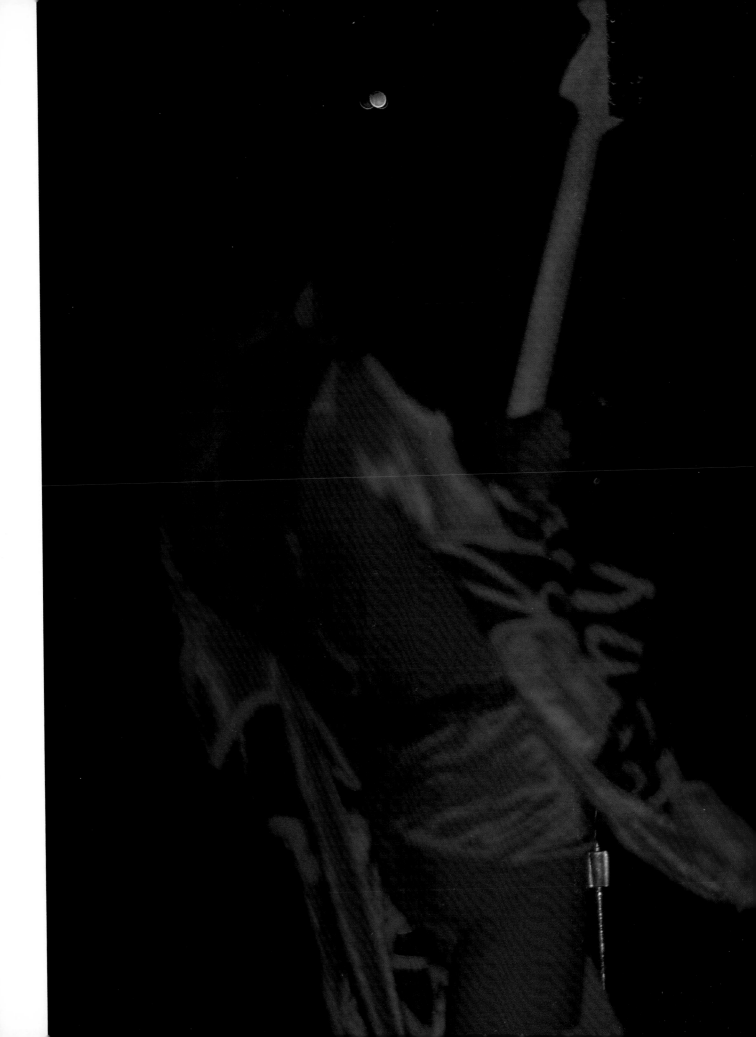

Friday, November 21, 1969

New York, Record Plant. Engineer: Tony Bongiovi. Second engineer: Tom Erdelyi.

With Hendrix having struck absolute bottom the previous evening, Bright and Douglas endeavored to redirect his sagging spirits. "We specifically brought in Tony Bongiovi to engineer 'Izabella,'" explains Bright. "Jimi would say things about Tony like, 'What the fuck is this kid doing in the studio?,' because Tony, at that time, looked very young. Tony gave Jimi's sound a groove which, we felt, hadn't been done before. With 'Izabella,' the sound of the bass and drums was so funky. Tony had worked in Motown, and he went for that element in his sound."

As intended, "Izabella" was reconstructed from the bottom up, beginning with a very loose initial take. Subsequent takes increasingly took shape. Via the talkback microphone, Alan Douglas could be heard directing the session, along with Bright and Bongiovi. Of the nineteen attempts made on this reel, takes 1, 2, 4, 10, 12, 16, and 19 were complete.

Following a tape change, one last attempt at "Izabella" was recorded, and this take, the twentieth of the evening, delivered the basic track. Even in its raw, unfinished form, this working master sounded very close to the finished mix briefly issued in February 1970 as a Band of Gypsys single. The focus then turned to "Burning Desire." This effort, however, was not as successful. As "Izabella" had done, "Burning Desire" gradually improved over the twenty-four takes recorded, but none captured the intensity Hendrix was searching for. Not having fully defined the song's rhythmic pattern caused some confusion for Buddy Miles, who struggled with some of the tempo changes. A ver-

sion of "Machine Gun" was also attempted, but its arrangement had varied only slightly from the primitive demo Hendrix had recorded during the August 1969 sessions at the Hit Factory. Four takes were recorded, and only the fourth and final take was complete. Nothing in this unrealized demo even hinted at Hendrix's evolving vision for this powerful song.

Unable to make progress at this stage with "Machine Gun," Hendrix turned to "Power of Soul," described here as "Paper Airplanes." Twenty-four takes were attempted, with no vocals from Jimi. At this stage, the group was still honing the song's complex arrangement. Apart from the main riff, Hendrix liberally experimented with his rhythm and solo parts. Of the many takes recorded, only take 2 could be described as complete. That version was immediately superseded as Hendrix, Cox, and Miles performed the song repeatedly in an attempt to learn each other's parts.

Friday, November 28, 1969

A quarter-inch, two-track recording was made on this day, although it is not known where the actual recording took place. The only legend marked on the tape box was "Buddy Miles/Billy Cox." This may have been a recording made at Baggy's rehearsal studios or simply a rough mix of a recording done this day at the Record Plant.

These November sessions would mark the conclusion of Douglas's stint as a producer for Hendrix. In a December 4, 1969, letter to Hendrix, citing his own busy schedule, constant pressure from Michael Jeffery, and Hendrix's own disinterest, Douglas parted company from Jimi.

While Douglas has made innumer-

able statements to the contrary over the past two decades, none of the sessions he supervised yielded as much as a single finished master. Save for the basic rhythm track for "Room Full of Mirrors," which Hendrix would later overhaul at Electric Lady Studios in August 1970, none of these November 1969 session tapes was recognized by Hendrix as a candidate for his long-overdue fourth studio disc. Even Douglas could not make use of these tapes. Instead, when he began assembling the controversial *Crash Landing* album in 1974, he opted to overdub rhythm parts onto other unfinished Hendrix tapes, using session musicians to replace the original contributions of Hendrix's sidemen.

Monday, December 15, 1969

New York, Record Plant. 3:00 A.M. Engineer: Bob Cotto. Second engineer: R. Beekman.

An upbeat session that yielded some surprises, most notably the lengthy rendition of Albert King's "Born Under a Bad Sign" later released as part of the 1994 compilation *Jimi Hendrix: Blues.* Following "Born Under a Bad Sign," the session took on the appearance of a rehearsal. A spirited "Lover Man" came next, albeit without a vocal from Jimi. Seemingly satisfied with the group's handle on that song, Jimi suggested that they try "Izabella." What followed was a sped-up rendition, with only occasional vocals from Jimi. Hendrix then

Jimi leads the Band of Gypsys at the Fillmore East, December 13, 1969.

(Joe Sia)

shifted to "Earth Blues," treating this single take in a similar fashion. Two promising takes of "Message to Love" followed, again with only casual vocal accompaniment from Jimi. These two renditions sported a different arrangement than either of the versions issued as part of *Band of Gypsys* or *Crash Landing*. Buddy assumed center stage for "Them Changes," enhanced by some strong rhythm and lead playing from Jimi. The group managed to complete a single, effective take before abandoning the track.

With the group in a groove, seven takes of "Lover Man" came next. These versions, rather surprisingly, never quite jelled. Switching to "Burning Desire," the group was beset by the same problems as with "Lover Man."

Thursday, December 18, 1969
New York, Record Plant. Engineer: Jack Adams. Second engineer: Tom Erdelyi.

The group made significant progress on "Message to Love," "Ezy Ryder," and "Bleeding Heart." "Ezy Ryder," still known at this stage as "Easy Rider," began this session on a high note, providing the basic track that would be expanded and completed at Electric Lady Studios the following summer. "We started 'Ezy Ryder' here at the Record Plant," explains Cox, "but it wasn't finished until the following summer at Electric Lady. Jimi had come up with the main pattern, but I had *da da da dum, da da did da da* and didn't know what to do with it. Jimi built on it from

there, and it became a living, breathing song, rather than just a combination of patterns."

The group then turned its focus to "Message to Love." The early takes revealed problems the group was having establishing the desired tempo. "We toyed with the tempo on that song," admits Cox. "Buddy wanted to slow it down, but Jimi wanted it more upbeat. Jimi would say, 'If you can't see little kids skippin' on your fast songs, you got nothing.'" Eighteen takes were recorded, with the eighteenth denoted the master.

Three takes of "Bleeding Heart" were also attempted, with the third complete but not identified as a master. Rough mixes were also prepared of "Ezy Ryder" (marked here as "Easy Rider") and "Message to Love."

Friday, December 19, 1969
New York, Record Plant. 3:00 A.M. Engineer: Bob Cotto. Second engineer: R. Beekman.

Building on the momentum created the previous evening, the Band of Gypsys completed basic tracks for both "Message to Love" and "Earth Blues." A single take of "Message to Love" captured the working master for that song, while "Earth Blues" required sixteen takes. Ultimately, Hendrix chose take 11 to serve as the basic track. Hendrix's lyrics for "Earth Blues" at this stage differed from later versions, although the arrangement would remain the same. Hendrix would also superimpose both a lead vocal and lead guitar part onto this

recording, both of these efforts later replaced by new overdubs. Backing vocals from Buddy Miles and the Ronettes were also recorded.

Tuesday, December 23, 1969
New York, Record Plant. Engineer: Bob Cotto. Second engineer: Tom Erdelyi.

Sadly, technical failures brought this spirited Band of Gypsys session to an abrupt close. "Honey Bed," a lively hybrid of "Bleeding Heart" and "Come Down Hard on Me," was debuted this evening. Jimi was in fine spirits, remarking, in his best Pigmeat Markham manner, that the track was called "Honey Bed, Sweetnin's, and a Yam!," which filled the control room with laughter. Three funky, albeit incomplete, takes were recorded, with Jimi alternately singing and humming the lyrics.

Of the lyrics Jimi did sing — which included such phrases as "Do I live or do I die?" and "You got me sitting up on your shelf" — the majority were later grafted to other Hendrix compositions. As take 3 wound down, Hendrix guided Cox and Miles through a primitive instrumental rendition of "Night Bird Flying." Just past the two-minute mark, a terrifying noise caused Jimi to shout, "Hey guys, what's that noise?" The squelch rapidly grew louder before the recording cut out and the session came to a halt. No other recording was attempted.

Wednesday, January 7, 1970

New York, Record Plant. Engineer: Bob Hughes. Second engineer: Tom Erdelyi.

Three complete takes of "I'm a Man" were recorded, as well as a single, complete take of "Cherokee Mist." Take 3 of "I'm a Man" provided the basic track onto which final overdubs were recorded on January 20, 1970. This new master, coupled with "Izabella," would be mixed and issued as a Reprise single in April 1970.

Friday, January 16, 1970

New York, Record Plant. Engineer: Bob Hughes. Second engineer: Dave Ragno.

Jimi presented yet another promising new song — a rough sketch of the medium-tempo ballad "Send My Love to Linda." Paced by Jimi's guitar and live vocal, Cox and Miles established the tempo. Though Jimi had developed only the song's rudiments, one take evolved into a lively, extended jam session.

Twelve takes of "Paper Airplanes," better known as "Power of Soul," were also recorded. Take 6, which came after five incomplete takes, was strong, but it still somewhat resembled a jam. Takes 11 and 12 were also complete, but again, an acceptable basic track eluded Hendrix. The group then tried "Burning Desire," but the five takes also left Jimi without a basic track.

Monday, January 19, 1970

New York, Record Plant. Engineer: Bob Hughes. Second engineer: Dave Ragno.

More work on "Burning Desire" was attempted, but Hendrix was still unable to realize a basic track from his effort. Additional overdubbing, as well as some experiments with backward guitar tracks, was also tried.

Tuesday, January 20, 1970

New York, Record Plant. Engineer: Bob Hughes. Second engineer: Dave Ragno.

A vibrant session, with Hendrix in good spirits. Overdub work was completed on the December 19, 1969, recording of "Message to Love." Jimi added a new lead guitar part to this master.

Take 11 of "Earth Blues" — from the same December 19, 1969, session as "Message to Love" — was also the recipient of a series of new overdubs, as Hendrix added new guitar and lead vocal parts. These would be replaced at Electric Lady Studios on June 26, 1970.

Take 3 of "I'm a Man," recorded on January 7, was rechristened "Sky Blues Today" and received guitar overdubs from Jimi, as did the December 18, 1969, recording of another promising, albeit unfinished, Band of Gypsys rocker, "Ezy Ryder."

Jimi's acquittal on drug charges and his recent progress with the Band of

Preparing another Stratocaster for action.

(Chuck Boyd/Flower Children Ltd.)

Gypsys had brightened his mood considerably. "You really could see that Jimi had turned the corner," says engineer Dave Ragno. "Jimi cut back on the party crowd and was trying to focus on his work. He came in alone on a lot of nights, just wanting to do guitar overdubs or experiment with some mix ideas that he had. His creativity was on the upswing, because he didn't have all of these people around him. His own drug use, just by what we could see, had also diminished. It was a healthier situation. I got to see a different side of him, as compared to when the Experience was falling apart during the spring. He was a sensitive, gentle person who was creative and enjoyed a genuine laugh. We would often go up to the roof of the Record Plant with Jack Adams and make paper airplanes. We would have contests to see who could throw them farther across the street. Chris Stone must have wondered where all the stationery was going!"

Rough mixes were prepared for all the songs completed on this evening. "Earth Blues," "Sky Blues Today," and "Ezy Ryder" (still titled "Easy Rider" at this stage) would each be reconstructed at Electric Lady Studios during the summer of 1970. "Message to Love," however, would not. While Hendrix had, for all intents and purposes, completed "Message to Love," he would issue a superior live version first, as part of *Band of Gypsys*. After he earmarked the song for that album, this studio recording was never again considered part of *First Rays of the New Rising Sun*, his projected double album.

In 1974, when Alan Douglas and engineer Les Kahn undertook a full review of the tape library, this studio version represented one of Douglas's strongest finds, as the recording was essentially finished. Apart from some incidental percussion added by Jimmy Maeulen in 1974, no additional overdubs were required to complete the track. It was ultimately remixed and added to *Crash Landing*.

■

Wednesday, January 21, 1970
New York, Record Plant. Engineer: Bob Hughes. Second engineer: Dave Ragno.

Fourteen takes of "Power of Soul," still known at this stage as "Crash Landing," were recorded. Of the fourteen recorded takes, numbers 2, 4, and 6 were complete, but no master take was achieved.

Hendrix then presented the

evening's most pleasant surprise: six intriguing attempts at "Astro Man." Though Jimi had never before tackled this song with Cox or Miles, these versions held surprisingly close to the finished master later recorded at Electric Lady Studios and released as part of *Cry of Love*. While only takes 5 and 6 are complete, the playing was upbeat and inspired throughout. Between takes, Hendrix informed Billy Cox that he was looking to inject more of a Spanish beat into the song's rhythm. While not listed on the tape box as among the staff for the session, engineer Tony Bongiovi can be heard offering take counts and occasional instructions. A complete take 5 displayed considerable promise, although no lead vocal was recorded. The sixth and final take started strongly but soon fell apart, and the song was abandoned. The last effort of the evening was a single uneventful take of "Valleys of Neptune." This version, while complete, lacked even a guide vocal from Jimi. At its conclusion, Jimi remarked, "We'll just pack it up," which signaled the close of the session.

The complete take 4 of "Paper Airplanes" was later pulled by Alan Douglas in 1974 and added to *Crash Landing*. Retitled "With the Power" for that album, this recording, like the January 20, 1970, rendition of "Message to Love," had been largely completed by Hendrix. Douglas then added percussion from Jimmy Maeulen and remixed the track.

■

Thursday, January 22, 1970
New York, Record Plant. Engineer: Bob Hughes.

Rough mixes of "Izabella" and "Sky Blues Today" were prepared, but both missed the mark and were later re-

placed. Considering the many attempts made at trying to craft a final mix for both songs, Hendrix was obviously searching for a specific sound. He would continue this work through February, hoping to capture the exact sound balance he desired.

■

Friday, January 23, 1970
New York, Record Plant. Engineer: Bob Hughes. Second engineer: Dave Ragno.

A wild evening of inspired jamming by Jimi. One of the evening's many highlights was a remarkable "Villanova Junction Blues" that lasted over fifteen minutes.

Another lengthy jam, which has enjoyed some notoriety as "MLK," began on reel one and continued on reel two. A loose, impromptu jam entitled "Slow Time Blues" followed, before giving way to a noteworthy stab at "Burning Desire." This version incorporated the group's live arrangement of the song, principally the hypnotic opening pattern that prefaced it. Though this adaptation vastly improved their effort, the rhythm section had problems accommodating to the song's intricate tempos. Furthermore, Hendrix did not record a vocal track, no doubt indicating that he felt more work was required before such steps could be taken.

Hendrix, Cox, and Miles, joined by an unnamed harmonica player, launched into a lengthy workout of Carl Perkins's rockabilly classic "Blue Suede Shoes," prefaced by some clowning from Jimi. In a blues groove, Jimi and Billy provide some tantalizing clues to the early development of "Freedom," while Jimi sang a spontaneous blues best described as "Highways of Desire." Partway through, Cox and Miles slowed the tempo by half, much to Jimi's approval. He then began "Seven Dollars in My Pocket," another impromptu blues original. As Jimi sang of a lost love from Sugar Hill, the rhythm section struggled to maintain the tempo, causing him to react. "C'mon. C'mon, keep it," he ordered. Jimi's concentration was broken, however, and the jam slowly came apart. Holding to the blues groove they had established, Jimi later sang the lyrics for "Midnight Lightning." An embryonic rendition of "Freedom" was also done, which, though not fully developed, was energetically performed. Unfortunately, the recording was marred by the unnamed harmonica player, who droned on incessantly throughout.

Two other blues originals, the instrumental titled "Country Blues" and "Once I Had a Woman," which featured a live vocal from Jimi, were also recorded. Though "Country Blues" has never been commercially released, a tape copy was lent by Alan Douglas to producer Elliot Mazer for use in a National Public Radio series based on Jimi's life that aired in the early 1980s. "Once I Had a Woman" was overhauled in 1974 with new overdubs, including a new harmonica part performed by Buddy Lucas. An edited version was later added to 1975's *Midnight Lightning*. A differently prepared version of the original recording, lasting an additional 2:05, was also released as part of 1994's *Jimi Hendrix: Blues*.

While "Country Blues" was an interesting recording compared to Jimi's other blues jams, neither version of "Once I Had a Woman" was particularly convincing. Jimi had, on many occasions, recorded more effective representations of his love for the blues.

A disastrous performance by Hendrix at Madison Square Garden on January 28 brought the future of the Band of Gypsys to a sudden halt. Hen-

drix lurched painfully through two numbers, "Who Knows" and "Earth Blues," before withdrawing from the stage. The public debacle infuriated Michael Jeffery, who promptly fired Buddy Miles backstage and brought the group's brief tenure to a close. "What went down was very embarrassing, and it left Jimi angry and disillusioned," says Cox. "It was unfortunate. Buddy and I walked over to Madison Square Garden, went into the dressing room, and there was Jimi. He was not in the best shape. Jimi was sitting next to Jeffery, and we *knew* it wasn't going to work. Jimi was in bad shape. We thought about not going out there, because someone was trying to make assholes out of us, but we did. We thought Jimi might be able to make it, but we only got through that one song before it started coming apart."

Though the relationship between Jeffery and Miles had always been strained, the notion that race may have played a role in their demise left Cox with a bitter taste. "Buddy and I thought that because they had successfully marketed the Jimi Hendrix Experience as being these two white guys, with Jimi in the middle, they didn't want to change horses midstream and go with three black guys up there. Who knows? I saw that I wasn't wanted, so I came back to Nashville and decided to do something else."

With the Band of Gypsys formally disbanded, Miles was left to reassemble the Express and resume his solo career. Disheartened, Billy Cox returned to Nashville. Miles extended an invitation to Cox to join his reformed group, but Cox declined. He did, however, fly to Chicago to lend fuzz bass to Miles's studio version of "Them Changes."

With the studio project on the brink of bankruptcy, and anxious to repair

Jimi's public image in light of the Madison Square Garden debacle, Michael Jeffery pressured Hendrix to support his wish that the original Experience reunite and resume touring. An interview with *Rolling Stone* reporter John Burks was staged in Jeffery's East 37th Street office, where Hendrix was joined by Mitchell and Redding. In the days following the interview, however, Jimi got cold feet, and Redding was again replaced by Cox, who reluctantly rejoined after some heavy persuasion. "I got a phone call from Jimi and Michael Jeffery telling me, 'Billy, things are different. It's not what you think.' They convinced me to come back to New York, but the scene still wasn't too good, so I came back to Nashville again. I said, 'This is it. I'm through with this shit.'"

With his band in total disarray, Hendrix huddled with Eddie Kramer at Juggy Sound, where the engineer had begun to review the remote recordings from the Band of Gypsys' recent Fillmore East performances. Juggy Sound was a small, predominantly R&B studio that, ironically, had once been owned by legendary Sue Records chief Juggy Murray — to whom Hendrix had been under contract in July 1965.

Staff engineer Kim King was very familiar with Jimi Hendrix. King, formerly the guitarist with Lothar & the Hand People, had jammed with Hendrix, known then as Jimmy James, on many occasions in the Village. "Juggy Sound had just installed a sixteen-track machine, but it was still a funky old R&B studio," King recalls. "Eddie and Jimi told me that they were tired of the Record Plant and wanted to work elsewhere. Eddie, in fact, was doing a few other things at Juggy, including a Buzzy Linhart album and some demos for a band from Queens called the Rosicrucians. The first Hendrix sessions I did with Eddie was preparing rough mixes of the Band of Gypsys' live material. Kramer said, 'Let's see how good you are at editing. What I want is all of the guitar solos left in and all of the drum solos left out.' That was how we started. We also did a couple of oddball things with Jimi there. There was one session where Jimi was really into something good. Unfortunately, we ran out of tape, but I had found some hubs with bits of blank tape on them. After the session, one of them dropped out in the middle, and I had to hand-spool twenty-four hundred feet back onto the reel. Fortunately, this was out of the view of Eddie and Jimi!

"On other occasions, Jimi would show up, and we would do some bizarre guitar experiments or work on overdubs for things he had recorded at other studios, but the focus was on the live album, and the push was on to finish Electric Lady [studios]. I had developed a rapport with Eddie, and he offered me a job at the new studio during the sessions."

From the four Fillmore East performances, Hendrix selected six songs to make up the album. Excluded were versions of such Experience favorites as "Fire" and "Voodoo Child (Slight Return)." Hendrix also chose to hold back stirring performances of "Ezy Ryder," "Burning Desire," and "Earth Blues," perhaps wanting to perfect studio versions instead. In their place, Hendrix put forward four new songs: "Message to Love," "Machine Gun," "Power of Soul" (listed as "Power to Love"), and "Who Knows." " 'Who Knows' was something Jimi started," recalls Cox. "Buddy thought up the stops, but it was really just a pattern that Jimi had that was great to play." Save for preconcert rehearsals at Baggy's Studios, the group had never dedicated a great deal of studio time to the song. The resulting live

performance suffered accordingly, sounding underdeveloped, despite the infectious interplay between Cox and Hendrix.

Where the contagious "Message to Love" and "Power of Soul" were engaging examples of Hendrix's unique blending of rock, R&B, and blues, his live performance of "Machine Gun" would ultimately be recognized as one

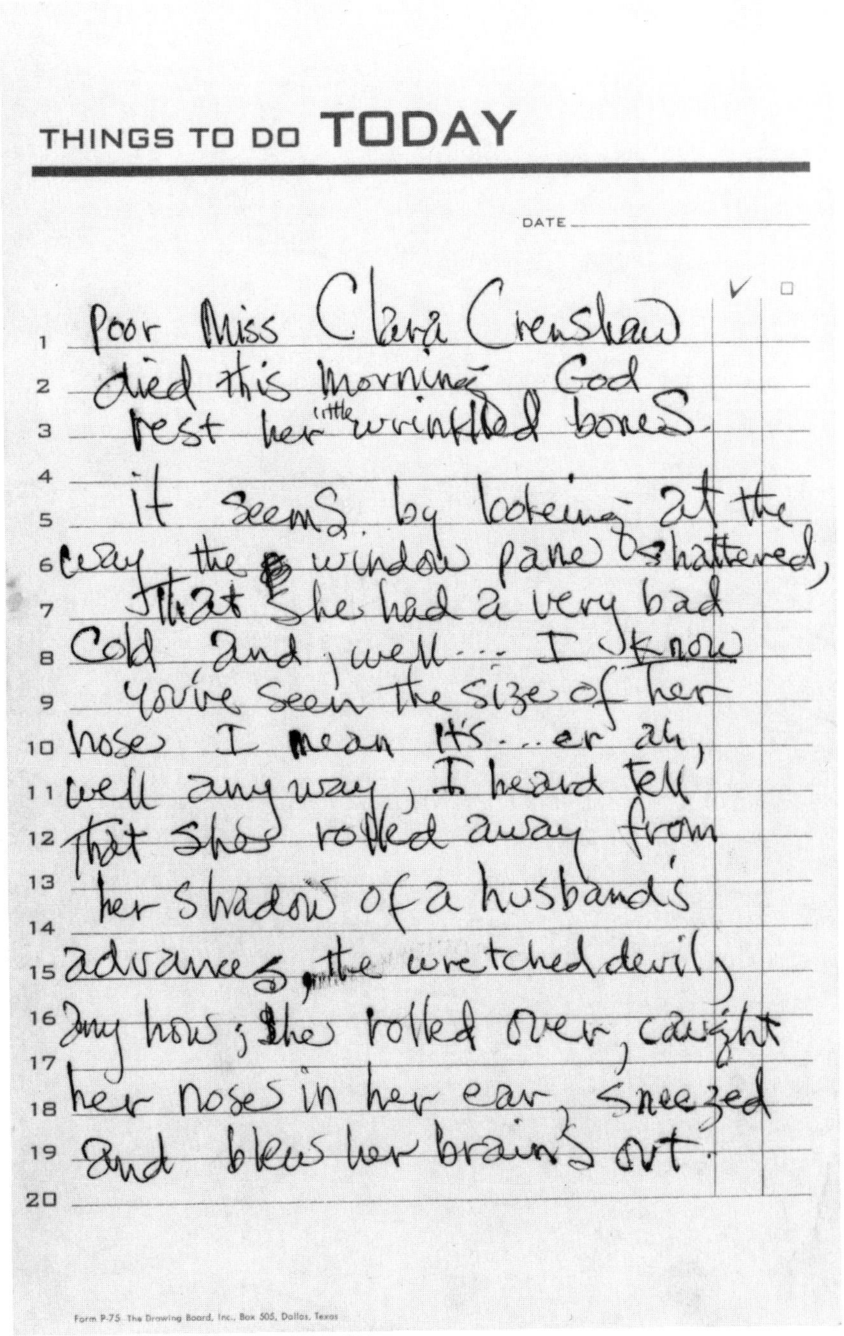

THINGS TO DO **TODAY**

DATE _____

1 Poor Miss Clara Crenshaw
2 died this morning, God
3 rest her little wrinkled bones.
4
5 it seems, by lokeing at the
6 way the window pane shattered,
7 That she had a very bad
8 Cold and, well... I know
9 you've seen the size of her
10 nose, I mean it's... er ah,
11 well anyway, I heard tell
12 That she rolled away from
13 her shadow of a husbands
14
15 advances, the wretched devil,
16 any how, she rolled over, caught
17 her noses in her ear, sneezed
18
19 and blew her brains out.
20

Form P-75 The Drawing Board, Inc., Box 505, Dallas, Texas

Hendrix loved to write and did not restrict his talents to songwriting. "Poor Miss Clara Crenshaw" provides a wonderful glimpse of Jimi's sense of humor.
(James A. Hendrix)

to disc. "We Got to Live Together"s grand, final crescendo had originally brought the second January 1 show to its pre-encore close, hence its positioning as the album's final track.

"When *Band of Gypsys* came out, we both wished we had done it in the studio," Cox remembers. "We would have loved to have done some overdubs and correct some of the mistakes that we had made. These were mistakes that *we* were aware of, not the public. We had reached that point where we wanted everything to be perfect. Overall, the feeling was, 'What the heck, the album doesn't belong to us anyway. Let's just move on and forget it.'"

■

Monday, February 2, 1970
New York, Juggy Sound. Engineer: Eddie Kramer.

Taking a break from mixing sessions for *Band of Gypsys,* Jimi engaged in two casual jam sessions with the Rosicrucians, a Queens-based group Kramer had been producing at the studio. The first jam lasted approximately five minutes, while the second was considerably longer and more cohesive.

■

Tuesday, February 3, 1970
New York, Record Plant. Engineer: Bob Hughes.

A rough mix of the January 21, 1970, studio version of "Power of Soul" was prepared. While this mix was never used, it was later cut to a reference master by Electric Lady engineer Andy Edlin on June 13, 1972, and was a contender for what would ultimately become *Loose Ends.*

Jimi adjusts volume levels as he prepares a rough mix. Though he lacked formal training, Jimi demonstrated a surprising ability behind the recording console.
(Chuck Boyd/Flower Children Ltd.)

of his greatest achievements. Seeking to be equitable, Hendrix included two of Buddy Miles's songs, "Changes" and "We Got to Live Together," on the final album. Both had to be shortened considerably, as Buddy's in-concert call-and-response vamping translated poorly

Sunday, February 8, 1970

Record Plant, Los Angeles. Engineers: Stan Agol. Second engineer: Dan Turbeville.

Although Jimi was not present, a four-track mixing session of "Star Spangled Banner" was completed. Take 7 was chosen the master and included in the forthcoming *Woodstock* album and film.

Wednesday, February 11, 1970

New York, Record Plant. Engineer: Bob Hughes. Second engineer: Dave Ragno.

Rough mixes of the Band of Gypsys' studio version of "Izabella" were completed.

Thursday, February 12, 1970

New York, Record Plant. Engineer: Bob Hughes.

Rough mixes of "Izabella" and "Sky Blues Today" were prepared. A master of "Izabella" was achieved on this session.

Sunday, February 15, 1970

New York, Record Plant. Engineer: Bob Hughes.

A master mix of "Sky Blues Today" was finally achieved during this session. This mix would later be coupled with "Izabella" and issued as a short-lived Reprise single in early April 1970.

Monday, February 16, 1970

New York, Record Plant. Engineer: Bob Hughes. Second engineer: Tom Flye.

Joined by Juma Sultan and Buddy Miles, Hendrix recorded two muscular, instrumental attempts at "Blue Suede Shoes," both vastly different from the extended jam Hendrix had recorded on January 23. Jimi then shifted into a loose "Hey Baby (Land of the New Rising Sun)." Singing live, Jimi evoked some gorgeous touches of Spanish flamenco stylings. When this jam broke down, Jimi kicked off a true gem — an impish, instrumental rendition of "Summertime Blues." With Buddy locked in the groove, Jimi rode the guitar's whammy bar with wonderful effect. This is a fabulous bit of unrehearsed fun, followed by another — a funky, impromptu original reminiscent of the Beatles' "Day Tripper."

One other reel recorded this evening was nowhere as inventive, since the three — with Sultan now on maracas — were mired in a series of uneventful jams thoroughly without direction.

Monday, March 23, 1970

New York, Sound Center. Studio A. 7:00 P.M. to 12 midnight. Producer: Noel Redding. Engineer: Skip Juried.

With the *Band of Gypsys* album delivered to Capitol and construction having resumed at Electric Lady, two of Hendrix's most pressing concerns had been lifted from his shoulders. He had signed a series of agreements for performances to commence in April, but Jimi balked at reuniting with Redding, with whom his relationship remained fragile. He wanted to bring Billy Cox back into the fold. Cox, who had left Hendrix for Nashville twice in the previous ten months, was disillusioned. "After the business at Madison Square Garden, I was real suspect," recalls Cox. "I agreed to come back in February, but that fell apart as well. I didn't hear from Jimi for about a month. Then I got a phone call from him saying, 'C'mon Bill. Let's get it on!' I said, 'Hey man, you ain't gettin' nothin' on. I'm here in Nashville, and I'm happy. I don't want to go through all that shit I went through again.' He promised and promised that I would have no hassles, so, like a fool, I came back for the third time."

While Hendrix had designated Cox his bassist, he still felt some loyalty toward Redding, and so agreed to help with Noel's record. His tenure in the Experience having come to a close, Redding had begun work on a solo album whose working title, appropriately enough, was *Nervous Breakdown*. Recording at Sound Center, Noel gathered vocalist Roger Chapman, of Family, and Paul Caruso, as well as drummer Steve Angel and organist Gerry Guida, formerly of the Big Three, a group managed by Jeffery associate Bob Levine.

Nervous Breakdown sessions began Friday, March 20, and continued through March 23, with Redding calling in favors from friends to contribute to the hastily organized project. Redding completed a remake of "Walking through the Garden," which Fat Mattress had previously recorded. Also recorded was a cover of Eddie Cochran's "Nervous Breakdown," "Everything's Blue," "Highway," with vocals by Fat Mattress's Neil Landon, and "Eric the Red," complete with bagpipes performed by the doorman at the Penn Garden Hotel. Lee Michaels added piano and organ to "Wearing Yellow" and "Blues in 3/4." Hendrix

At work in the Record Plant.

(Linda McCartney/Star File)

stopped by on March 23 to lend guitar to Redding's "My Friend."

Ever industrious, Redding quickly organized material for these sessions. "I started getting some demos together after Jimi and Mitch began rehearsing with Billy Cox," remembers Redding. " 'My Friend' was a song I had written. It was a tune in the key of E. Jimi also had a song by that name, but I think he stole the title from me. Jimi came over to the studio and offered to play guitar. I think he was trying to make up with me, because he had never spoken to me or even called to say that he was going to be playing with another guy. Jimi played guitar on 'My Friend.' I got as far as putting a rough vocal on it."

■
Monday, March 23, 1970
New York, Record Plant. Engineer: Jack Adams. Second engineer: Dave Ragno.

A short solo session, with Jimi recording three incomplete takes of "Midnight Lightning," singing and playing live as he sat on a chair. The song's slow beat was accented, in the tradition of such bluesmen as Lightnin' Hopkins and John Lee Hooker, by the steady tapping of his foot on the floor.

The beginning of the reel captures some chat between Jimi and the control room. Jimi remarks, "Instant coma. Instant coma, you know what I mean?," no doubt making a pun on John Lennon's recently issued single "Instant Karma." While none of the three takes that followed was complete, each — especially take 3 — recalled the deep

blues stylings of John Lee Hooker and Lightnin' Hopkins.

Initially, Hendrix had wanted to record the track live, and the tape captured a brief portion of Jimi's discussion with engineer Jack Adams, a disagreement regarding the recording of Jimi's vocal. After take 2 broke down, Jimi changed his mind. "I'll tell you what. I'm not going to do the words," Jimi remarked. "I can't get no feeling with this thing only in my ear. I'm going to do the vocals over again anyway, so this vocal here won't be any good." Sensing his discomfort, Adams relented and offered to record the track as Jimi had originally wished. "Could you get the feel of the vocal if we opened the door again?" Adams asked. "Because we can manage it if we got to do it. Open the door. Open it wide." A third take was attempted, although it too fell incomplete. Sounding tired and depressed, Hendrix called the session to a close with a weary, "Yeah, I'm going to give up on this one." No other recording was attempted.

■

Tuesday, March 24, 1970
New York, Record Plant. Engineer: Jack Adams. Second engineer: Dave Ragno.

An unusual session, which began with Jimi accompanied by an unknown drummer. Working without a bass player, a loose, energetic take of "Bleeding Heart" was recorded. "Call that right there 'Bleeding Heart,' " says Jimi directly after the take. This was followed by three takes of "Midnight Lightning," but none of these efforts was put forward with much spirit from Hendrix, and no finals were achieved.

At this point, it appears that the session has ended. Recording resumed, however, with Billy Cox joining the proceedings. Some rehearsing may also have taken place, as only four takes of "Bleeding Heart" were required before the fourth was marked the master take. Unlike the version recorded earlier, Hendrix's concentration and intensity level had improved considerably.

Like many similar Record Plant efforts, this reel would later be transferred to Electric Lady Studios, where Jimi would take steps toward completing the track to his satisfaction. Additional guitar parts were overdubbed there, and Mitch Mitchell would replace the existing percussion tracks with new drum parts of his own. While Hendrix was unable to finish "Bleeding Heart" before his death, take 4 was pulled to the *Rainbow Bridge* master on March 11, 1971.

■

Band of Gypsys
Capitol Records STAO-472. U.S. album release. Wednesday, March 25, 1970. Producer: Jimi Hendrix. Engineer: Eddie Kramer.
Who Knows/Machine Gun/Changes/Power of Soul/Message to Love/We Gotta Live Together

Having waited so long for Hendrix to deliver this album, Capitol rushed the disc to stores as quickly as possible. Michael Jeffery delivered the finished master to Capitol executives in Los Angeles on February 25, 1970, soon after postproduction had been completed. The album was mastered on March 4, 1970. Just three weeks later, Capitol had product in the shops to service Hendrix's fans, who awaited the release with eager anticipation. Despite the dramatic shift in Hendrix's sound and style — especially when compared to *Electric Ladyland* — *Band of Gypsys* nonetheless met with overwhelming approval. Though *Band of Gypsys* would peak at number 5, by the time of Hendrix's death in September 1970, its sales had already surpassed those of all Hendrix's Reprise albums save for *Are You Experienced?*

■

"Stepping Stone"/"Izabella"
Reprise 0905. U.S. single release. Wednesday, April 8, 1970.

These two tracks, mixed in February 1970 by Hendrix and Record Plant engineer Bob Hughes, were briefly issued as a single before being almost immediately recalled. Capitol Records expressed its concern that airplay and sales of the single would interfere with the *Band of Gypsys* release. Eager to avoid another confrontation with Capitol, Reprise simply pulled the disc from the market and made no other effort to rerelease either of the two songs. Though limited copies of the single were pressed and still exist, it is unknown just how wide the original circulation actually was, as the disc did not register on the *Billboard* chart.

■

Thursday, May 14, 1970
New York, Record Plant. Engineer: Eddie Kramer. Second engineer: Tom Flye.

After the two March sessions at the Record Plant, no evidence exists to suggest that any further recording was attempted until May 14. In the interim, the re-formed Experience gathered to begin rehearsals for their upcoming U.S. tour, which was to begin in Los Angeles on April 25. Hendrix expanded the group's stage repertoire, incorporating such unfinished studio works as "Hey Baby (Land of the New Rising Sun)" and "Room Full of Mirrors," as well as "Message to Love" and "Machine Gun" from the *Band of Gypsys* album. Despite the tumultuous events of the past nine months, Billy Cox remembers no animosity between him, Hendrix, and Mitchell. "Mitch was cool," says Cox. "There were no problems at all. He didn't even talk about the Band of Gypsys. He just went about his business and never mentioned it. There was a real respect between Mitch and Jimi. We just got down to playing, which is what it was all about."

The tour kicked off with a superb, sold-out engagement at the Forum in Los Angeles. It was further buoyed by the dramatic success of *Band of Gypsys*,

Los Angeles Forum, April 25, 1970. Opening night of Jimi's final U.S. tour.

(Chuck Boyd/Flower Children Ltd.)

whose impressive sales showing earned Hendrix his fifth consecutive U.S. *Billboard* Top 10 disc.

While the Experience would again be headlining a mixture of theaters, college auditoriums, and sports stadiums, this venture, billed as the "Cry of Love Tour," would be unlike any previous Experience jaunt. With Electric Lady Studios nearly operational, Hendrix won a bitterly contested compromise with Michael Jeffery to limit the tour engagements to a series of three-day weekends throughout the summer. The cash generated by these dates would keep the studio project solvent, affording Hendrix sufficient time to recuperate and record throughout the week at his new facility. Hendrix eagerly anticipated the opportunity to record at his own studio, and opted to wait, rather than return to other facilities such as the Hit Factory and the Record Plant.

At Electric Lady Studios, Kramer and studio president Jim Marron built a staff. Maintenance engineer Shimon Ron, a hard-nosed former Israeli paratrooper, was recruited from A&R Studios, where his work there during Kramer's sessions with Led Zeppelin had made a distinct impression. Kim King, the former guitarist from Lothar & the Hand People, had worked as an assistant engineer to Kramer at Juggy Sound while Hendrix and Kramer compiled the *Band of Gypsys* album. Kramer had also lured drummer Dave Palmer from Ted Nugent and the Amboy Dukes to join the team as an assistant engineer. While a $300,000 loan secured from Warner Bros. Records, guaranteed against Jimi's future royalty earnings, had infused the project with much-needed cash to operate, a seemingly endless string of technical complications tested Hendrix's patience.

In early May, the first test recordings were made, with Kramer on piano.

These revealed that more work was required before Hendrix could begin. Originally, he intended to begin recording at Electric Lady on May 14; however, technical problems forced Kramer and the group to move to the Record Plant, where two days of recording were booked on Thursday and Friday, May 14 and 15.

Despite their setback at Electric Lady, the mood inside the Record Plant's Studio C — the third and most recent addition to the storied facility — was spirited and upbeat. While Kramer's name was not listed on the tape boxes, the session tapes clearly reveal that he directed the session.

The group began with three takes of "Come Down Hard on Me," followed by rough instrumental attempts at "Straight Ahead." At this stage, the song's tempo was noticeably slower and the arrangement quite unlike the version later released as part of *Cry of Love*. Take 4 evolved into a jam of "Night Bird Flying." When this broke down, a short discussion between Jimi, Mitch, and Billy was briefly audible. Jimi then announced, "L.A." Over the talkback, Kramer asked, "What in L.A.?" "L.A. — without the bullshit or the words," was Hendrix's sly reply, which resulted in laughter in both the control room and studio. Off microphone, Mitch then suggested "Lower Alcatraz," which Jimi repeated, followed by Billy's suggestion of "Lower Alabama." "Yeah, Lower Alabama," Hendrix echoed. A false start caused Kramer to remark "Get it together" over the talkback microphone. Hendrix briefly mimicked Kramer's request on the guitar, composed himself, and kicked off a unique hybrid of "Midnight Lightning" and "Keep on Groovin'." The track began with an instrumental introduction before, midway through, Jimi signaled an unusual tempo change,

which seemed momentarily to confuse Mitch and Billy. Though they carried the song to a finish, it lacked a strong ending and remained, at this early juncture, another inspired demo teeming with potential. "That [untitled front part] was a pattern we had worked out in Los Angeles," Cox remembers. "That was all we had, was that first part. We weren't playing by notes, we were playing by patterns. It was kind of weird, but that's how we thought. We were always trying to hook these patterns together to make songs. Jimi would just give you a look, and Mitch and I would know where he was going."

After strumming the distinctive introductory notes to "Power of Soul," Hendrix started an infectious instrumental workout of "Straight Ahead." In direct contrast to the versions that began the evening, this rendition was much more compact, with a faster tempo and an arrangement nearly identical to the finished master. Hendrix was exuberant, and his playing provided several highlights throughout.

"Freedom" followed next, with Jimi supplying a charged lead vocal, singing live as the three recorded the basic track. "Freedom" had been one of the stronger songs to emerge from the March and April rehearsals for the Cry of Love tour. Impressed with its progress, Hendrix had inserted the song into the group's stage repertoire, where it made its debut at the April 25 L.A. Forum performance. In this early incarnation, girlfriend Devon Wilson's voracious appetite for heroin was the primary focus of Jimi's lyrics. His intent was obvious, as Jimi, with great conviction, sang of his desire to "take the junk out of her hand." While uneven in spots, this particular attempt at "Freedom" was still first-rate, fueled by Jimi's rampant emotion. Perhaps to counter the intensity of "Freedom," Hendrix

Billy Cox onstage during the 1970 U.S. Cry of Love tour.

(Chuck Boyd/Flower Children Ltd.)

then lurched into a high-pitched, woefully out-of-key rendition of Frankie Laine's "Catastrophe." At its conclusion, Kramer deadpanned, "At a hundred and fifty dollars an hour, that's pretty good." As the laughter subsided, recording continued with an inspired single take of "Hey Baby (Land of the New Rising Sun)."

■

Friday, May 15, 1970
New York, Record Plant. Engineer: Eddie Kramer. Second engineer: Tom Flye.

"Freedom" again dominated the focus, as Hendrix was keen to develop this exceptional track to its full potential. The group attempted nineteen new takes, with take 15 particularly strong, bolstered by Jimi's tremendous enthusiasm. Despite an exceptional effort, no masters were achieved, as Hendrix would continue to make a series of minor refinements over the coming weeks before finally succeeding at Electric Lady in late June.

The group also attempted a promising instrumental "Valleys of Neptune," but it fell incomplete, causing Hendrix to admit that he hadn't actually devised an appropriate ending yet. "Peter Gunn" and a short reprise of "Catastrophe" (both later issued as part of 1972's *War Heroes*), kept spirits loose before Hendrix directed the group through a muscular stab at "Freedom." Not quite satisfied, Jimi again shifted gears, kicking off a slower-paced "Hey Baby (Land of the New Rising Sun)." Styled similar to the arrangement on *Rainbow Bridge*, Hendrix's extended solo was marvelous. An energetic "Lover Man" followed, after which Jimi remarked, "Philadelphia," which elicited a laugh from Mitch, perhaps referring to their gig at that city's Temple Stadium the following day.

Even though Electric Lady still lacked a number of essentials, like a freight elevator, Hendrix was eager to make use of his new studio. His enthusiasm was shared by Eddie Kramer, studio president Jim Marron, and the engineering staff. Though its lengthy construction had exacted an emotional and financial toll, Electric Lady represented an impressive achievement for Jimi Hendrix. While his sole design request had been round windows, Electric Lady Studios had been crafted with great care. "We were committed to creating an artist's environment at the studio," explains Jim Marron. "This would not be a facility dominated by technical types who had wires and cables all over the place. This was to be Hendrix's creative home." Echoes Kramer, "We built that studio for Jimi to work and feel comfortable in, contrary to the antiseptic boxes then in vogue."

To foster such an environment, architect John Storyk, with direct input from Hendrix, incorporated a host of ideas, including the soundproofed, curved walls that shaped the exterior of Studio A's control room and studio. There were white carpeted walls and colored lights, complete with an instrument panel for Hendrix to control, allowing him to match his mood with the colors he desired. These were small touches, yet they drove home the point that this facility had been tailored for him exclusively. "He just loved being in the studio," Kramer remembers. "He would say, 'Give me red lights or yellow lights tonight,' and wash the walls in a rainbow of different colors. It had always been his intent to have the studio loose and casual, yet at the same time we worked hard to maintain a high standard of professionalism."

With Studio A inching closer to becoming operational, Kramer and the engineering staff tested the facility by making a number of experimental recordings. Rather than raise Jimi's hopes prematurely, these practice efforts were done without him present. "We did a lot of testing," recalls Kim King. "I brought in a band I would later produce, and Michael Jeffery brought in a couple of bands that he was considering for his management company."

■
Woodstock
Cotillion SD350. U.S. album release. Wednesday, May 27, 1970. Producer: Eric Blackstead. Engineers: Eddie Kramer, Lee Osbourne.

Star Spangled Banner/Purple Haze/Instrumental Solo

Timed to coincide with *Woodstock's* massive Memorial Day weekend opening in cinemas throughout the country, this triple-disc set enjoyed widespread popularity, *entering* the *Billboard* album chart at number 4 before claiming the magazine's coveted top position for four weeks.

While the soundtrack album was filled with highlights from the likes of Sly & the Family Stone and the Jefferson Airplane, Jimi's stunning rendition of "Star Spangled Banner" provided one of the film's defining moments.

■
Berkeley Performance Center, Berkeley, California
Saturday, May 30, 1970. Engineer: Abe Jacob.

Both of Hendrix's superb performances at this three-thousand-seat venue were filmed and recorded. Undersized for Hendrix's considerable following in the San Francisco/Oakland area, more than a thousand empty-handed fans were turned away from the venue. When the doors opened for the first concert, a mass of unruly gate-crashers stormed the building. Local police and promoter Bill Graham's security staff were overrun. Angry fans scaled the building's walls and roof; others lobbed rocks at those with tickets trying to gain legitimate entrance. After the concert began, in an effort to pacify the hostile crowd outside the building, engineer Abe Jacob swung open the rear doors of the remote sound truck, filling the street with the sounds of the Experience.

Nearly all of the great moments from these two concerts were later released in one form or another. Many were issued as part of the film *Jimi Plays Berkeley,* while others, such as "Johnny B. Goode," formed the backbone of such posthumous compilations as *Hendrix: In the West.* Reworking cover material for his live performances was a time-honored Hendrix tradition, and "Johnny B. Goode" was no exception. Billy Cox explains: "Two weeks earlier, we were playing Temple University, and just before we went onstage, Jimi said we were going to start the show with 'Sgt. Pepper's Lonely Hearts Club Band' and 'Johnny B. Goode.' I just looked at him. 'Sgt. Pepper' and 'Johnny B. Goode'? He laughed and said, 'C'mon man, you know all that old shit!' "

The group's late afternoon sound check was also recorded and filmed, yielding the spontaneous "Blue Suede Shoes," later issued as part of *Hendrix: In the West.* The Experience's two 12-song sets were recorded as follows: "Fire," "Johnny B. Goode," "Hear My Train A Comin'," "Foxey Lady," "Machine Gun," "Freedom," "Red House," "Message to Love," "Ezy Ryder," "Star Spangled Banner," "Purple Haze," and "Voodoo Child (Slight Return)." The second set began with "Pass It On" (an early version of what would later become "Straight Ahead"), "Hey Baby (Land of the New Rising Sun)," "Lover Man," "Stone Free," "Hey Joe," "I Don't Live Today," "Machine Gun," "Foxey Lady," "Star Spangled Banner," "Purple Haze," and a hybrid of "Voodoo Child (Slight Return)" and "Midnight Lightning."

■

Late May/June 1970
New York, Electric Lady Studios.

Electric Lady Studios was a source of tremendous pride for Hendrix — tangible proof that his talent had not only paid off but had created a facility that would allow him to do what he loved best: write and record his music. Hendrix's closest friends were equally impressed. "I was awed," admits Cox. "I had never seen a studio like that in my life. It was both unique and very personal."

The first order of business at the new studio was to evaluate the piles of multitrack tapes Hendrix had recorded over the previous nine months. Hendrix and Kramer dedicated a considerable amount of time to selecting which masters warranted overdubs, which would need to be recut, and which would be scrapped entirely. Kramer explains: "When Studio A had been completed and Jimi wanted to start working, all of the tapes from the previous year, when he had been jamming and writing stuff at places like Record Plant and Hit Factory, were dumped in our laps. We started to listen to them, trying to make some sense out of this huge backlog of stuff. Jimi knew exactly what was on those tapes, and he knew which tapes he wanted to work on first. We would listen to them, define whether the song was worth recutting — which we did

on many occasions — or overdubbing, which we also did." One of the first songs Hendrix tackled at Electric Lady was the Band of Gypsys funk masterpiece "Ezy Ryder." " 'Ezy Ryder' was one of the first things we did," agrees Cox. "That had begun at the Record Plant, but Eddie pulled out the tapes, and Jimi spent a lot of time doctoring up and trying to improve those tracks we had already recorded. We spent a bunch of time doing this before we started creating new material."

Enhancing previously recorded tracks only whetted Jimi's appetite to begin recording new material. "Jimi was so enthused about recording again," says Kramer, "he would arrive at sessions right on time — even early, on occasion — something he rarely did. We would spend up to ten or twelve hours at a time, recording take after take. Unlike in the past, where, through jamming, he would try to develop the germ of an idea into a song, Hendrix came into Electric Lady with a distinctive idea as to how he wanted each track to sound."

It was during this evaluation process that Jimi began to realize just how considerable an upgrade in overall recording quality the studio offered him. "Jimi immediately recognized Electric Lady's significance when we started recording again," says Kramer. "Having come from working on all of his old tapes — where people at other studios clearly were intimidated by him or just didn't give a shit — Jimi could hear that *his* studio offered him a better bass sound, better drum sound, better everything. I think Jimi relished the challenge that the studio represented."

While Hendrix's enthusiasm had been renewed by the possibilities Electric Lady now afforded him, his vacillating moods were still the driving force behind his creativity. "There were times

when he would say, 'I'm not into this,' and bail out and go home," says Kim King. "Then there were the nights when he was *on*. Even if Jimi was like that for only one night during the week, it made up for everything."

Hendrix's mood swings, acknowledges Billy Cox, indeed played a primary role in the outcome of each session. "Jimi's spirit had to be flowing in order for him to be creative," Cox explains. "If there were things on his mind — and there was plenty — dampening his spirit, then we were in for an unproductive evening. If there was nothing bothering him, then we were in for a helluva night. Man, we'd get in there and just go on and on."

Hendrix's stormy relationship with his girlfriend, Devon Wilson, directly affected his concentration. Their volatile arguments tended to darken his mood considerably. "If his old lady had pissed him off, things weren't going to be too good," admits Cox bluntly. These disputes, however, were internalized by Hendrix, as he was not prone to airing his personal problems, even to close friends like Cox and Mitchell. Instead, they respected Hendrix's unspoken language, recognizing when to push and when to lay back without addressing the issue or verbally confronting him. "If you were around Jimi, you could tell when something was bothering him," states Cox. "We would try to do something to take his mind off of his situation. Mitch or I would crack a joke or do something silly, while Eddie would try to divert Jimi's attention into the music. He'd say, 'Let's mix that track we did last night.' Pretty soon, Jimi's head would be back into it, and he'd want to do an overdub or go out in the studio to try something new. Mitch, Eddie and I would look at each other like, 'Phew, worked that one out.' "

Over the summer, Electric Lady

"Room Full of Mirrors," "Hey Baby (Land of the New Rising Sun)," and "Freedom" were among

the new songs Jimi performed on the 1970 U.S. tour.

(Chuck Boyd/Flower Children Ltd.)

A backstage conference with the police interrupts Jimi's study of the latest *National Examiner* and *Mad* magazine. Left to right: Gerry Stickells, Michael Goldstein, unnamed police officers.

(Michael Ochs Archives)

often served as a safe haven for Hendrix. He would leave the apartment he shared with Wilson at 59 West 12th Street and walk the few blocks to the studio. "Jimi enjoyed recording at Electric Lady, but there were also times when he just wanted to cool out there," recalls Jim Marron. "Devon was giving him a bitch of time, so he would stay at the studio and listen to playbacks. He

used to let Kramer go home to catch a few hours' sleep while he would just cool out. Eddie would offer to stay and keep working, but Jimi just wanted some playtime. It was part of the reason why we built the place for him. He would just sit in the control room and have one of Kramer's assistants thread up the tapes he wanted to hear."

While Hendrix's closest associates

knew that Devon's relationship with Jimi was a double-edged sword, no one dared pry into the intimate details of his private life. "*Hell* no," says Cox. "You just accepted that that was part of the whole experience. Jimi had to work that out alone. Advice wasn't offered because it was not asked for."

The escalating tide of this emotional intrigue was something the newly hired staff at Electric Lady was utterly unprepared for. "We were kept in the dark about a lot of stuff," admits Kim King. "Rumor was rampant in the studio; much of it was unconfirmed. What was going on upstairs in the office, which did not necessarily have anything to do with what was going on downstairs — and yet it did — had an impact."

And what of the Experience? Were they still a viable group or simply Jimi's backing musicians? "Initially it was strange," says Kim King, "because Mitch was back in the band, and when we weren't cutting new tracks, we would be working with tapes which had Buddy Miles on drums."

Understandably, Mitchell's enthusiasm had no doubt been tempered by his ongoing battle with Michael Jeffery for back royalties and tour receipts. "At that time, we didn't get paid as session players," explains Cox. "There was really no reward other than finishing these songs and trying to get the album together. My obligation was to myself first, and to Jimi, so I was always there and always punctual. If Jimi called me and said we were all going to meet at the studio at seven-thirty, I would be there at seven o'clock, waiting on him. I would sit around in the control room with Eddie until he came in. He knew he could count on me. But there were a lot of times early on when Mitch would show up late or not show up at all. That got Jimi very frustrated. He would want

to cancel the session, and I would say, 'Don't worry about it. That will give us a chance to tighten up our shit.' There were times when we would try to do some things without Mitch and overdub his part later, but that never worked, as our time would either fluctuate up or down without Mitch acting as our timekeeper. After a while, though, Mitch got into what we were doing. It was something different for him, because it was more of a creative process. When he got into the spirit of things, his attitude changed."

Another crucial change was the increased security afforded Hendrix via the studio's locked front door and twenty-four-hour security. Kramer seized the opportunity to enforce a new set of rules aimed at stopping the hordes of hangers-on who jammed the control room and lobbied for Hendrix's attention. "The control room was the inner sanctum, and Eddie, especially, was very strict," explains Kim King. "On any given night, there were instructions from Jimi as to who to let in and who was to be excluded."

These changes had to be enforced, argues Kramer, if Jimi was going to maximize the opportunities the new studio presented. "It had been impossible trying to get work done during those sessions at the Hit Factory and the Record Plant," remembers Kramer. "At one point, I remember there were thirty people in the control room. That would never happen at Electric Lady. I wouldn't allow it. I knew he enjoyed this carnival atmosphere at times, because he still occasionally would bring in a bunch of people, but if I felt they were imposing, I would turn to him and say, 'Jimi, we can't get any work done.'"

Kramer's call for heightened security was not the only one. Billy Cox had endured far too many frustrating sessions disrupted by Jimi's 'guests.' "The

only people who would be in the control room at Electric Lady would be Devon, whomever I wanted, and Lynn Mitchell," states Cox simply. "Stella and Colette were welcome, as were Emmeretta Marks, the twins, Juma Sultan, Gerry Stickells, Eric Barrett, and Gene McFadden. It was a tight-knit group."

As Electric Lady was his studio, Hendrix would occasionally liberalize the rules. "There definitely was a different atmosphere in the studio when Kramer wasn't around," remembers King. "Jimi was like a schoolboy playing hooky. On one of these nights, I was engineering a session he was producing for the Patterson Singers. There were people all over the control room, and Jimi was bouncing around between the studio and the console. It was almost more than I could handle."

■

Band of Gypsys

Track Records 2406 001. U.K. album release. Friday, June 12, 1970. Producer: Jimi Hendrix. Engineer: Eddie Kramer. Who Knows/Machine Gun/Changes/Power of Soul/Message to Love/We Gotta Live Together

Track and Polydor Records had not yet reached a settlement in their long-standing legal battle with Ed Chalpin and PPX Industries over ownership rights to Jimi's master recordings. Therefore, the British release of *Band of Gypsys* was delayed nearly three months. The wait served to whet the appetite of Jimi's legion of fans, as the album jumped to number 6 during a lengthy, thirty-week stay on the album chart.

Once again, Track's choice of cover artwork was the subject of controversy, because their version featured an unflattering puppet of Jimi flanked by similar dolls made to resemble Bob Dylan and Brian Jones. Whatever their original intent, Track eventually succumbed to public pressure and substituted a new cover: a photo of Hendrix performing at the massive Isle of Wight festival.

■

Monday, June 15, 1970

New York, Electric Lady Studios. Engineer: Eddie Kramer. Second engineer: Dave Palmer.

Traffic's Chris Wood and Steve Winwood paid a visit to the studio, and the two were so impressed with the facility that they decided to jam. With Mitch Mitchell unavailable, a drummer was needed on short notice. Kramer volunteered Dave Palmer, the onetime member of Ted Nugent's Amboy Dukes turned Electric Lady engineer. Palmer, who lived across the street from the studio, was rousted out of bed by a telephone call from Kramer. Palmer explains: "Kramer called me at two A.M. saying, 'Hendrix is down at the studio and we need a drummer. Get your ass over here and bang on those tubs.' When I got there, Hendrix and Kramer were showing Steve Winwood the place. Nothing was really set up, but Jimi and Stevie had the itch to play, so Eddie set up a couple of microphones and I got behind the drums and jammed with the two of them."

Prior to Palmer's arrival, Hendrix had previewed some of his recent recordings for Winwood and Wood. The two were, in fact, coaxed into providing backing vocals for "Ezy Ryder," one of Jimi's most promising works-in-progress.

The first jam — a spirited workout founded loosely on Traffic's "Pearly Queen" — would feature Hendrix on bass, Winwood on electric piano, and Palmer on drums. Palmer then returned to the control room, and Hendrix took over on guitar. After some discussion, Hendrix and Winwood began a slow, soulful rendition of "Valleys of Neptune." In addition to his electric piano, Winwood's "Rhythm Ace," an electronic metronome device, provided a steady backbeat for the two to play against. The pairing of these two special talents clicked instantly, as Winwood quickly grasped Hendrix's arrangement and began to provide not just a simple accompaniment but his own accents as well. While the quality of this recording is raw — just room microphones quickly set up — several brilliant moments were captured on tape. Kramer, who enjoyed the distinct privilege of recording both Hendrix and Traffic, especially appreciated the limitless possibilities of any such collaborative effort. "Steve was the perfect foil for Jimi and one of the very few musicians who could have kept up with him," muses Kramer.

Where Chris Wood had not partaken in Winwood's jam with Jimi, Winwood did not take part in Wood's wild, free-form jazz jam with Hendrix, which filled an entire reel of tape. There were no takes of any kind — just exuberant, unstructured jamming, much to the pleasure of all involved. Later jams intermittently involved Winwood, as well as Jenny Dean, a mutual friend who lent vocals to a similar free-form effort entitled "Slow Blues." In all, a wild night to remember.

■

Tuesday, June 16, 1970

New York, Electric Lady Studios. Engineer: Eddie Kramer. Second engineer: Kim King.

An extremely productive evening, arguably Jimi's strongest studio performance since the closing days of the *Electric Ladyland* album. Joined by percussionist Juma Sultan, the group began the evening by debuting "Nightbird Flying," a superb new Hendrix original.

"Nightbird Flying" had been in development for some time. Small elements of the song's rhythm pattern can be traced to jams staged at TTG Studios in October 1968. In early 1969, the song began to take form as "Ships Passing in the Night." Hendrix revisited the song on a number of occasions throughout 1969, weaving selected portions into various jam sessions. Demos were also recorded, with the first known recording made on April 14, 1969, at the Record Plant. Later demos were also put to tape, but none could be described as definitive. On this evening, Hendrix began anew, recording thirty-two takes before the final master was achieved. While take 7 held together until just prior to the close, a complete take 12 provided the first real glimpse of the song's vast promise. Take 17 was appropriately listed as "good," but Hendrix was not satisfied. Take 23 narrowed the margin even further, but it, too, was rejected. A marvelous take 24 was listed as "good" and timed at 3:45. Following a playback, however, a new reel of tape was installed, and work resumed. Takes 29 and a particularly robust take 30 were marked "good," but Jimi pressed on. Finally, a superb take 32 confirmed his vision. A tremendous track had been achieved. Following a playback, three edits were attempted, with the second ultimately inserted into the final master. At the close of the master take, after the song had been faded out, Hendrix and Kramer can be heard discussing how and where to fade out the song to create a proper ending.

While much time over the following weeks was dedicated to recording over-

Eddie Kramer engineering at Electric Lady Studios.

(Eddie Kramer)

Flying' was truly a superlative effort," lauds Kramer. "Mitch was great on that track, really on the mark." As complex as the basic rhythm track had been, recording Jimi's overdubs was equally challenging. "That song was a bastard to mix because we had so many guitar parts," remembers Kramer. "There's one bit in there [beginning at 2:22 and lasting until 2:30] where Jimi displayed his country influence. He did it as a piss-take and was laughing when he played it. I loved when Jimi would throw bits like that in."

With "Nightbird Flying" completed to his satisfaction, Jimi initiated work on "Straight Ahead." The versions recorded here showcased the group tightening their grasp on the song's arrangement, honing the various rhythm patterns in preparation for more formal takes.

After "Straight Ahead," Hendrix debuted a brand-new instrumental. "Messing Around," as the recording was described on the tape box, was a funky, medium-to-fast-tempo instrumental whose arrangement evolved gradually over multiple takes. Prior to take 17, Hendrix made some specific refinements, instructing Cox to try playing his bass line with simpler notes. While Cox responded accordingly, Hendrix was unable to bring the song to an effective close. Despite such structural problems, the remaining three takes brimmed with promise. Hendrix, however, seemed to recognize that more work would be required before a proper master could be achieved. After take 20, he abandoned the track entirely.

Next was "Beginnings," the instrumental originally conceived as "Jam Back at the House" at the guitarist's Shokan retreat in July 1969. While some takes were highly charged, the four appeared to be working the parts out as they went, Jimi intermittently

dubs and preparing a final mix for "Nightbird Flying," everyone involved in this special evening knew that Jimi had created a masterwork indicative of his growth as a musician and composer and certainly a worthy representation of his new musical direction. " 'Nightbird

addressing each musician with thoughts and instructions. None of these versions was complete or formally slated as a take. They did, however, serve to rally the group, as an extremely potent instrumental rendition of "Freedom" followed. While the song's structure was immediately recognizable, the pacing was noticeably slower. The gritty texture of Jimi's guitar tone was also dissimilar, as Hendrix adopted a higher-pitched, jangling tone not featured anywhere on the finished master. Especially noteworthy were Hendrix's exceptional chord stylings — earthy and raw, like the demo itself. While no match for the finished master, which would be recorded nine days later, on June 25, this sparkling demo provided a fascinating window into the song's evolution. At its conclusion, a tired Hendrix remarked, "That's good enough for tonight. We'll come back and do that tomorrow."

■
Wednesday, June 17, 1970
New York, Electric Lady Studios. Engineer: Eddie Kramer. Second engineer: Kim King.

An exceptional evening session that began with an enthusiastic reprise of "Straight Ahead." Following some twenty-five rehearsal "takes," take 1, the first "formal" take, was complete and timed at 4:20. After a playback, Hendrix asked Kramer, "What guitar tone was I using, this one [demonstrates with a quick burst of treble notes] or the one with more bass?" "The one with more bass," Kramer replied. Sounding confident and with all three musicians in obvious good spirits, work progressed steadily. Take 7 was listed as having a "nice feel," while take 11 was cited as complete. Following take 18, an edit of the song's front part was at-

tempted. Two takes were done, and the second was kept. After a playback and evaluation of their efforts, Jimi added a lead guitar overdub.

Next, Hendrix, Cox, and Mitchell concentrated on creating a section of "Straight Ahead" to be edited into the new master take. Various sections were recorded, showcasing superb performances from all three. Jimi's enthusiasm was in full display, creating a momentum that had been conspicuously absent from far too many of Jimi's sessions the previous year.

Similar edit sections were then recorded for "Astro Man." This effort featured Hendrix and Cox playing the same part simultaneously — a driving, distorted rhythm pattern. While this, too, was extremely well performed, there is no evidence that this overdub — unlike the edit sections created for "Straight Ahead" — made the final master.

With "Straight Ahead" deemed finished for the time being, Hendrix's interpretation of Bob Dylan's "Drifter's Escape" came next. Hendrix had originally decided to begin the song alone, but he suggested that Cox initiate the track on bass. As Cox pumped the song's distinctive opening notes, Hendrix countered with quick, sparse strokes on the guitar. This won his immediate approval, as his excited "Yeah!" was also captured on tape. Having seized the idea, Jimi abruptly brought the group to a halt. "Run the tape! Run the tape!" he demanded. "We are, we are, we are," Kramer reassured him. Jimi then began to sing 'Help me in my weakness' in a high-pitched voice, then "Help me in my . . . aah!" in an even higher octave, his voice on the verge of cracking. Straining, Jimi's voice finally does give in on the third, and highest, "aah!," which brings a laugh from Kramer. "Oh fuck!" laughs Jimi. "The

Devil made me sing like that!" When Jimi announced the song, Kramer asked him to sing along live. "You want me to sing it?" Jimi asked with a laugh. A promising, albeit incomplete, "Drifter's Escape" then followed. Take 2, also incomplete, was even stronger, with Jimi supplying a charged live vocal throughout the song's first half. At the conclusion of this take, Hendrix teased roadies Eric Barrett and Gene McFadden, who wanted to make some equipment changes. "Don't worry, Eric Barrett and Gene McFadden." "Eric says he's dying a death out here," added Kramer in a mock cockney accent. "Well, listen," Hendrix joked, "I'm going to save him right this very instant . . . if we can just get it right this time." "Just play!" bellowed Mitch. "You have three minutes," advised Kramer. "Oh, three minutes — no wonder we have so much time," Hendrix added with a laugh. His misfiring of the song's introduction caused him to remark, "Oh fuck! Two and a half minutes," which brought general laughter. Eric Barrett continued the horseplay with a remark about Mitch's earphones falling off his head. "We'll have to get you a special pair of cans [headphones] Mitch," Kramer deadpanned. "Ones weighted with lead." "No, the kind with the gum on the insides," suggested Hendrix, which broke everyone up. As Barrett and McFadden changed amplifiers, installing a new Ampeg for Billy Cox, the group took a break in the control room. After the work was completed, they returned to the studio to record the third take, an exceptional effort that yielded the working master. Hendrix, at a later, undocumented session, would overdub additional lead and rhythm guitar parts as well as a lead vocal.

Beginning with the two May dates at the Record Plant, Kramer's role had evolved, now encompassing dual re-

Mitch Mitchell.

(John Gardiner)

sponsibilities as engineer and co-producer. Hendrix was still in charge of each session, deciding which songs to record and what arrangements to utilize, but the working relationship between the two had matured, allowing Kramer to maximize his contributions without clashing with Hendrix's eager attitude and desire to try to do everything. "Except for Gary Kellgren, the other engineers we had worked with at the Record Plant gave us very little input," explains Cox. "They just figured that Jimi knew what he was doing, so they left him alone. They would make suggestions like changing the batteries in the wah-wah pedal or replacing a Fuzz-Face unit if it was causing problems, but none of them would get into a song like Eddie would do. Kramer got totally absorbed into what we were doing. Jimi appreciated that. Eddie wasn't the type of guy who would come over the talkback and say, 'Guys, you were playing an F# there instead of an F.' He never got into that. He stayed on top of Jimi's tuning and every now and then would say, 'What's that I hear?' and Jimi would say, 'Yeah, I hear that too. Let's change or fix that.' "

For Kramer, the key to maximizing their working relationship was simply maintaining a clear understanding of each other's strengths and responsibilities. "At this point, now that we had started working together again, his sense of involvement behind the console was not as heavy as it had been before," recalls Kramer. "He left it more or less up to me and was showing more interest in what was happening out in the studio rather than the control room. However, we still mixed songs together, and the old team feel came back immediately."

"Kramer was like a director," explains Kim King. "There was no telling Jimi *what* to play, but if he was on, Kramer would channel him into some-thing productive, because if he hadn't, Hendrix would have gone on all night long recording some marvelous jam that was simply unusable."

Kramer's complete commitment to Jimi's music endeared him to Hendrix. "We felt that a lot of the engineers we had worked with at the Record Plant had been nice guys, but Eddie had his head into what we were all about," remembers Cox. "We were all comfortable with Eddie and knew that he could help us make magic out of what we put down on tape. Eddie was into our music and would add direction to our creativity. He would hear something we'd play and want to try something backwards or make adjustments to Jimi's guitar sound. Here was an engineer who was really concerned. Heretofore, the other engineers we had used would ask us whether or not to use EQ or which tracks the drums should be recorded on. We didn't want the engineer to ask *us* — we wanted him to feel it and get involved. Kramer got involved. You needed that with Jimi Hendrix, because he was such a perfectionist. There were many times when I would say, 'Damn, that's good! You can't improve that,' but he would keep trying. He would record a great guitar overdub, and Eddie would tell him that it was great. He'd think we were all putting him on and that he could do it better. There were times — even at Electric Lady — when he would take two hours to come to the conclusion that what he was playing now was great, but not better than the take we had thought was great."

After concert dates in Albuquerque (June 19), San Bernardino (June 20), Ventura (June 21), and Denver (June 23), Hendrix returned to New York and to Electric Lady eager to build on the encouraging progress he had made. The group's efforts on this evening did not disappoint, as Hendrix focused squarely on "Astro Man." Hendrix had frequently incorporated portions of the rhythm pattern from "Astro Man" — or "Asshole Man," as he would occasionally label the song — in a number of his Record Plant jams during 1969. Previously, the most developed attempt at recording the track was made by the Band of Gypsys in January 1970. That version, however, never progressed past the demo stage. The song's inspiration was simple, drawing its roots from Hendrix's love for animated cartoons. "That's what 'Astro Man' was all about," says Cox with a laugh. "We used to love watching cartoons at his apartment. He enjoyed Mighty Mouse and especially loved Rocky and Bullwinkle."

Capturing the song's infectious groove was Hendrix's primary task on this evening, and the group filled two reels of tape with instrumental takes, each new effort inching gradually closer to the arrangement eventually featured on the finished master. "We were in a groove that night," remembers Cox. " 'Astro Man' was such a fun song to play. By that time, we knew those patterns extremely well. We enjoyed building on them." Reel three began with a loose run-through of Muddy Waters' "Rollin' Stone," marked incorrectly on the tape box as "I Just Want to Make Love to You." Six incomplete takes of "Astro Man" followed. An extended take 7 was spectacular, with Cox and Mitchell firmly interlocked, teaming with Hendrix to expand the boundaries of the arrangement. An edited version of this jam was originally slated for *Bootleg,* the 1985 compilation album prepared by Reprise Records but never released.

At the conclusion of this expanded take 7, Hendrix shifted gears, guiding Cox and Mitchell through an effective workout of "In from the Storm." With its final structure still undetermined, some passages were uneven. At its conclusion, Cox led Hendrix through a short burst of Cream's "Politician." Four additional takes of "Astro Man," numbering 11 through 14, came next. Though none would yield a finished master, Jimi's playing was, nevertheless, especially noteworthy. With the band in full flight, lost within another electrifying take, the reel of tape abruptly ended, forcing assistant engineer Dave Palmer to hurriedly change reels. As soon as the new reel was installed, Palmer snapped on the record button, capturing the final forty seconds of the jam. Hendrix then tore into a stunning medley that lasted — without pause — nearly twenty-six minutes. His incredible flight began with a slow, blistering, seven-minute rendition of "Beginnings," with Mitchell and Cox swinging tightly behind him. This evolved into an up-tempo "Hey Baby (Land of the New Rising Sun)," which boasted several thrilling moments. Jimi then downshifted, cruising into a spirited jam that evolved as "Keep on Movin'," a spontaneous hybrid of "Straight Ahead" and "Midnight Lightning." A furious instrumental take of "Freedom" followed, carried to a close with a rousing flourish. Kramer's enthusiasm came immediately over the talkback, and applause from guests seated in the control room was audible. Hendrix seemed genuinely surprised by the reaction and called for

the band to come in and listen to what remains today, more than twenty-five years later, a fascinating document of his magnificent talent.

Sessions such as these emphatically underscored Hendrix's creative rejuvenation. Electric Lady had sparked Jimi's creativity, challenging him to maximize his immeasurable gifts as both a musician and composer. Within the confines of his new studio, Hendrix had successfully refocused his energy and concentration on his music. "Inside the studio, we were never bothered by outside influences," remembers Cox. "Even Michael Jeffery stayed away. I only saw him come down once, and that was just to see what was going on. He didn't have any input whatsoever. We were left to create music, and that's what we loved to do. That made Jimi so happy. He would say, 'Man, we don't fish or go bowling like other people do. We make music, and *this* is fun.' I said, 'It sure is. I feel sorry for a whole lot of musicians who can't do this.' Electric Lady was home to us. Even when we would be out on the road — we'd be thinking up little patterns, showing them to each other and saying, 'We'll have to try that at the studio when we get back.' "

■
Thursday, June 25, 1970
New York, Electric Lady Studios. Engineer: Eddie Kramer. Second engineer: Dave Palmer.

Work continued on "Astro Man," with the group, joined by Juma Sultan, applying finishing touches to the new basic track. More overdubs, as well as a number of rough mixes, would follow, but the version recorded on this day would serve as the final master for *Cry of Love.*

"Drifting," a superlative new ballad, made its recorded debut. The group re-

corded a backing track, with Hendrix playing through a Leslie organ speaker while simultaneously contributing a guide vocal track. Following that successful take, the song's introduction was also recorded. Both these efforts would be marked 'master.'

Putting "Drifting" aside, Hendrix turned to "Freedom." After an incomplete initial take, take 2 was especially lively. A brief conference between Hendrix and Kramer ensued, because Kramer felt the entry of the bass guitar needed to be repositioned. The group came back into the control room for a listen. The meeting was clearly beneficial, as — following a false start marked take 3 — take 4 was especially strident. Having missed an occasional note, Hendrix knew he could improve on his own performance. After a false start on take 5, an exceptional sixth take captured the master.

"Originally, all Jimi had was just that opening riff," recalls Billy Cox. "I remember him playing it to me at his apartment during the time of the Band of Gypsys. We spent a lot of time working that song out before we finally recorded it at Electric Lady. Back then, what we did was to always record a work track. A work track was simply a basic track — just the basic guitar, bass, and drum parts down on tape. With that work track, the possibilities were unlimited. You could go over that guitar, you could erase that bass part, because you already had the basic ingredients of a dynamic song recorded. We did not work with paper and pen or bars and time signatures. We had all this in our head. With a work track down, we could build something, and that's how 'Freedom' finally came about."

One other track, described on the tape box as "Cherokee Mist," was also put down during this productive session, but the sole take recorded was edited out of the multitrack master tape and transferred to a compilation reel prepared by Alan Douglas in 1974. That work reel has either been lost or stolen, and the whereabouts of a safety copy, if one even exists, is unknown.

Having satisfied the terms of his settlement with Capitol Records and PPX Industries by means of the recent *Band of Gypsys* album, Hendrix's plan was to prepare *First Rays of the New Rising Sun*, a double album of new material. Some time on June 24, Hendrix took stock of his progress, composing a memo to himself that listed the following tracks as "having backing tracks completed, Ezy Ryder, Room Full of Mirrors, Earth Blues Today, Have You Heard ["Straight Ahead"], Freedom, Stepping Stone, Izabella — complete, needs new mix, Astro Man and Nightbird Flying." Also listed were "Drifter's Escape" and "Burning Desire," but Jimi had placed questions marks beside them. He also made a note to get the tape of "Highway Chile."

■
Friday, June 26, 1970
New York, Electric Lady Studios. Engineer: Eddie Kramer. Second engineer: Kim King.

A busy evening dedicated to revisiting and overdubbing previously recorded masters. The December 19, 1969/January 20, 1970, Record Plant recording of "Message of Love" was reviewed, but no overdubbing was attempted. This decision, says Kramer, was made because Hendrix felt that songs such as "Message to Love," "Machine Gun," and "Power of Soul" had been given over to *Band of Gypsys*. Issuing studio versions — however different in style or arrangement — seemed regressive and not in keeping with his plans for the projected double album.

The December 19, 1969/January 20, 1970, Record Plant recording of "Earth Blues," however, received an extensive overhaul. Rather than simply recut the track, Hendrix chose to reconstruct the song from within, replacing the bulk of the original recording with new overdubs. A decision was made to replace Buddy Miles's original drum parts with a new overdub by Mitchell. Billy Cox improved upon his original bass line, and Hendrix was busy as well, overdubbing a new rhythm guitar line as well as two new lead tracks. The backing vocals from Buddy Miles and the Ronettes were retained, but Jimi also added a new background vocal to complement their original effort.

Though considerable time and effort had been invested in revamping "Earth Blues," Hendrix stopped short of designating this track finished, believing that he might still be able to improve on his performance. "While 'Earth Blues' very much fit musically into the framework of his new direction, we were never certain that it was ever going to make the final record," states Kramer. Of all Jimi's new material, "Earth Blues," with its overt R&B influence, seemed to best exemplify the deepening creative divide between Hendrix and manager Michael Jeffery. "Earth Blues" was a good track," explains engineer John Jansen. "But nobody upstairs wanted to hear those 'Everybody!' chants on a record by Jimi. When Jimi wasn't around and Jeffery heard us working on it, he would wave his hands in the air and roll his eyes."

"Stepping Stone" was another Band of Gypsys staple retooled at Electric Lady. On this evening, Hendrix would overdub additional rhythm and lead guitar parts. Later undocumented sessions would result in more guitar overdubbing from Jimi, a vocal overdub, and new drum parts from Mitch Mitchell, replacing those originally re-

corded by Buddy Miles. Nevertheless, Eddie Kramer feels that Jimi would have continued to tinker with "Stepping Stone" had he lived. "The tempo was always the problem with this song," explains Kramer. "Both Buddy and Mitch had trouble staying with Jimi on that one."

Additional work on "Valleys of Neptune," another promising track making encouraging strides at the studio, was also completed. The origins of "Valleys of Neptune" took shape during Hendrix's summer retreat at the Shokan house during the summer of 1969. Beginning at the Hit Factory in September 1969, Hendrix, clearly aware of the song's potential, recorded a number of unrealized versions over the following nine months. In spite of this extraordinary effort, he had been unable to complete a master take to his satisfaction. "I loved that song," states Cox. "Jimi spent a lot of time at his apartment trying to tighten it up. He kept adding to his original idea. We almost completed that song at Electric Lady, and if we had, it would have been a monster."

Also on this evening, marbled within overdub attempts by Hendrix and Cox for "Valleys of Neptune," strains of another intriguing Hendrix original were debuted, a sparse, solo demo entitled "Heaven Has No Sorrow." Building on this skeletal take, Hendrix labored closely with Cox in an attempt to establish an appropriate bass line and further develop the song's existing rhythm pattern. "'Heaven Has No Sorrow' was an idea of Jimi's that we never really got to do," states Cox. "The demo we cut was nothing of any real significance, but it probably could have evolved into a pretty dynamic song, something along the lines of 'Angel.'"

With the studio becoming more functional each day, Hendrix's enthusiasm grew. "That studio was like our

**Percussionist Juma Sultan. Even after the breakup of Gypsy Sun &
Rainbows, Juma continued to guest on Jimi's recordings. He often sat in on
sessions at Electric Lady, performing on such tracks as "Dolly Dagger."**
(Jim Cummins/Star File)

laboratory," says Cox. "We'd be out on
the road just playing in our hotel room,
and if we came up with a good pattern,
we would say, 'We've got to try that
when we get back to the studio.' That's
what the studio meant for Jimi. We
would go out on the road and work, so
that he could *create* back at Electric
Lady."

While Kramer's presence may have
served to sharpen Jimi's focus, minimiz-
ing the many distractions suffered elsewhere played a critical role in Hendrix's
creative rejuvenation. Kramer and studio president Jim Marron lectured both
the employees and engineering staff to
allow Jimi whatever distance he desired.
"Beyond the front door to the studio,
Jimi did not exist for any of the assistant
engineers," explains Kim King. "His private life was absolutely separate from
the studio. That was one of the things
about Electric Lady — Jimi would be
able to walk through the door and be
someplace else. The real world would
stop once he came in the front door."

The studio's twenty-four-hour,
closed-circuit camera security system
quickly justified its expense, as each
person who arrived at the new facility's
locked front door had to be announced.
No longer could uninvited guests simply walk into the studio and disrupt the
control room, as had become the policy
at the Record Plant. Electric Lady's
new policy of restricting visitors met
with strong approval from Billy Cox.
"When I first came onboard, Jimi's sessions were nothing but a big party,"
states Cox. "He saw that I would get
uptight when a lot of those strangers
would come in and disrupt our sessions. It just wasn't productive. I wasn't
a party person, so I didn't want to waste
all that time standing around doing
nothing. I would let off some bad vibes
when all those people would crowd our
sessions. The studio was the place
where you could experiment and make

mistakes while you were getting songs together. The studio was not our stage. Jimi knew what was happening. He would privately say, 'If I was a janitor, do you think all of these people would want to watch me mop the floor?' But then he wouldn't throw anybody out, because he didn't want to create a scene. All that changed at Electric Lady. We were finally able to get our work done without being disturbed. As a result, Jimi's spirits were higher, and the recordings sounded better. We accomplished so much that summer, and keeping away those distractions was a major reason why."

While the majority of his previous sessions at the Record Plant had usually begun after midnight, Hendrix's sessions at Electric Lady usually started at 7:00 P.M. "We would know when Jimi had arrived, because he would have to be buzzed in at the front door," remembers King. "Jimi rarely came down the stairs and walked straight into the control room. He generally would head to the office upstairs. Eddie usually had a rough mix of something set up and ready to go, but often it would turn out that Jimi would want to work on something else. When Jimi would come into the control room, he would have a private meeting with Eddie, and assistant engineers were not party to that. When they were finished, Jimi would head out to the studio, and Eddie would tell us what we would be doing that night. But even then, Jimi's sessions were almost entirely directed by his mood and whims. Some nights we would stick to the game plan; other nights he would want to change midstream and get into something else."

Although the elimination of the hordes of hangers-on had improved the creative climate within the studio, it did little to comfort the delicate condition of Hendrix's private life. The vola-

tility of his relationship with Devon Wilson, coupled with his many battles with Michael Jeffery, extracted a heavy toll. "There were also some nights where Jimi would arrive, head upstairs, and not come down at all," remembers King. "We would wait, and sometimes Eddie would get a phone call from upstairs saying that Jimi was not going to work that night. There were some serious politics going on up there, but Eddie forbade us from getting involved with it in any way. We were *not* to put our two cents in."

Devon Wilson cast a large shadow within Electric Lady. Her standing as Jimi's girlfriend lent considerable weight to her criticisms and observations. "Devon was just as cunning as Michael Jeffery," remembers Jim Marron. "She was intensely into anything that she perceived as being good for Jimi. Jeffery would not take any shit from her, but at the same time, she used to try and see just how far she could push him."

Devon's reach extended right through to the control room, where she was a frequent spectator throughout the long summer. "She used to hang around a lot," recalls engineer Dave Palmer. "She wanted to be there all the time, saying once, 'If you're going to be making music or mixing music with Jimi, I've got to be there.' That was weird — a necessary evil for Hendrix, I guess. Kramer got along well with her, but I always sensed he would have just preferred she not be there."

The depth of Devon's influence within Electric Lady fluctuated wildly, tightly bound to the present status of her relationship with Jimi. Their relationship was so volatile that Hendrix would occasionally bar her from the studio. "Devon was more often part of the scene than not, but there were times when she was not allowed in," ex-

plains Kim King. "On some evenings, as per Jimi's instructions, we were not to answer the door to Devon."

■

Monday, June 29, 1970
New York, Electric Lady Studios. Engineer: Eddie Kramer. Second engineer: Kim King.

A session dedicated to recording overdubs, with "Drifting" the subject of Hendrix's concentration. Jimi would overdub a lead vocal and experiment with a number of interesting ideas, including a recording of his breathing superimposed backward as an effect. A number of various electronic sound effects were also tried, including an attempt to recapture the 'seagull' sound originally featured as part of *Electric Ladyland*'s "1983 (A Merman I Should Turn to Be)." Save for the song's lead vocal part, none of the ideas presented on this evening would ultimately be included on the master prepared for *Cry of Love*.

■

Wednesday, July 1, 1970
New York, Electric Lady Studios. Engineer: Eddie Kramer. Second engineer: Dave Palmer.

For many years, this date has often been inaccurately referred to as Electric Lady's unofficial opening date. While that claim is untrue, this lengthy session was, arguably, Hendrix's most productive there. On this evening, "Dolly Dagger," one of Hendrix's most promising new songs, came to life. Unlike the majority of Hendrix's other compositions from this period, "Dolly Dagger" did not evolve through repeated jam sessions at the Record Plant during 1969. "Hendrix cut 'Dolly Dag-

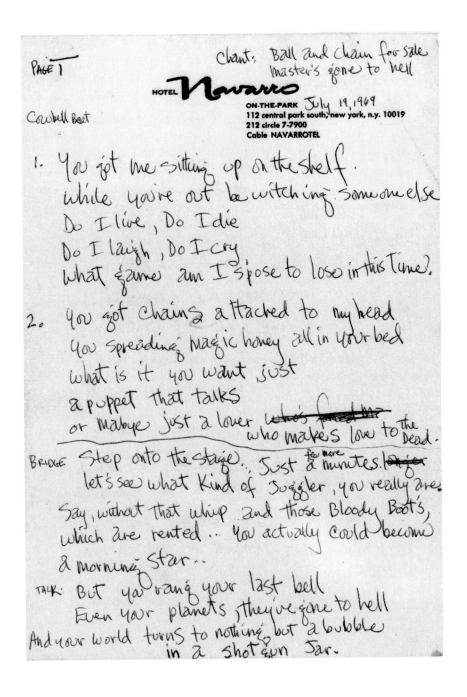

Chant: Ball and chain for sale
master's gone to hell

HOTEL Navarro
ON-THE-PARK   July 19, 1969
112 central park south, new york, n.y. 10019
212 circle 7-7900
Cable NAVARROTEL

Cowbell Beat

1. You got me sitting up on the shelf.
while you're out be witching some one else
Do I live, Do I die
Do I laugh, Do I cry
What game am I spose to lose in this Time?

2. You got chains attached to my head
You spreading magic honey all in your bed
what is it you want, just
a puppet that talks
or Mabye just a lover ~~who's forced to~~
who makes love to the dead.

BRIDGE Step onto the stage.. Just a ~~few more~~ minutes.
let's see what kind of Juggler, you really are.
Say, without that whip and those Bloody Boot's,
which are rented .. You actually could become
a morning Star ..

TALK: But you rang your last bell
Even your planets, they've gone to hell
And your world turns to nothing, but a bubble
in a shot gun Jar.

"Ball and Chain." An unreleased song
inspired by Jimi's relationship with girlfriend
Devon Wilson.

(James A. Hendrix)

ger' twice," recalls Kramer. "He had recorded a rough demo at the Record
Plant [in November 1969], but that
was scrapped entirely. We cut the new
basic track [during this session] but
spent three or four days overdubbing
guitars and finishing the background
vocals."

Where Billy Cox's bass line had
originally inspired Hendrix to develop
the song's rhythm pattern, "Dolly
Dagger"'s colorful lyrics, says guitarist

Arthur Lee, were inspired by Devon
Wilson. "The lyric 'She drinks her blood
from a jagged edge,'" Wilson explained
to Lee, drew its origins from Hendrix's
November 27, 1969, birthday party,
when Mick Jagger accidentally pricked
his finger. When he asked for a band-
aid, Devon rushed to him and told him
that wouldn't be necessary. Then, in
full view of Hendrix, she sucked the
blood from his finger.

The group joined again by percussionist Juma Sultan, recording began
with six rehearsal takes of "Dolly Dagger," performed without Mitchell on
drums. These six takes revealed Hendrix and Cox, supported by Sultan's in-
sistent conga work, developing the
song's distinctive groove. After the sixth
rehearsal, Hendrix and company re-
treated to the control room to assess
their progress. When recording resumed, Mitch Mitchell was now seated
behind his Gretsch double drum kit,
contributing to a charming interpretation of "Bolero." "Bolero" was actually
marked take 1, followed by an ineffec-
tive complete take of "Dolly Dagger."
With the group not entirely in sync,
Hendrix shifted gears, guiding them
through the more familiar "Hey Baby
(Land of the New Rising Sun)." Jimi
sang the first line off-key, which caused
him to remark "flat" unceremoniously
before continuing the song as an instrumental. Their next attempt was considerably upgraded, creating the version
later issued as part of *Rainbow Bridge*.
An instrumental stab at "Drifting" followed, closing out the reel.

With a fresh roll of tape installed, a
hearty "Dolly Dagger" opened reel two,
ignited by Hendrix's energy and enthusiasm. Singing and playing live, Jimi
can be heard improvising the song's lyrics as he shaped the infectious rhythm
track.

Their focus sharpened, work on

"Dolly Dagger" began in earnest. A series of takes, numbered 3 through 17, followed, but each was incomplete. Though it would not yield the master, an encouraging take 18 finally turned the corner. With the band primed for success, take 19 provided the master and also "Slow Part," an unexpected delight. "As 'Dolly Dagger' began to come apart," explains Kramer, "Billy Cox started playing the bass line to 'Gimme Some Lovin','" the Spencer Davis Group song, and that developed into a jam lasting nearly ten minutes."

" 'Dolly Dagger' had broken down," remembered John Jansen, "but the band continued to play. After three minutes or so, Hendrix began playing this beautiful melody, and the rest of the guys fell in behind him."

"When the jam started, Jimi was just fucking around," remembers Kramer. "The tone he was using was just his quiet jam tone, with the amplifier turned down some, and not the full-bore Marshall sound he had used to cut the basic track. Afterwards, when he realized that there might be something in this after all, he overdubbed a second guitar and a new solo, with the Marshall back at full volume. He did these with the Uni-Vibe, as well as a Leslie at the end."

Marked on the tape box as "Slow Part" by second engineer Dave Palmer, an edited version of this instrumental would be posthumously retitled "Pali Gap" and join "Dolly Dagger" as part of the *Rainbow Bridge* film and its accompanying soundtrack album. The title "Pali Gap" was coined by Michael Jeffery in an attempt to further wed the song to the film's Hawaiian locale. While Hendrix had taken the additional step of adding overdubs to "Slow Part," Kramer recalls that there was no plan ever to include the instrumental as part of *First Rays of the New Rising Sun*.

Next would be two attempts at the blues-based "Midnight Lightning," neither of which was complete. Considering his many attempts throughout 1969 and 1970 to record this song, it was obvious that Hendrix was keen to develop the definitive rendition and include it as part of the projected double album. At this stage, however, a suitable arrangement still eluded him. "There was a point in time where 'Midnight Lightning' got kind of repetitive," admits Cox. "It was a good song, but we were just bogged down with it. When we started touring, we got some new, refreshed ideas as to how to try and do it, but the process still wasn't complete."

A jam based on an entirely new pattern followed, but Hendrix soon directed this into "Beginnings." Five exceptional takes were recorded, the fifth later edited and released as part of 1972's *War Heroes*.

At the session's conclusion, it was obvious to all that in "Dolly Dagger," Jimi had created a special work, wholly indicative of both his impressive abilities and his new musical direction. While additional work on "Dolly Dagger" would be completed over the following weeks, the music made on this evening emphatically reinforced Jimi's confidence and reaffirmed the promise that Electric Lady Studios would foster such achievements.

■

Sunday, July 2, 1970
New York, Electric Lady Studios. Engineer: Eddie Kramer. Second engineer: Kim King.

Important work on "Ezy Rider" would be completed on this evening. "Ezy Ryder," says Kim King, was one of a number of older recordings from the Record Plant that were reserved for nights when Jimi would come in alone

and just want to replace lead vocal or guitar parts. On this night, Jimi prefaced his lead vocal overdub with his own risqué variation of bluesman Chick Willis's "Stoop Down Baby": "Old Mother Hubbard went to the cupboard to find her poor dog a bone. But when she bent over, Rover took over, because Rover had a bone of his own. Shakespeare! Page 35!" "I thought it was hilarious," remembers Kramer, "but Jimi thought it too vulgar and instructed me to keep it out of the mix."

Hendrix had invested heavily in "Ezy Ryder," dedicating hours searching for the exact guitar sounds he desired. "Jimi would come up with a riff, and we would dub it down to two-track," remembers King. "That idea would lead to something else, as he would come back and want to change one of the guitar tracks or replace a specific measure on one of the lead guitar tracks. The fight for open tracks had been a bear on some of the songs we had added overdubs to, but this was a guitar song, a *symphonic* guitar song. It was handled like string quartet parts, although nothing was written on paper — it was all improvised. We overdubbed eight tracks of guitars. Everything in pairs — four tracks of lead and four tracks of rhythm — all at Electric Lady. This work took weeks and involved a number of intricate punch-ins. There were no tape counters or auto locators or anything like that, so I was tape jockey. We settled into a unit, and we didn't have to talk about what to punch in or keep."

Preparing the song's final mix proved to be equally eventful. King explains: "During the song's final mixing session, we were using two tape machines, and Eddie and Jimi were doing a four-handed mix on the console while I was doing the flanging — actually holding my thumb on the tape reel and

varying the pressure on the flange of the tape reel, you're controlling the speed, which is controlling the pitch. By varying the pitch by microcycles, you're varying the angle of phase between those two notes. The actual sound you are hearing is the two notes beating against each other. I was playing the flange, and Jimi and Eddie were doing these very elaborate pans, where sounds were changing sides and coming out of the middle. I had terrible blisters on my thumb, but the sound was fantastic — in fact, the entire mix

Rockin' and rollin' in the streets of **Hollywood. Buddy Miles.**
(Robert Fitzpatrick Archives)

SESSIONS

was magical. Eddie, Jimi, and I were rocking and leaning back in our chairs throughout. Right near the end of the song, we leaned back too far and all fell over. We were scrambling around the floor before Eddie got to the board, grabbed the master fader, and brought it up full to make sure we had hit the end of the tune correctly. Actually, we hadn't — there was some garbage there at the end — but the mix worked, and Jimi thought the whole thing was hilarious, so we left it in!"

Also recorded on this day was an unrelated four-track demo by flautist Jeremy Steig. While the session was engineered by Kramer, Hendrix does not make an appearance.

■
Atlanta Pop Festival
Saturday, July 4, 1970.
Fire/Lover Man/Spanish Castle Magic/Red House/Room Full of Mirrors/Hear My Train A Comin/Message to Love/All Along the Watchtower/Freedom/Foxey Lady/Purple Haze/Hey Joe/Voodoo Child (Slight Return)/Stone Free/Star Spangled Banner/Straight Ahead/Hey Baby (Land of the Rising Sun)

After the July 2 session for "Ezy Ryder," the Experience resumed their touring schedule, with Hendrix's next engagement at the massive Atlanta Pop Festival on July 4. His fine set there, later released, in part, as *Stages*, showcased a number of songs currently in development at Electric Lady, including "Room Full of Mirrors," "Freedom," and "Straight Ahead."

When Hendrix's touring commitments pulled him from the recording studio, he continued to write on the road, exchanging and recording ideas with Billy Cox within the confines of his hotel suites. Conversely, serious work on new material was never ac-

complished during pre-concert sound checks — a formality that Hendrix loathed. "Sound checks were the worst time in the world to work on songs," explains Cox. "Jimi especially hated them. We both felt that they were intimidating and unnecessary. People would be there looking for him to put on a show, and it wasn't time for that. It was time to check our monitors and amplifiers, which we could do by running through one or two songs. Even then, I would basically strum my E and G strings back and forth just to make sure we had a good sound. Once we did, we'd call it a day."

Rather than tinker with such songs as "Straight Ahead" during sound checks, Hendrix instead preferred to perform them in front of his audiences. "We'd get in the dressing room and Jimi would say, 'Hey, let's try this song or that song tonight,'" Cox remembers. "And the people loved it. Now he always had to do 'Fire,' 'Foxey Lady,' and 'Purple Haze,' if he didn't do anything else. Sometimes, if the crowd pushed, he'd do 'All Along the Watchtower.' On the whole, he got tired of playing every one of those songs except 'Foxey Lady.' He loved playing that song, because it wasn't too cluttered and it allowed him to do his splits and all of his stage things. But after the show, he'd talk about how the new songs went down."

From Atlanta, the Experience traveled to Miami, performing two shows at the Jai Alai Fronton on July 5. In Miami, Hendrix extended his time there to accommodate some additional rest and relaxation. During his stay, he also hooked up with jazz bassist Jaco Pastorius, although no recording was attempted.

Despite the considerable role Electric Lady — even in its unfinished state — had in renewing Hendrix's creative spirit, new problems emerged,

raising questions hidden beneath the recent euphoria. Although Hendrix had given over *Band of Gypsys* to Capitol Records as per the negotiated settlement of his bitter lawsuit with Ed Chalpin's PPX Industries, the demands placed by Michael Jeffery upon Jimi never diminished. He had insisted on the Cry of Love tour, to keep both the studio and the entire company solvent. While Jeffery had, so far, honored his concession to limit Jimi's schedule of engagements to a series of three-day weekends, the thorny issue of Hendrix's having to alter his recording schedule to facilitate sessions by paying clients rankled him. The philosophical divide between the two men could not have been more distinct. Electric Lady Studios — or, at the very least, Studio A — was to have been Hendrix's creative space. With only one functional room available, Hendrix felt Jeffery had breached their unspoken agreement — namely, that the profit generated by the rental of Studio B would cover the facility's operating costs, service the outstanding loan to Warner Bros., and allow Hendrix to maintain a private, creative space available twenty-four hours a day. Jeffery, however, soon succumbed and was eager to market the studio's state-of-the-art equipment and artist-friendly environment. Prospective clients peppered Jeffery and Marron with requests for studio time. Where the locked doors, security cameras, and closed sessions had vastly improved the creative atmosphere for Jimi's sessions, it directly contributed to Electric Lady's mystique. Hendrix, just two short years earlier, had single-handedly put the Record Plant on the map with his extended booking shortly after the studio opened. Now, with operational costs at Electric Lady mounting and the debt to Warner Bros. outstanding, the offers and requests

proved too tempting to ignore. Jeffery eventually relented, accepting bookings during the profitable daytime hours and during weekends when Hendrix was on the road.

While Hendrix had established his own schedule at the studio, preferring to begin in the early evening, maintenance and booking by outside clients continued at other hours. While Jimi worked with Kramer in Studio A, Shimon Ron worked feverishly to com-

Berkeley Community Center, Berkeley.
May 30, 1970, second show.
(Richard Peters)

plete Studio B. Many minor technical issues remained unresolved, leaving Kramer, Ron, Palmer, and King with innumerable tasks. By July, with Studio B still unfinished, Jimi was occasionally denied time or was forced to curtail his session so the studio could be reset for incoming, outside clients. Such interruptions infuriated Hendrix. "While it didn't happen that often, there were times when Jimi had to leave the studio because there would be a morning session booked," recalls Kim King. "That pissed him off. There was one big flap in particular, where I recall him complaining, 'This is my studio. Why do I have to leave?'"

King was not the only Electric Lady employee who witnessed such incidents. "Jimi would complain that he could never get in to record," echoes Linda Sharlin. "There were times when he would have to wait until the daytime sessions were finished so that he could get in. He wanted to know if *his* studio was for him or if it was to make money. Other times, he'd come in unannounced, and if the studio was booked, he'd leave. He just wanted to plug in his guitar and play — that's all he ever wanted to do."

"Deep down in his heart, Jimi knew that the studio was not his to claim solely," says Cox. "But he accepted that. He wasn't naive enough to think that he could own a recording studio in Greenwich Village all by himself. He knew that he had to have powerful people behind him."

In addition to early clients like Jeremy Steig, studio president Jim Marron actively recruited work from Madison Avenue, creating a lucrative cash flow that required relatively short sessions and few technical demands. Weekend sessions, usually while the Experience was on the road, were frequently staged, so that Michael Jeffery could audition new talent or have staff engi-

neers record demos for groups he was considering. "That's how I got to sit in the big chair," adds Dave Palmer with a laugh. "Michael Jeffery would arrange these sessions for his management company. He would bring in bands to cut demos and tracks with the hope of landing them a record deal."

While Hendrix and Jeffery may have been equal partners in the venture, their goals for the studio couldn't have been more different. To Hendrix, Electric Lady represented an impressive achievement and a tangible measure of his success and hard work. The studio was to be his creative haven, a home created by the fruits of his music and forever supported by it. For Jeffery, the rental of the studio was necessary to keep the facility solvent. Despite their standing as partners, Hendrix and Jeffery simply did not share the same operating philosophy.

In just two months, as many of the final touches were completed, Electric Lady blossomed to heights Hendrix may never have imagined. The studio, in all its celebrated splendor, was nothing like the simple, creative workspace he had originally requested. And while the release of *Band of Gypsys* had helped to ease the oppressive grasp of the PPX lawsuit, the pressure to produce had not subsided. The stakes had, in fact, grown even higher. In addition to owing Reprise a long-overdue sequel to *Electric Ladyland*, Hendrix was beholden to Warner Bros. for its $300,000 loan, guaranteed against any royalties he might earn. Electric Lady was more than just a workspace for Hendrix: Jeffery's headquarters controlled the entire second floor, a not-so-subtle reminder that the studio would accommodate both work and play. "Michael Jeffery had removed all of whatever existed in a sleazy old nightclub and built this plastic spaceship," recalls Kim King. "And now, Jimi had to deliver.

There was a real push/pull dynamic at work there. Hendrix had to show up to go to work, and he didn't want to go to work. On any given day, he'd play hooky, he'd show up begrudgingly, or he'd show up and things would click and we would record some magical, high-quality music. Jimi wanted a place to record where he could leave everything set up and walk in and walk out. He wanted it to be *his* studio. Suddenly, the whole thing had snowballed so far away from whatever his original idea had been that there was a certain resentment at Michael. Then there was the dynamic between Michael and Eddie. Electric Lady was not Jimi's studio — it was Eddie's studio. Eddie wanted Jimi to have the best damn studio in the world, with everything state-of-the-art. Jimi appreciated the studio's complexity and the lengths that people went to so that he would be able to deliver product. But much to the consternation of everyone upstairs, Jimi obviously didn't give a shit about product. Eddie was in a very tough position. It was his responsibility to see that product was delivered, and there was resentment in general on Jimi's part in that he had to deliver it at all. That was a constant undercurrent."

Kramer's relationship with Jeffery started poorly and never improved. Jeffery openly mistrusted Kramer and remained wary of his relationship with Hendrix. "Jeffery always wanted to limit Kramer's role at Electric Lady," explains Jim Marron. "The right way of doing it, had Eddie not been in such an adversarial position with Michael, would have been to bring him into the family and make a mutually beneficial deal. That's not how things were handled. Jeffery was leery of Kramer's relationship with Hendrix. He always wanted to be kept abreast of what Eddie was up to downstairs."

Tuesday, July 14, 1970

New York, Electric Lady Studios. Engineer: Eddie Kramer. Second engineer: Dave Palmer.

Eighteen takes of "Jam," later titled "Comin' Down Hard on Me Baby" and, finally, "Come Down Hard on Me," were recorded. While no complete takes were recorded, takes 11 and 18 were marked as having "good front sections." These renditions featured a slightly altered arrangement and a more intricate rhythm guitar pattern from Hendrix. Timing problems, however,

A rare shot of Hendrix recording at Electric Lady Studios.

(Eddie Kramer)

repeatedly hampered the group's progress. Hendrix can be heard offering instructions to Mitchell, Cox, and Sultan throughout, leading what clearly resembled, at this stage, a rehearsal.

"Jam" followed, but this was actually a rough sketch of "Bolero," with Hendrix guiding Cox and Sultan through the song's chord changes. Mitchell did not participate, and no masters, or even formal takes, were achieved. When recording resumed once more, Mitchell had returned, and "Midnight Lightning" was attempted. Despite its promising start, Hendrix had still not fully developed the song; this effort came apart shortly after the four-minute mark. At this stage, "Midnight Lightning," despite its engaging rhythm pattern and novel adaptation of Chick Willis's risqué classic "Stoop Down Baby," was abandoned. After making a series of technical adjustments, Hendrix shifted to "Bolero." These takes represent a vast improvement over the group's earlier effort, showcasing several highlights from Hendrix.

From "Bolero," Hendrix returned to "Comin' Down Hard on Me." These, too, were vastly improved. Incredibly, earlier, discarded takes can be heard between these newly recorded takes. These early rehearsals and takes were erased by engineer Dave Palmer, who simply wound the tape back to the start of the reel when formal takes were initiated. Hendrix obviously thought little of the entire night's work — both erased and recorded — as the tape box was marked "Do Not Use." These versions would be superseded by new takes and overdubs recorded the following evening.

■
Wednesday, July 15, 1970
New York, Electric Lady Studios. Engineer: Eddie Kramer. Second Engineer: Dave Palmer.

Hendrix successfully reprised "Comin' Down Hard on Me" here, recording several new basic tracks, followed by overdubs and a rough mix. The version later issued as part of 1973's *Loose Ends* compilation was drawn from these takes, edited posthumously by Electric Lady engineer John Jansen. Jansen did not use a single, complete take, instead combining two separate takes with the guitar overdubs and lead vocal Hendrix recorded on this evening. Ironically, when Alan Douglas and Tony Bongiovi were preparing *Crash Landing* in 1974, they could not locate the actual multi-track tape master. As none had ever existed, Bongiovi and Douglas simply overdubbed onto Jansen's composite master, adding a rhythm guitar line from Jeff Miranov and replacing Cox's and Mitchell's original contributions with new overdubs from bassist Bob Babbit and drummer Alan Schwartzberg.

■
New York Pop Festival
Downing Stadium, Randall's Island, N.Y. Friday, July 17, 1970.

The Experience's uneven performance at this chaotic and utterly disorganized outdoor event staged just across the river from Manhattan was both filmed and recorded. The group performed "Stone Free," "Fire," "Red House," "Message to Love," "Lover Man," "All Along the Watchtower," "Foxey Lady," "Ezy Ryder," "Star Spangled Banner," "Purple Haze," and "Voodoo Child (Slight Return)."

An edited version of "Red House," strangely bathed in echo, was later added to the 1982 compilation *Jimi Hendrix Concerts*. Save for sections of "Foxey Lady" and "Star Spangled Banner" included in *Free* or *Freedom* — the rarely seen documentary of this event — no other selections from this performance have ever been released.

■
Sunday, July 19, 1970
New York, Electric Lady Studios. Engineer: Eddie Kramer. Second Engineer: Kim King.

Work was completed on "Nightbird Flying," "Straight Ahead," "Astro Man," "Freedom," and "Dolly Dagger."

■
Monday, July 20, 1970
New York, Electric Lady Studios. Engineer: Eddie Kramer. Second engineer: Dave Palmer.

An earnest attempt to record the definitive studio rendition of "Lover Man." A master take was achieved, but it was curiously devoid of the energy and enthusiasm that had made it a staple of the Experience's stage repertoire. Fourteen takes were recorded, with the Experience opting to feature the arrangement used during their recent performances, such as the version recorded May 30, 1970, in Berkeley and later released on *Hendrix: In the West*. Take 10, timed at 3:00 and recorded without a vocal from Jimi, was briefly considered a master. Two guitar overdubs were attempted. The first was deemed "no good," while the second was apparently successful. Following a review of the new master, Hendrix chose to scrap this rendition and try again. Four more takes were done, with

take 14 now deemed best. Fourteen, however, was only marginally better than take 10, both surprisingly uninspired by recent Electric Lady standards. A rough mix was completed, but work on "Lover Man" was shelved. No available documentation suggests that Hendrix ever reprised the song before his death.

Additional overdubbing for "Angel" was also attempted, with Hendrix, Mitchell, and Cox all completing a series of subtle refinements. At Electric Lady, guitar and bass overdubs like these were undertaken in the control room, with Cox and Hendrix sitting close to the console, rather than out in the studio. This practice, while common today, was not the custom in 1970. The primary benefit, explains Cox, was

that the artist could hear the full recording played through the control-room speakers rather than through headphones. Moreover, Hendrix and Cox could receive immediate, face-to-face feedback from Kramer, who would be seated at the console. "Jimi and I were most comfortable doing our overdubs at the board," admits Cox. "You didn't have the obstruction presented by those earphones. You could get right into it when you heard the music through those speakers. That was another benefit of working at Electric Lady. Eddie understood that this was our way of doing overdubs. We didn't have to fight or explain *why* we were doing. We just did them."

As Hendrix's music had evolved, so had Mitch Mitchell's style. Mitch's

playing now reflected a more subtle and intricate approach rather than his previous display of power, speed, and dexterity. New songs, such as "Freedom," "Straight Ahead," and "Hey Baby (Land of the New Rising Sun)," steeped in rhythm and blues, dictated such a shift. "Mitch certainly did contribute a lot to Jimi's music," says Cox. "Even though we all played different instruments, we were united in making this work as a three-piece. Jimi and I were thinking about the patterns we were playing, but Mitch came at the music from a different perspective. He would hear something and say, 'That's good, but when you come to the end of the bar, let me try *this*.' He did that on all the stuff we recorded there."

"Jimi and Mitch were always throwing each other curveball riffs," remembers Kim King. "Mitch's role was to play lead drums, not to supply rhythm. On bass, Billy Cox kept everything moving straight ahead while Jimi and Mitch would battle it out."

While Hendrix accepted suggestions from Cox, Mitchell, and Kramer, the one area closed to scrutiny was his lyrics. "That was an area we all left alone," explains Cox. "Jimi's lyrics were sacrosanct. If there was something that obviously didn't fit, he knew and we knew. We would never say anything, but he would remark, 'Well, this is all I have written down right now. I'll put the rest on tomorrow.' I would ask him who he was singing about in some of those songs, but he would just fall out laughing and never tell me."

■

Tuesday, July 21, 1970

New York, Electric Lady Studios. Engineer: Eddie Kramer. Second engineer: Dave Palmer.

"Tune X — Just Came In," better known as "In from the Storm," was the focus of this evening. "That song was put together in one session in Jimi's hotel room when we were on the road," explains Cox. "We had a little amplifier with us, and we worked out the whole song. Room service came up with some steaks and trays of food, and I said, 'Jimi, do you remember the times when we used to share chili in Indianapolis?' He grabbed one of the dishes and said, 'Yeah man. Look at us now, eating *horsie doors* [hors d'oeuvres]!' I couldn't help

but to break out laughing." After dinner and a few hours of concentrated effort, Cox and Hendrix had polished off a strong new original destined to become one of the highlights of both the fateful September 1970 European tour and *Cry of Love*.

While no master would be recorded over the course of this session, Hendrix, Cox, and Mitchell ran through thirty versions, honing the arrangement and making subtle changes to their individual parts.

■

Wednesday, July 22, 1970

New York, Electric Lady Studios. Engineer: Eddie Kramer. Second engineer: Dave Palmer.

Work on "Tune X — Just Came In" resumed, beginning with a series of advanced rehearsals sounding substantially stronger than those done the previous day. The first eight takes gradually improved, with the complete eighth take the most promising. A break was called so that the group could return to the control room and review their progress. Eleven new takes followed, with numbers 5, 6, 10, and 11 complete. The song's arrangement was clearly in place, as the complete takes sounded nearly identical. Hendrix, however, seemed particularly intent on upgrading his own performance before designating any of these takes finished. After one particularly strong take, Jimi exclaimed, "And your mama, too!," which broke everyone up. Take 10 was originally considered the master, and the group successfully inserted an edit section into the master. Following a playback, however, Hendrix opted to scrap this take and begin again. An inspired take 11 provided the new master, requiring no such edits.

While the song's basic track had been achieved, later overdub sessions were scheduled to accommodate additional rhythm and lead guitar parts. Jimi and Emmeretta Marks recorded backing vocals after an experiment with Cox and Mitchell joining their effort was rejected. Hendrix would also replace his lead vocal, and the comment which prefaced his effort — "Regardless of whether you can use it or not" — was preserved for posterity at the beginning of the finished master.

Rough mixes were also completed for both "Just Came In" and "Comin' Down Hard on Me." While Hendrix would supervise additional rough mixes of "Just Came In" over the next month, an approved final mix was never completed before his death. So that "Just Came In" could become part of *Cry of Love*, the finished master was cut from this reel on November 29, 1970, and mixed by Kramer and Mitch Mitchell. Retitled "In from the Storm," the song was added to the album's master reel on December 3, 1970.

■

Thursday, July 23, 1970

New York, Electric Lady Studios. Engineer: Eddie Kramer. Second engineer: Dave Palmer.

With two major engagements in San Diego on July 25 and Seattle's Sicks Stadium on the twenty-sixth looming, Hendrix rallied, making significant ad-

Jimi plays Berkeley Community Center. A moment from one of Hendrix's finest performances, May 30, 1970.
(Richard Peters)

vances on two of *Cry of Love's* most evocative ballads, "Drifting" and "Angel."

The evening began with a magnificent take of "Drifting," followed by two incomplete but equally inspired takes. "We didn't do much rehearsing of that song before we recorded the basic tracks," remembers Billy Cox. "That one just flowed from Jimi. It was very spiritual and didn't require many takes at all."

In addition to reprising the Leslie organ speaker he had prominently featured during the June 25 recording of "Drifting," Hendrix was also eager to realize a "watery" tone from his guitar. Kramer, intrigued by Jimi's fascination with water, sent Shimon Ron off to purchase a plastic speaker. When Ron returned, Kramer placed the device in a large pail of water, fed Hendrix's guitar to it, and set up a microphone to record the results. "It sounded like shit," laughs Kramer. Hendrix enjoyed far more success with another innovative yet far more familiar technique — the backward insertion of various guitar parts. These session tapes definitively document Hendrix's relative ease with this complicated technique.

"Drifting" directly merged into another Leslie guitar effort, "Angel." Hendrix had had "Angel" under wraps for quite some time, as evidenced by the recent surfacing of a charming acoustic demo recorded sometime in early 1968. Long before putting the song forward at Electric Lady, Jimi took pains to develop it. "Before we had gone in to cut 'Angel,' we had gone over and over it, because Jimi wanted to make it a nice, sweet song," explains Cox. "We made some adjustments here and there, just practicing in our hotel rooms on the road, but Jimi had it completed. The bass line for that track was inspired by an old record we loved called 'Cherry Pie' [recorded originally by Skip & Flip

in 1960]," Cox remembers. "That gave the record the feel of those great 1950s R&B ballads." The group recorded seven takes, with numbers 2 and 6 complete, and 7 considered the working master.

When the basic track had been completed to Jimi's satisfaction, Mitch overdubbed a series of percussion effects, each treated with VFO (Variable Frequency Oscillator) manipulation to create various effects. Despite this effort, these overdubs would be erased and replaced with new drum parts recorded by Mitchell after Hendrix's death.

Following Mitchell's overdubs, a series of rehearsals prefaced the recording of a single complete take of "Belly Button Window." Using just six of the available sixteen tracks, this version, quite unlike the finished master, was performed as a slow-to-medium-tempo blues shuffle. No further work was attempted, however, as Hendrix opted to fix his concentration on "Drifting" and "Angel," recording a series of guitar overdubs for each.

While overdubs for both songs would be completed on this evening, neither "Angel" nor "Drifting" was ever finished during Hendrix's lifetime.

Following two concerts in San Diego and Seattle, the group traveled to Hawaii to take part in the filming of *Rainbow Bridge*, on the island of Maui. The film's concert scenes were filmed on July 30. The Experience flew to Oahu to perform at the Honolulu International Center on August 1. Hendrix spent another ten days vacationing in Maui before returning to New York during the second week of August.

Once back at Electric Lady, Hendrix took stock of his progress in the studio, creating yet another list of songs he wanted to include on his next album. "Songs for the LP *Straight Ahead*,"

he titled the memo before proceeding to list the following: "Ezy Ryder, Room Full Of Mirrors, Earth Blues Today, Valley Of Neptune, Cherokee Mist — that's going to be an instrumental, Freedom, Stepping Stone, Izabella, Astro Man, Drifter's Escape, Angel, Bleeding Heart, Burning Desire, Nightbird Flying, Electric Lady — slow, Getting My Heart Back Together Again, Lover Man, Midnight Lightning, Heaven Has No Tomorrow — slow, Sending My Love — slow to medium, This Little Boy, Locomotion, Dolly Dagger and The New Rising Sun ['Hey Baby']."

So much progress had been made at Electric Lady that Hendrix even considered releasing a three-record set entitled *People, Hell and Angels*. From as far back as January 1969, Hendrix had stated a preference for the title *First Rays of the New Rising Sun*. At Electric Lady, *Straight Ahead* had emerged as a working title, although *First Rays of the New Rising Sun* had never been dismissed. While the the three-disc concept may have been overly ambitious, Hendrix fully intended to deliver a two-disc set to Warner Bros. to meet its request for a Hendrix album for the lucrative Christmas season.

Upon his return from Hawaii, with a framework now in mind for the shape of the album, Hendrix's August 1970 sessions were principally reserved for mixing. 'We spent a great deal of time overdubbing and mixing and trying to

Performing at the Atlanta Pop Festival, July 4, 1970.

(Joe Sia)

finish tracks," recalls Kramer. "Some of the material, such as 'Room Full of Mirrors,' required a great deal of work. I was never happy with the drum sound on the original master, as it sounded squashed; therefore, that track required a considerable amount of time. In a continuing series of overdubs and re-mixes, we added guitars and created some intricate panning effects before finishing."

■
Friday, August 14, 1970
New York, Electric Lady Studios. Engineer: Eddie Kramer.

Overdubs and rough mixes were com-pleted for "Dolly Dagger" and "Free-dom." While "Dolly Dagger" would be completed by Hendrix before his death, "Freedom" would fall just short, lacking a final guitar overdub. In its place, Kramer reveals, was a guide track — possibly recorded on this evening — lasting from 2:22 until 2:30 on the finished master. Hendrix had intended to replace the part, but he passed away before he could complete the work.

Mixing sessions were routinely at-tended by all three members of the Ex-perience. Kramer would begin these sessions by organizing a rough mix and presenting his ideas. Hendrix would follow in kind, remaining open to sug-gestions from Cox and Mitchell. "Jimi wanted Eddie to set mixes up, because he knew he had that ear," recalls Cox. "Eddie could hear things we couldn't. Mitch would occasionally want his

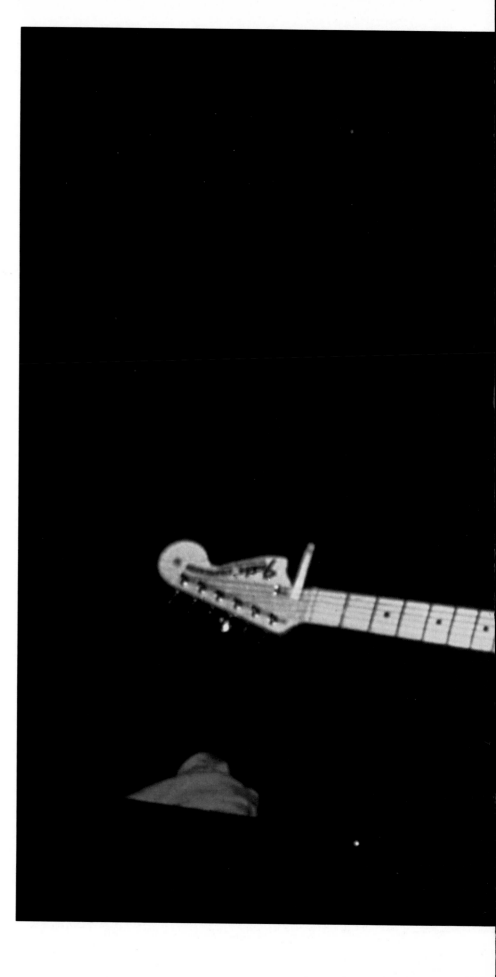

Bending the Stratocaster vibrato bar to create another unique sound.
(Barry Gruber Archives)

SESSIONS

drums to sound a certain way, or I might suggest an idea, but once Eddie got things started for him, Jimi could really do some things behind that board. Eddie would push Jimi, creating effects and always asking, 'What about this? How about that?,' and Jimi liked that. He knew exactly how he wanted the music to sound. Jimi would say that he wanted his guitar to sound like *that*, and Eddie could do *that*. They had worked together for so long that Jimi knew Eddie would get him what he wanted."

■
Tuesday, August 18, 1970
New York, Electric Lady Studios. Engineer: Eddie Kramer. Second engineer: Dave Palmer.

An evening of overdub work on "Dolly Dagger," with Hendrix recording a series of lead guitar parts. Jimi also overdubbed a new lead vocal. The background vocals of Albert and Arthur Allen, known professionally as the Ghetto Fighters, were also recorded on this evening.

Despite the privacy that Electric Lady now afforded him, Hendrix remained steadfast in his demand that he always record his lead vocal part from behind barricades, out of view of everyone in the studio. Ironically, while Kramer would routinely construct the barricades Jimi desired, Hendrix regularly sang during the recording of basic tracks. These spirited vocals, cautions Kramer, should not be mistaken for fin-

Performing at the Atlanta Pop Festival, July 4, 1970.

(Joe Sia)

ished vocals. To Hendrix, whose self-conscious qualms about the quality of his voice had never fully diminished, recording a lead vocal track required specific concentration. "When Jimi would sing while he was cutting basic tracks, he was *performing*," says Kramer. "He would *sing* when he was putting vocals on." "Jimi was self-conscious about his voice," explains Cox. "He had to have that wall up. I told him, 'Man, you don't need to have that.' But he wouldn't record his vocals unless it was. Mitch, Eddie, and I would crack up sometimes, because the irony was that even though he was hiding from us, we could still hear him. But that was his thing, and we didn't knock it. If he had to have that wall to make him comfortable, that's what would be done."

In addition to recording lead vocals and replacing guitar parts with new overdubs, Hendrix was also trying to catch up on his lyrics. "Because of all of the pressure he was under, Jimi had been a little behind getting his lyrics together," admits Cox. "Musically, he could count on support from Mitch and I, but lyrically, he had to rely on himself. If he didn't do it, it didn't get done. That's simply because we had no input regarding his lyrics. We let him handle that."

■
Thursday, August 20, 1970
New York, Electric Lady Studios. Engineer: Eddie Kramer. Second engineer: Dave Palmer.

The sole remaining reel of multitrack tape from this session captures a jam already in progress. Hendrix guides this gorgeous, slow blues jam, less than three minutes in length, with a warm, stinging guitar tone rarely featured.

Sadly, the recording inexplicably cuts out, and there is nothing more.

Whatever caused this interruption was presumably repaired, as an extensive mixing session followed. Additional work and rough mixes were completed for "Straight Ahead," "Room Full of Mirrors," "Ezy Ryder," "In from the Storm," "Drifting," "Angel," "Belly Button Window," "Dolly Dagger," and "Freedom."

■
Saturday, August 22, 1970
New York, Electric Lady Studios. Engineer: Eddie Kramer.

Rough mixes of "Straight Ahead," "Ezy Ryder," "Nightbird Flying," "Drifter's Escape," "Astro Man," "Comin' Down Hard on Me Baby," "In from the Storm," "Beginnings," and "Cherokee Mist (Valleys of Neptune)."

Working alone with Kramer, Hendrix also recorded a charming four-track demo of "Belly Button Window." "'Belly Button Window' was cut as a demo," Kramer remembers. "We both liked it so much." The song's simple beauty caused Kramer to remark enthusiastically that the track reminded him of Mose Allison's work. Intrigued, Hendrix continued, adding a second guitar. "I'm sure Jimi would have done something different had he lived," says Kramer. "But even in demo form, it was such a cool song."

While some have suggested that the inspiration for "Belly Button Window" was drawn from Jimi's own childhood experiences — or, worse, was a foreshadowing of his coming demise — Billy Cox heartily disagrees. "Jimi told me that 'Belly Button Window' had been written about the baby Mitch and his wife Lynn were expecting. He used to say that the baby was looking out

Lynn's belly button window at us."

As so much of Hendrix's time at Electric Lady had been dedicated to completing works already in progress, demos such as "Belly Button Window" were the exception rather than the norm. Yet, when the inspiration hit him, Jimi would put these ideas down on tape for future reference. "On a lot of sessions, Hendrix would come to the studio without Mitch Mitchell or Billy Cox," explains Dave Palmer. "He would just use the time to write. It wasn't, 'Okay, this is *the* tune for *the* record, let's *go*.' It was mainly, 'Okay, let's do some things and see what we have.'"

"We kept a half-inch, four-track machine loaded with tape in case Jimi was inspired to just do some writing," explains Kim King. "Rather than do it straight to sixteen-track or quarter-inch two-track, he would record demos on the four-track machine. His first two albums had been entirely recorded on four-track, so having this was a luxury for him."

Sadly, however, nearly all Jimi's four-track recordings from Electric Lady — save for the aforementioned "Belly Button Window" — have vanished, leaving no clues to such unrealized Hendrix ideas as "Locomotion," "Electric Lady — slow," and "This Little Boy."

■

Monday, August 24, 1970
New York, Electric Lady Studios. Engineer: Eddie Kramer. Second engineer: Kim King.

Another evening dedicated to enhancing the "Dolly Dagger" master. Billy Cox completed a fuzz bass overdub, another of the song's distinctive accents, while Hendrix attempted some final guitar overdubs, some of which were keyed in and out of the final mix by Kramer.

"Jimi and Eddie gave me a lot of freedom to try different ideas," remembers Cox. "I did the fuzz bass overdub in one take, punching in an occasional note to make sure it was just right."

In addition to his fuzz bass overdub, Cox was also asked to handle some faders on the console while Hendrix and Kramer began the intricate mixing of "Dolly Dagger." "I was in hog heaven," laughs Cox. "Eddie and Jimi put me in between them, and I got to do some fading while they were flying around the board doing the mix. It was great."

The song's final mix was completed on this evening, creating the master later issued on *Rainbow Bridge*. " 'Dolly Dagger' was a finished performance," explains Kramer. "It was well planned and thought out. Jimi eliminated everything he didn't like. The mix was complete. All of the perspectives were there. The sound of the lead guitar was exactly as he had wanted it. The bass had the right relationship to the guitar, which had the right relationship with the drums. And his voice was complete."

As his sessions at Electric Lady Studios had served to refocus Jimi's energies, "Dolly Dagger" represented the sweeping return of his artistic powers. To many, the song provided a shining example of just what Jimi could and would continue to achieve at the new facility. With the finest tools now at his disposal, the impressive results had already begun to flow. Sadly, following Jimi's untimely death less than a month later, "Dolly Dagger" instead became the symbol of unfulfilled promise, a bittersweet reminder of what might have been. "After Jimi had died," recalls John Jansen, "we used to play 'Dolly Dagger' a lot, especially during other mixing sessions — just to see if whatever we were doing was up to that." The difference, explains Kramer, was entirely due

to the unique perspective Hendrix provided. "When Jimi Hendrix was there, something extra always got done," says Kramer simply. "It was a mental thing. You would always push the faders differently with Jimi present than you would have if you were by yourself. He was so inspirational."

While it is possible that Jimi may have worked on August 25, no documentation exists to verify this. If he did not work at the studio, the August 24 session represents Jimi's last known session at Electric Lady.

■

Historic Performances Recorded at the Monterey International Pop Festival
Reprise MS 2029. U.S. album release. Wednesday, August 26, 1970.
Like a Rolling Stone/Rock Me Baby/Can You See Me/Wild Thing

More than three years after this milestone event actually took place, Reprise issued this collection of performances by Hendrix and Otis Redding.

Save for "Wild Thing," which had been included in the documentary film made at the festival and later broadcast by ABC, none of the other songs had been previously released. Despite the fine performances found throughout, the album's poor final mix did the collection little justice.

Backed by a modest promotional effort by Reprise, sales of the album began to escalate only after Jimi's death on September 18, 1970. Later that month, the album peaked at number 16, eventually spending twenty weeks on the album chart.

August 26 was also the date for the public unveiling of Electric Lady Studios. No recording was scheduled on this evening, as the studio staff franti-

A pensive Jimi.

(Jim Cummins/Star File)

content to remain with his own small band of friends. The party was a smash success, with guests enjoying a buffet of Japanese food and being entertained by recordings recently made at the studio. In addition to recordings by such Michael Jeffery–managed clients as the Patterson Singers and Jimmy & Vela, some of Jimi's new music was debuted. "We made a tape of three finished mixes to play at the party," remembers Kim King. "It was played over and over that night."

After leaving the party to fly to London, Hendrix would never return to Electric Lady. He died Friday, September 18, 1970, in the London flat of Monika Dannemann. The remarkable music Jimi Hendrix managed to create in less than four incredible years of recording continues to inspire and influence much of popular music today.

■

"Voodoo Child (Slight Return)" / "Hey Joe" / "All Along The Watchtower"

Track Records 2095 001. U.K. extended-play single. Friday, October 23, 1970.

This posthumously issued extended-play disc coupled *Electric Ladyland's* "Voodoo Child (Slight Return)" with "Hey Joe" and "All Along the Watchtower." "That single was a tribute to Jimi," explained Track executive Daniel Secunda. "We priced that record as close to actual cost as possible." The love and sympathy held by British record buyers for Jimi was clearly expressed when the single reached the top position on the U.K. chart, posthumously providing Jimi with his first British number 1 disc.

cally prepared for their gala opening party. Though Studio B was still unfinished, Shimon Ron plugged in the console to make the room appear fully operational. After much prodding from Jim Marron, Hendrix made an appearance, but he maintained a low profile,

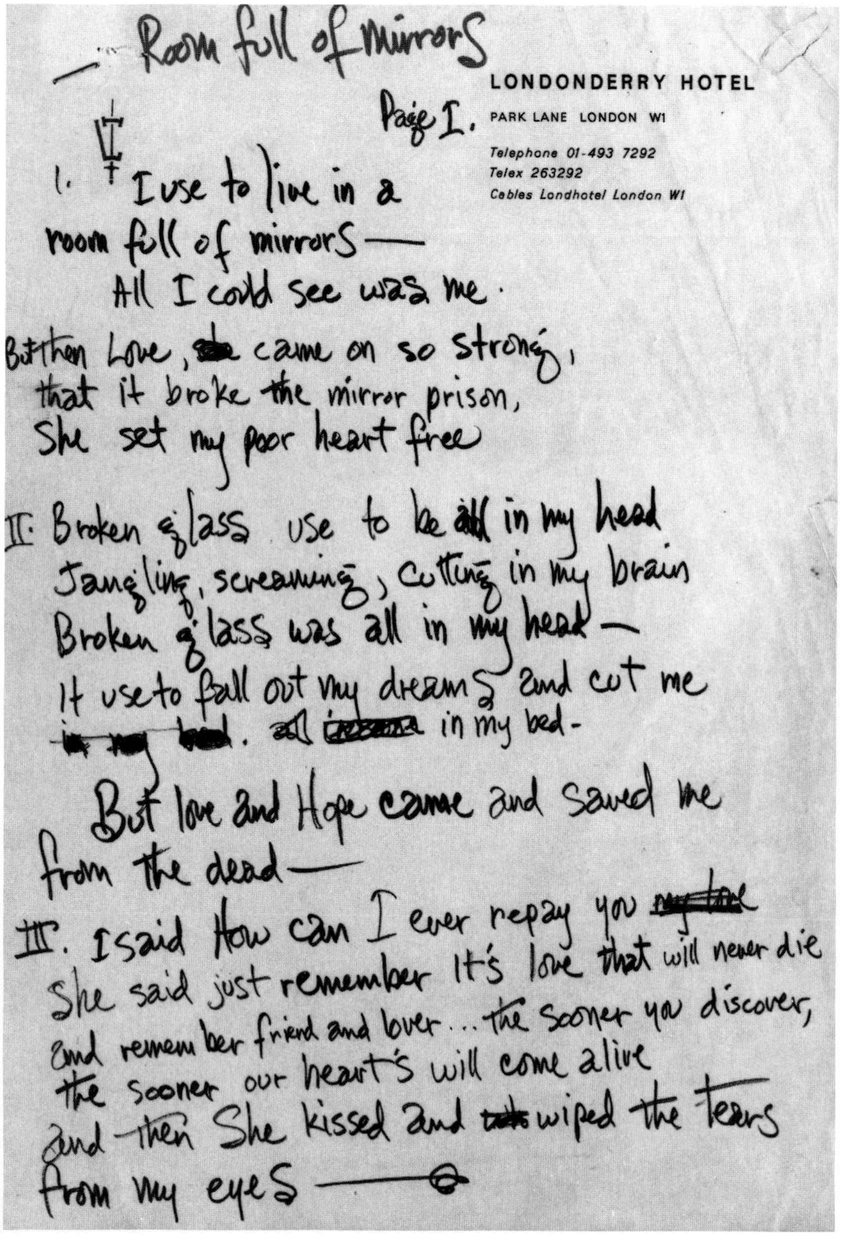

Room full of mirrors
Page I.

LONDONDERRY HOTEL
PARK LANE LONDON W1

Telephone 01-493 7292
Telex 263292
Cables Londhotel London W1

1. I use to live in a
room full of mirrors —
All I could see was me.
But then Love, ~~she~~ came on so strong,
that it broke the mirror prison,
She set my poor heart free

II. Broken glass use to be ~~all~~ in my head
Jangling, screaming, cutting in my brain
Broken glass was all in my head —
It use to fall out my dreams and cut me
~~in my bed. all inside~~ in my bed —

But love and Hope came and saved me
from the dead —

III. I said How can I ever repay you ~~my love~~
She said just remember It's love that will never die
and remember friend and lover ... the sooner you discover,
the sooner our heart's will come alive
and then She kissed and ~~tats~~ wiped the tears
from my eyes —

An early draft of Jimi's "Room Full of Mirrors."

(James A. Hendrix)

■
The Cry of Love

Reprise MS 2034. U.S. album release.
Wednesday, March 5, 1971. Producers: Jimi
Hendrix, Eddie Kramer, Mitch Mitchell.
Engineer: Eddie Kramer. Second engineers:
Kim King, Dave Palmer.
Freedom/Drifting/Ezy Ryder/Nightbird Flying/
My Friend/Straight Ahead/Astro Man/Angel/In
from the Storm

Despite the encouraging progress made
throughout the summer at Electric
Lady, all the material Jimi had recorded, overdubbed, and mixed had
been left in various stages of completion. Though he had narrowed his selections for the proposed double album,
his untimely death came before work
on the project could be completed.

Beginning in late October 1970,
Eddie Kramer and Mitch Mitchell began the painful process of compiling an
album from the remaining tapes.
Though Hendrix had been committed
to the double-album concept, after his
death, Michael Jeffery ordered Kramer
and Mitchell to construct two albums,
including one that would serve as the
soundtrack for his still-unfinished feature film *Rainbow Bridge*.

Save for "My Friend" and "Ezy
Ryder," all of the tracks featured on *Cry
of Love* had been recorded at Electric
Lady — with "Ezy Ryder" having been
virtually transformed at the studio by
the recording of new overdubs. While
"Dolly Dagger" and "Room Full of Mirrors" were held back at the last minute
for the forthcoming *Rainbow Bridge* album, the best of Jimi's new material
was mixed and put forward for the album. Some songs were more polished
than others — ranging from "Nightbird
Flying" and "Freedom," which lacked
only minor finishing touches, to "Angel"
and "Drifting," which required considerably more attention.

During what all involved recall as a
tense, emotional session, Mitch
Mitchell returned to Electric Lady's
Studio A and replaced all of his original
drum parts for "Angel." "Mitch was
around the control room listening to
playbacks, and I was wondering if he
was up to it," remembers John Jansen,
assistant engineer on the session.
"Then he got behind his kit and
doubled his original drum line in one
take. It was amazing." "I remember that
we applauded him for doing so," con-
curs Kramer.

Mitchell's heartfelt effort, says

Kramer, added a special significance to the track. "Mitch had always intended to overdub tom-tom [drums] with mallets, because that was a sound we were particularly good at getting. This was an idea that had been discussed originally, something we all — Jimi included — felt would embellish the track. Therefore, I had no problem with Mitch adding the overdub at all."

Where Mitchell's drum overdub for "Angel" solidified an existing rhythm pattern, "Drifting" posed a more intricate challenge, requiring considerable reconstruction. While the song's basic track had featured the combined efforts of Hendrix, Mitchell, and Cox, its delicate melody was framed by just two guitar lines and buttressed by generous insertions of Jimi's backward guitar. Kramer then fused portions from the June 25 recording to the July 23 master in order to further develop the song's basic track. To match the guitar sound, Kramer was forced to improvise. "I was working on 'Drifting' late one night in Studio A when I realized that I only had a DI [direct injection] guitar track for this very important lead-rhythm part. Originally, wanting a very clean guitar sound, Jimi had put this part on tape to act as a guide. There was no amplifier

track, so in order to create the amplifier sound, I ran the DI out of the console, through the cue system into the studio, fed it through a transformer into Jimi's Marshall stack, and miked it up. All of the lights were out in the studio, save for the glow of the Marshall headstack, and it sounded just as if Jimi were playing through the amplifier. The back door to the studio had been open, and in the midst of transforming the sound to tape, an assistant engineer was startled to hear Jimi's screaming guitar in Studio A. He came running into the control room, flustered, his face white as a sheet, sure that he had heard Jimi playing again, before he realized what I had been doing."

With Hendrix's guitar tracks in place, Mitch Mitchell replaced his drum parts. "Mitch just shined at this type of playing," explains Kramer. "It was perfectly within his scope, with gentle playing, a lot of cymbal work, double stops, and smashes on the downbeats. A superb performance." To add a final touch, vibraphonist Buzzy Linhart was recruited to contribute a charming, tastefully muted overdub. "It was a difficult session," remembers Kramer. "Buzzy Linhart was deadly serious about what he was to play." "Eddie

Kramer and Mitch Mitchell called me up and told me they had one track where Jimi hadn't been sure if he wanted vibes playing the song's chords or an additional rhythm guitar, and would I play on this song for them? It was just so touching to be in the studio he built, playing back this tape and hearing Jimi's beautiful voice."

Hendrix's untimely death also robbed Cox of his due, as no publishing credit was given to Cox. "Those songs were a part of my soul. I enjoyed the camaraderie and I enjoyed helping Jimi create those songs, but my name is nowhere in sight. Had Jimi lived, I know my name would have appeared on some of them, but who do I complain to? Mitch and Buddy can verify to what I contributed, but we also did a lot in private. I also felt slighted when I wasn't asked to help put *The Cry of Love* together. I might have been quiet in the studio, but that didn't diminish the contributions that Jimi himself acknowledged."

The Cry of Love was warmly received by critics and fans, and the album peaked at number 3, spending a total of thirty-nine weeks on the *Billboard* chart.

THE ALBUMS

Are You Experienced?

Track Records 612 001

Release date: May 1967

Producer: Chas Chandler

Engineer: Eddie Kramer

Additional engineering: George Chkiantz, Mike Ross, Dave Siddle

Studios: CBS, DeLane Lea, Olympic, Pye, Regent [London]
Foxey Lady/Manic Depression/Red House/Can You See Me/Love or Confusion/I Don't Live Today/May This Be Love/Fire/Third Stone from the Sun/Remember/Are You Experienced?

Are You Experienced?

Reprise RS 6261

Release date: August 1967

Producer: Chas Chandler

Engineer: Eddie Kramer

Additional engineering: George Chkiantz, Mike Ross, Dave Siddle

Studios: CBS, DeLane Lea, Olympic, Pye, Regent [London]
Purple Haze/Manic Depression/Hey Joe/Love or Confusion/May This Be Love/I Don't Live Today/The Wind Cries Mary/Fire/Third Stone from the Sun/Foxey Lady/Are You Experienced?

Axis: Bold as Love

Reprise RS 6281

Release date: January 1968

Producer: Chas Chandler

Engineer: Eddie Kramer

Second engineers: George Chkiantz, Andy Johns, Terry Brown

Studio: Olympic [London]
EXP/Up from the Skies/Spanish Castle Magic/Wait Until Tomorrow/Ain't No Telling/Little Wing/If Six Was Nine/You Got Me Floatin'/Castles Made of Sand/She's So Fine/One Rainy Wish/Little Miss Lover/Bold as Love

Electric Ladyland

Reprise 2RS 6307

Release date: October 1968

Produced & directed by: Jimi Hendrix

Additional production: Chas Chandler

Engineers: Eddie Kramer, Gary Kellgren

Second engineers: Tony Bongiovi, George Chkiantz, Andy Johns

Studios: Olympic [London], Record Plant, Mayfair, Bell Sound [New York]
And the Gods Made Love/Have You Ever Been (to Electric Ladyland)/Crosstown Traffic/Voodoo Chile/Little Miss Strange/Long Hot Summer Night/Come On (Part 1)/Gypsy Eyes/Burning of the Midnight Lamp/Rainy Day Dream Away/1983 (A Merman I Shall Turn to Be)/Moon, Turn the Tides . . . Gently Gently Away/Still Raining, Still Dreaming/House Burning Down/All Along the Watchtower/Voodoo Child (Slight Return)

Smash Hits

Track Records 613 004
Release date: April 1968
Producer: Chas Chandler
Engineers: Eddie Kramer, Mike Ross, Dave Siddle
 *Purple Haze/Fire/The Wind Cries Mary/Can You See Me/51st
 Anniversary/Hey Joe/Stone Free/The Stars That Play with
 Laughing Sam's Dice/Manic Depression/Highway Chile/The
 Burning of the Midnight Lamp/Foxey Lady*

Smash Hits

Reprise MS 2025
Release date: July 1969
Producers: Chas Chandler, Jimi Hendrix
Engineers: Eddie Kramer, Dave Siddle, Mike Ross
 *Purple Haze/Fire/The Wind Cries Mary/Can You See Me/Hey
 Joe/All Along the Watchtower/Stone Free/Crosstown Traffic/
 Manic Depression/Remember/Red House/Foxey Lady*

Band of Gypsys

Capitol STAO–472
Release date: April 1970
Producer: Heaven Research Unlimited [Jimi Hendrix]
Engineering & remixing supervision: Eddie Kramer
Additional remote engineers: Wally Heider, Jimmy Robinson
Live recording: Fillmore East, New York, January 1, 1970
Edited & mixed: Juggy Sound [New York]
 *Who Knows/Machine Gun/Changes/Power of Soul/Message to
 Love/We Gotta Live Together*

Woodstock

Cotillion SD 3500
Release date: June 1970
Producer: Eric Blackstead
Engineers: Eddie Kramer, Lee Osbourne
Live recording: Woodstock Festival, Bethel, N.Y.,
 August 19, 1969
 Star Spangled Banner/Purple Haze/Instrumental Solo

Historic Performances Recorded at the Monterey International Pop Festival

Reprise MS 2029
Release date: August 1970
Producers: Lou Adler, John Phillips
Engineers: Wally Heider, Eric Weinbang
Live recording: Monterey Pop Festival, Monterey, Calif.,
 June 18, 1967
 *Like a Rolling Stone/Rock Me Baby/Can You See Me/Wild
 Thing*

Woodstock II

Cotillion SD 2400
Release date: March 1971
Producer: Eric Blackstead
Engineers: Eddie Kramer, Lee Osbourne
Live recording: Woodstock Festival, Bethel, N.Y.,
 August 19, 1969
 *Jam Back at the House/Izabella/Getting My Heart Back Together
 Again*

The Cry of Love

Reprise MS 2034
Release date: March 1971
Producers: Jimi Hendrix, Eddie Kramer, Mitch Mitchell
Engineer: Eddie Kramer
Second engineers: Dave Palmer, Kim King, John Jansen
Additional engineering: Jack Adams
Studios: Electric Lady, Record Plant [basic tracks: Ezy Ryder],
 Sound Center [basic tracks: My Friend]
 *Freedom/Drifting/Ezy Ryder/Night Bird Flying/My Friend/
 Straight Ahead/Astro Man/Angel/In from the Storm/Belly Button
 Window*

Experience

Ember 5057 [not Released in U.S.]
Release date: August 1971
Producer: Jerry Goldstein
Additional production: Chas Chandler
Live recording: Royal Albert Hall, London, February 24, 1969
 *Sunshine of Your Love/Room Full of Mirrors/C# Blues [Bleeding
 Heart]/Smashing Amps*

More Experience

Ember 5061 [not released in U.S.]
Release date: March 1972
Producers: Jerry Goldstein, Chas Chandler
Live recording: Royal Albert Hall, London, February 24, 1969
 *Little Ivey [Little Wing]/Voodoo Chile [Voodoo Child (Slight
 Return)]/Room Full of Mirrors/Fire/Purple Haze/Wild Thing/
 Bleeding Heart*

Jamming backstage at
Madison Square Garden,
May 18, 1969.

(Eddie Kramer)

The First Great Rock Festivals of the Seventies: Isle of Wight/Atlanta Pop Festival

Columbia G3X 30805
Release date: September 1971
Producer: Ted Macero
Engineers: Don Puluse, Stan Tonkel, Russ Payne
Live recording: Isle of Wight Festival, August 30, 1970
   Power to Love [actually *Message to Love*]/*Midnight Lightning*/
   Foxey Lady

Isle of Wight

Polydor 2302 016 [not released in U.S.]
Release date: November 1971
Producer: Michael Jeffery
Mixing engineers: Eddie Kramer (Electric Lady Studios),
   Carlos Olms (Polydor Studios, London)
Live recording: Isle of Wight Festival, August 30, 1970
   *Midnight Lightnin'/Foxey Lady/Lover Man/Freedom/All Along
   the Watchtower/In from the Storm*

Rainbow Bridge

Reprise MS 2040
Release date: October 1971
Producers: Jimi Hendrix, Eddie Kramer, Mitch Mitchell, John
   Jansen
Engineer: Eddie Kramer
Additional engineering: John Jansen, Abe Jacob, Dave Palmer,
   Kim King, Tony Bongiovi, Gary Kellgren, Angel Balestier,
   Bob Cotto, Ron Beekman
Studios: Electric Lady, Record Plant [basic tracks: Star
   Spangled Banner, Room Full of Mirrors, Earth Blues], TTG
   [basic tracks: Look Over Yonder]
Live recording: Hear My Train A Comin', Berkeley,
   May 30, 1970, first show
   *Dolly Dagger/Earth Blues/Pali Gap/Room Full of Mirrors/Star
   Spangled Banner/Look Over Yonder/Hear My Train A Comin'/
   Hey Baby (The Land of the New Rising Sun)*

Hendrix in the West

Reprise MS 2049
Release date: February 1972
Producers: Eddie Kramer, John Jansen
Engineers: Eddie Kramer, John Jansen
Live recordings: Berkeley, San Diego, London, Isle of Wight
   Johnny B. Goode [Berkeley, 5/30/70, first show]/*Lover Man*
   [Berkeley, 5/30/70, second show]/*Blue Suede Shoes* [Berkeley,
   5/30/70, afternoon rehearsals]/*Voodoo Child (Slight Return)*
   [Royal Albert Hall, London, 2/24/69]/*God Save the Queen/Sgt.*

Pepper's Lonely Hearts Club Band [Isle of Wight, 8/30/70]/
Little Wing [Royal Albert Hall, London, 2/24/69]/*Red House*
[San Diego, 5/24/69]

War Heroes

Reprise MS 2103
Release date: December 1972
Producers: Jimi Hendrix, Eddie Kramer, John Jansen
Engineers: Eddie Kramer, John Jansen, Dave Palmer, Kim
   King
Additional engineering: Gary Kellgren, Tony Bongiovi, Bob
   Hughes, Jack Adams, Dave Ragno
Studios: Electric Lady, Record Plant [basic tracks: Izabella,
   Stepping Stone, Three Little Bears, Bleeding Heart, Tax
   Free, Izabella, Stepping Stone], Olmstead [Midnight],
   Olympic [Highway Chile, Tax Free]
   *Bleeding Heart/Highway Chile/Tax Free/Peter Gunn/Catastro-
   phe/Stepping Stone/Midnight/Three Little Bears/Beginning/
   Izabella*

Soundtrack Recordings from the Film: *Jimi Hendrix*

Reprise 2RS 6481
Release date: June 1973
Live recordings: Berkeley, Monterey, Isle of Wight, Fillmore
   East, London, Woodstock [as well as interviews with
   Hendrix and other associates]
   Rock Me Baby [Monterey, 6/18/67/*Wild Thing* [Monterey,
   6/18/67], *Machine Gun I* [Isle of Wight, 8/30/70]/*Interviews I/
   Johnny B. Goode* [Berkeley, 5/30/70, first show]/*Hey Joe*
   [Monterey, 6/18/67]/*Purple Haze* [Berkeley, 5/30/70, first
   show]/*Like a Rolling Stone* [Monterey, 6/18/67]/*Interviews II/
   Star Spangled Banner* [Woodstock, 8/19/69]/*Machine Gun II*
   [Fillmore East, 1/1/70, first show]/*Hear My Train A Comin'*
   [London, 12/19/67]/*Interviews III/Red House* [Isle of Wight,
   8/30/70]/*In from the Storm* [Isle of Wight, 8/30/70]/
   Interviews IV

Loose Ends

Polydor 2310 301 [not released in U.S.]
Release date: February 1974
Producer: Michael Jeffery
Engineer: Alev Trevor [John Jansen]
Additional production: Jimi Hendrix, Chas Chandler
Additional engineering: Eddie Kramer, John Jansen, Dave
   Palmer, Kim King, Gary Kellgren, Jack Adams, Tom Flye,
   Bob Hughes, Dave Ragno
Studios: Electric Lady, Record Plant [basic tracks: Blue Suede
   Shoes, Jam 292], Baggy's Studios [Burning Desire, I'm Your

Berkeley Community Center, May 30, 1970, first show.

(Richard Peters)

SELECTED DISCOGRAPHY

During his Los Angeles stay, Jimi deepened his ties with the Buddy Miles Express, jamming with the group and writing the liner notes to *Expressway to Your Skull,* their debut album.

(Jim Marshall)

Hoochie Coochie Man], Mayfair [The Stars That Play with Laughing Sam's Dice], Olympic [Electric Ladyland]
Coming Down Hard on Me/Blue Suede Shoes/Jam 292/The Stars That Play with Laughing Sam's Dice/Drifter's Escape/Burning Desire/I'm Your Hoochie Coochie Man/Electric Ladyland

Crash Landing

Reprise MS 2204

Release date: March 1975

Producers: Alan Douglas, Tony Bongiovi

Arranger: Brad Baker

Engineers: Les Kahn, Tony Bongiovi, Ron Saint Germain

Studios (1974): Shaggy Dog [Stockbridge, Mass.], Track
  [Washington, D.C.], Media Sound [New York]
  Message to Love [Record Plant, 12/19/69]/*Somewhere Over the
  Rainbow* [Sound Center, 3/68]/*Crash Landing* [Record Plant,
  4/24/69, 4/29/69]/*Come Down Hard on Me* [Electric Lady,
  7/14/70]/*Peace in Mississippi* [TTG, 10/24/68]/*With the Power*
  [Record Plant, 5/15/69]/*Stone Free Again* [Record Plant,
  4/9/69]/*Captain Coconut* [composite pieces from recordings
  originally made at Electric Lady, Record Plant, TTG, and the
  Hit Factory]

Crash Landing

Unreleased version
  Crash Landing [H-256, Record Plant, 4/24/69]/*Somewhere*
  [H-124, 3/68]/*Anything Is Possible (with the Power)* [H-36,
  Record Plant, 1/21/70]/*New Rising Sun* [H-264, TTG,
  10/22/68]/*Message to Love* [H-34, Record Plant, 1/20/70]/*Scat
  Vocal-Lead 1-Scat Vocal 2-Lead Vocal 2* [H-273, Hit Factory,
  8/28/69]/*Stone Free* [H-255, Record Plant, 4/7/69]/*Peace in
  Mississippi* [H-282, TTG, 10/24/68]/*Here Comes Your Lover
  Man* [H-248, TTG, 10/29/68]

Midnight Lightning

Reprise MS 2229

Release date: November 1975

Producers: Alan Douglas, Tony Bongiovi

Arranger: Brad Baker

Engineers: Les Kahn, Tony Bongiovi, Ron Saint Germain

Studios (1974–75): Shaggy Dog [Stockbridge, Mass.], Track
  [Washington, D.C.], Media Sound [New York]
  Trash Man [Olmstead, 4/4/69]/*Midnight Lightning/Hear My
  Train* [Record Plant, 4/9/69]/*Gypsy Boy* [Record Plant,
  3/18/69]/*Blue Suede Shoes* [Record Plant, 1/23/70]/*Machine
  Gun* [Hit Factory, 8/29/69; Record Plant, 9/23/69]/*Once I Had
  a Woman* [Record Plant, 1/23/70]/*Beginning* [Electric Lady, 7/
  1/70]

Multicolored Blues

Unreleased version
  Seven Dollars in My Pocket/Hootchie Cootchie Man [Record
  Plant, 12/18/69]/*Midnight Lightning/Lee Blues* [H-396, Hit

Factory, 8/28/69]/*Izabella Blues* [H-276, Hit Factory, 8/29/69]/
Blue Suede Shoes [H-38, Record Plant, 1/23/70]/*Farther On
Down the Road* [Electric Lady]/*Winter Blues* [H-309, Record
Plant, 5/7/69]/*Slow Time Blues* [H-39, Record Plant, 1/23/70]/
Blues for Me and You [H-242, Hit Factory, 9/6/69]/*Last
Thursday Morning* [H-83, Electric Lady, 7/20/70]/*Comin'
Down Hard* [Electric Lady]

Essential Jimi Hendrix Volume One

Reprise 2RS 2245

Release date: July 1978
  *Are You Experienced?/Third Stone from the Sun/Purple Haze/
  Little Wing/If Six Was Nine/Bold as Love/Little Miss Lover/
  Castles Made of Sand/Gypsy Eyes/Burning of the Midnight
  Lamp/Voodoo Child (Slight Return)/Have You Ever Been (to
  Electric Ladyland)/Still Raining, Still Dreaming/House Burning
  Down/All Along the Watchtower/Room Full of Mirrors/Izabella/
  Freedom/Dolly Dagger/Stepping Stone/Drifting/Ezy Ryder*

Essential Jimi Hendrix Volume Two

Reprise 2293

Release date: April 1979
  *Hey Joe/Fire/Foxey Lady/The Wind Cries Mary/I Don't Live
  Today/Crosstown Traffic/Wild Thing/Machine Gun/Star
  Spangled Banner/Gloria* [Unreleased studio track: TTG,
  10/29/68]

Nine to the Universe

Reprise HS 2299

Release date: March 1980

Producer: Alan Douglas

Assistant producer: Les Kahn

Engineer: Ron Saint Germain
  *Nine to the Universe/Jimi-Jimmy Jam/Young-Hendrix/Easy
  Blues/Drone Blues*

Jimi Hendrix Concerts

Reprise 22306-1

Release date: August 1982

Producer: Alan Douglas

Associate producers: Daniel Secunda, Albert Koski

Engineers: Bob Potter, John Porter, Les Kahn, Buddy Epstein,
  Rino Roucco

Recorded live: Winterland, San Diego, New York, London,
  Berkeley
  Fire [Winterland, 10/12/68, first show]/*I Don't Live Today* [San
  Diego, 5/24/69]/*Red House* [Randall's Island, N.Y., 7/17/70]/
  Stone Free [Royal Albert Hall, London, 2/24/69]/*Are You*

Experienced? [Winterland, 10/10/68, first show]/*Little Wing* [Winterland, 10/11/68, second show]/*Voodoo Child (Slight Return)* [Winterland, 10/10/68, first show]/*Bleeding Heart* [Royal Albert Hall, London, 2/24/69]/*Hey Joe* [Berkeley, 5/30/70]/*Wild Thing* [Winterland, 10/12/68, first show]/*Hear My Train A Comin'* [Winterland, 10/10/68, first show]/*Foxey Lady* [San Diego, 5/24/69 — CD bonus track only]

Kiss the Sky

Reprise 25119

Release date: October 1984

Compilation producers: Kevin Laffey, Chip Branton, Alan Douglas

Are You Experienced?/I Don't Live Today [recorded live: San Diego, 5/24/69]/*Voodoo Child (Slight Return)/Stepping Stone/ Killing Floor* [recorded live: Monterey, 6/18/67]/*Purple Haze/ Red House/Crosstown Traffic/Third Stone from the Sun/All Along the Watchtower*

Jimi Plays Monterey

Reprise 25358-1

Release date: February 1986

Producer: Alan Douglas

Associate producer: Chip Branton

Original production: Lou Adler, John Phillips

Original engineers: Wally Heider, Eric Weinbang

Remix engineer: Mark Linett

Killing Floor/Foxey Lady/Like a Rolling Stone/Rock Me Baby/ Hey Joe/Can You See Me/The Wind Cries Mary/Purple Haze/ Wild Thing

Johnny B. Goode

Capitol MLP 15022

Release date: June 1986

Producers: Alan Douglas, Chip Branton

Remix engineer: Mark Linett

Voodoo Child (Slight Return) [Atlanta Pop Festival 7/4/70]/ *Johnny B. Goode* [Berkeley, 5/30/70, first show]/*All Along the Watchtower* [Atlanta Pop Festival, 7/4/70]/*Star Spangled Banner* [Atlanta Pop Festival, 7/4/70]/*Machine Gun* [Berkeley, 5/30/70, second show]

Band of Gypsys 2

Capitol SJ-12416

Release date: October 1986

Producers: Alan Douglas, Chip Branton

Hear My Train A Comin' [Fillmore East, 12/31/69, first show]/ *Foxey Lady* [Fillmore East, 1/1/70, first show]/*Stop* [Fillmore

East, 1/1/70, first show]/*Voodoo Child (Slight Return)* [Atlanta Pop Festival, 7/4/70]/*Stone Free* [Berkeley, 5/30/70]/*Ezy Ryder* [Berkeley, 5/30/70]

Live at Winterland

Rykodisc RCD 20038

Release date: May 1987

Producer: Alan Douglas, Chip Branton

Mixing engineer: Mark Linett

Prologue/Fire [10/11/68, first show]/*Manic Depression* [10/12/68, second show]/*Sunshine of Your Love* [10/10/68, second show]/*Spanish Castle Magic* [10/12/68, second show]/ *Red House* [10/11/68, first show]/*Killing Floor* [10/10/68, second show]/*Tax Free* [10/11/68, second show]/*Foxey Lady* [10/11/68, second show]/*Hey Joe* [10/12/68, first show]/*Wild Thing* [10/12/68, first show]/*Epilogue*

Radio One

Rykodisc RCD 20078

Release date: November 1988

Production supervisor: Alan Douglas

Remix engineer: Mark Linett

Mono BBC Radio Recordings

Stone Free [2/13/67]/*Radio One* [12/15/67]/*Day Tripper* [12/15/67]/*Killing Floor* [3/28/67]/*Love or Confusion* [2/13/67]/*Catfish Blues* [10/6/67]/*Drivin' South* [10/6/67]/*Wait Until Tomorrow* [12/15/67]/*Hear My Train A Comin'* [12/15/67]/*Hound Dog* [10/6/67]/*Fire* [3/28/67]/*I'm Your Hoochie Coochie Man* [10/17/67]/*Purple Haze* [3/28/67]/*Spanish Castle Magic* [12/15/67]/*Hey Joe* [2/13/67]/ *Foxey Lady* [2/13/67]/*Burning of the Midnight Lamp* [10/6/67]

Red House: Variations on a Theme

Hal Leonard HL00660040

Release date: November 1989

Producer: Alan Douglas

Red House [Berkeley, 5/30/70, first show]/*(Electric Church) Red House* [TTG, Studios, 10/29/68]/*Red House* [L.A. Forum, 4/26/69]/*Red House* [Randall's Island, N.Y., 7/17/70]/*Red House* [Royal Albert Hall, London, 2/24/69]/*Red House* [Winterland, 10/10/68, first show]

Lifelines

Reprise 9 26435

Release date: December 1990

Producer: Bruce Gary

[Radio Program]

Introduction/Testify/Lawdy Miss Clawdy/I'm a Man/Like a

**Cutting tracks at the
Record Plant, 1969.**
(Willis Hogans, Jr./Bill Nitopi
Collection)

*Rolling Stone/Red House/Hey Joe/Hoochie Coochie Man/Purple
Haze/The Wind Cries Mary/Foxey Lady/Third Stone from the
Sun/Rock Me Baby/Look Over Yonder [Mr. Bad Luck]/Burning
of the Midnight Lamp/Spanish Castle Magic/Bold as Love/One
Rainy Wish/Little Wing/Drivin' South/The Things That I Used
to Do/All Along the Watchtower/Drifter's Escape/Cherokee Mist/
Voodoo Child (Slight Return)/1983 (A Merman I Should Turn to
Be)/Voodoo Chile/Come On (Part I)/Manic Depression/Machine
Gun/Room Full of Mirrors/Angel/Rainy Day Shuffle/Valley of*

*Neptune/Send My Love to Linda/South Saturn Delta/Dolly
Dagger/Night Bird Flying*
[L.A. Forum Concert: April 26, 1969]
*Tax Free/Foxey Lady/Red House/Spanish Castle Magic/Star
Spangled Banner/Purple Haze/I Don't Live Today/Voodoo Child
(Slight Return)/Sunshine of Your Love*

SELECTED DISCOGRAPHY

Jamming at TTG Studios: Buddy Miles lays down the groove while Mitch Mitchell (*in background*) adds the cymbal.

(Chuck Boyd/Flower Children Ltd.)

Stages

Reprise 9 26732
Release date: November 1991
Producer: Alan Douglas
[Stockholm, 9/5/67]
    Sgt. Pepper's Lonely Hearts Club Band/Fire/The Wind Cries
    Mary/Foxey Lady/Hey Joe/I Don't Live Today/Burning of the
    Midnight Lamp/Purple Haze
[Paris, 1/29/68]
    Killing Floor/Catfish Blues/Foxey Lady/Red House/Drivin'
    South/The Wind Cries Mary/Fire/Little Wing/Purple Haze
[San Diego, 5/24/69]
    Fire/Hey Joe/Spanish Castle Magic—Sunshine of Your Love/Red

House/I Don't Live Today/Purple Haze/Voodoo Child (Slight Return)

[Atlanta, 7/4/70]

Fire/Lover Man/Spanish Castle Magic/Foxey Lady/Purple Haze/ Hear My Train A Comin'/Stone Free/Star Spangled Banner/ Straight Ahead/Room Full of Mirrors/Voodoo Child (Slight Return)

■
HIGHLIGHTS OF HENDRIX AS GUEST AND/OR PRODUCER

Lonnie Youngblood

Fairmont Records F-1002
   Go Go Shoes/Go Go Place
Fairmont Records F-1022
   Soul Food (That's What I Like)/Goodbye Bessie Mae

Isley Brothers

Atlantic 2263
   Testify (Part I)/Testify (Part II)
   The Last Girl/Looking for a Love
Atlantic 2303
   Move Over and Let Me Dance/Have You Ever Been Disappointed?

Rosa Lee Brooks

Revis Records 1013
   My Diary/Utee

Little Richard

Vee Jay 698
   I Don't Know What You've Got but It's Got Me (Part 1)/I Don't Know What You've Got but It's Got Me (Part 2)

King Curtis

Atco 6402
   Help Me (Part 1)/Help Me (Part 2)

Curtis Knight & the Squires

RSVP 1120
   How Would You Feel/Welcome Home
RSVP 1124
   Hornet's Nest/Knock Yourself Out

Get That Feeling

Jimi Hendrix Plays and Curtis Knight Sings
Capitol ST 2856
Release date: December 1967
Producer: Ed Chalpin
Engineer: Mickey Lane
Studio: Studio 76 [New York]
   How Would You Feel/Simon Says/Get That Feeling/Hush Now/ Welcome Home/Gotta Have a New Dress/No Business/Strange Things

Flashing

Jimi Hendrix Plays and Curtis Knight Sings
Capitol ST 2984
Release date: October 1968
Producer: Ed Chalpin
Engineer: Mickey Lane
Studio: Studio 76 [New York]
   Gloomy Monday/Hornet's Nest/Fool for You Baby/Happy Birthday/Flashing/Day Tripper/Odd Ball/Love Love/Don't Accuse Me

Hundreds of compilations have been fashioned — far too many to list individually — from the relatively few studio recordings Jimi made with Curtis Knight. These tapes were made during sessions held in October and December 1965, as well as July 17, 1967, and August 8, 1967. Producer Ed Chalpin incorporated another Knight/Hendrix recording as the backing track for "Suey," an obscure single featuring actress Jayne Mansfield.

An almost equal number of albums has been fashioned from primitive recordings of the group's December 26, 1965, performance at George's Club 20, in Hackensack, N.J., as well as a second, undetermined New York or New Jersey venue.

   Drivin' South/California Night/On the Killin' Floor/What'd I Say/I'll Be Doggone/Bright Lights Big City/I'm a Man/Sugar Pie Honey Bunch (I Can't Help Myself)/Get Out of My Life Woman/ Ain't That Peculiar/Last Night/Satisfaction/Land of 1000 Dances/UFO/You Got Me Running/Money/Let's Go, Let's Go, Let's Go/You Got What It Takes/Sweet Little Angel/Walkin' the Dog/There Is Something on Your Mind/Hard Night

Billy Cox and Mitch Mitchell onstage at Boston Garden, June 27, 1970.

(Willis Hogans, Jr./Bill Nitopi Collection)

McGough & McGear

Parlophone PCS 7047
Release date: October 1968
Producer: Paul McCartney
Studio: DeLane Lea
So Much/Ex Art Student

Eire Apparent

Buddah Records 2011-117
Rock 'n' Roll Band/Yes I Need Someone

Eire Apparent

Sunrise
Buddah Records 2011-117
Release date: May 1969
Producer: Jimi Hendrix
Studios: Record Plant [New York], TTG [Los Angeles], Polydor
    [London}
Engineers: Eddie Kramer, Gary Kellgren, Tony Bongiovi
    [Record Plant], Jack Hunt [TTG], Carlos Olms [Polydor]
    The Clown/Let Me Stay/Magic Carpet,/Mr. Guy Fawkes/
    Someone Is Sure to (Want You)/Morning Glory/Captive in the
    Sun/Got to Get Away/1026/Yes I Need Someone

Cat Mother & the All Night Newsboys

The Street Giveth . . . and The Street Taketh Away
Release date: June 1969
Polydor 24-4001
Producers: Jimi Hendrix & Cat Mother
Studio: Record Plant
Engineers: Gary Kellgren, Tony Bongiovi
    Bad News/Probably Won't/Track in a (Nebraska Nights)/Favors/
    Can You Dance to It/Marie/Good Old Rock 'N' Roll/How I Spent
    My Summer/Bramble Bush/Boston Burglar

Buddy Miles Express

Electric Church
Mercury SR-61222
Release date: June 1969
Producer: Jimi Hendrix
Studios: Record Plant [New York], Mercury Studios [New
    York]
Hendrix-produced songs include
    Miss Lady/69 Freedom Special/Destructive Love/My Chant

Timothy Leary

You Can Be Anyone This Time Around
Douglas Records I
Release date: April 1970
Producer: Alan Douglas
Engineer: Stefan Bright
Studio: Record Plant
    Live and Let Live

Lightnin' Rod

Doriella Du Fontaine
Celluloid/Douglas Records CEL-166
Release date: July 1984
Producer: Alan Douglas
Engineer: Stefan Bright
Mixdown: Material & Dave Jerden
Studio: Record Plant [basic tracks], RPM [1984 mixing]
    Doriella Du Fontaine

Stephen Stills

Stephen Stills
Atlantic SD 7202
Release date: November 1970
Producers: Stephen Stills & Bill Halverson
Engineer: Andy Johns
Studio: Island [London]
    Old Times Good Times

Love

False Start
Blue Thumb BTS 22
Release date: December 1970
Producer: Arthur Lee
Session Date: March 1970
Studio: Olympic [London]
    The Everlasting First

Ghetto Fighters

Ghetto Fighters
Unreleased
Producers: Jimi Hendrix & the Ghetto Fighters [Albert &
    Arthur Allen]
Engineer: Eddie Kramer
Studio: Electric Lady

Leading the Band of Gypsys. Fillmore East, December 31, 1969.
(Bob Oleson)

acknowledgments

WITHOUT the kind assistance and contributions from the following people, neither this book nor *Hendrix: Setting the Record Straight,* its companion, could have been written. Leslie Aday, Tunde and Taharqa Aleem (Albert and Arthur Allen), Carmine Appice, Dan Armstrong, Bob Babbit, Angel Balestier, Frank Barselona, Jeff Baxter, Danny Blumenauer, Tony Bongiovi, Joe Boyd, Stefan Bright, Al Brown, Terry Brown, Baird Bryant, Randy California, Jim Capaldi, Paul Caruso, Jack Casady, Ed Chalpin, Chas Chandler, Neville Chesters, George Chkiantz, Larry Coryell, David Crosby, Monika Dannemann, Lillian Davis, Spencer Davis, Leon Dicker, Alan Douglas, Andy Edlin, Tom Edmonston, Tom Erdelyi, Kathy Etchingham, Mike Finnigan, Robert Fitzpatrick, Tom Flye, John Gardiner, Jerry Goldstein, Michael Goldstein, Keith Grant, Gerry Guida, John Head, Michael Hecht, John Hillman, Duane Hitchings, Elliot Hoffman, Tom Hulett, Abe Jacob, John Jansen, Andy Johns, Glyn Johns, Les Kahn, Henry Kalow, Steve Katz, Linda Keith, Marta Kellgren, Kim King, Al Kooper, Howard Krantz, Bob Krasnow, Bob Kulick, Kevin Laffey, Joe LaNostra, Arthur Lee, Bob and Kathy Levine, Mark Linett, Emmeretta Marks, Jim Marron, John Marshall, Paul Marshall, Dave Mason, Roger Mayer, Paul and Linda McCartney, Jim McCarty, Eugene McFadden, Terry McVey, Buddy Miles, Jeff Miranov, Mitch Mitchell, Tom Moffat, Nigel Morgan, Juggy Murray, Graham Nash, Mike Neal, Stevie Nicks, Dave Palmer, Peter Pilafian, Ken Pine, Faye Pridgeon, Dave Ragno, Noel Redding, Bill Rich, Barry Reiss, Jim Robinson, Roland Robinson, Shimon Ron, Mike Ross, Tony Ruffino, Ron Saint Germain, Don Schmitzerle, Abby Schroeder, Alan Schwartzberg, Daniel Secunda, Mickey Shapiro, Linda Sloman, Joe Smith, Chris Stamp, Jeremy Steig, Mark Stein, Gerry Stickells, Stephen Stills, Bill Stoddard, Chris Stone, John Storyk, Ron Terry, Ed Thrasher, Velvert Turner, Willie Vacarr, Larry Vaughan, Jerry Velez, John Veneble, Johanan Vigoda, Chuck Wein, Steve Weiss, Judy Wong, and Herbie Worthington.

Special thanks are also due to Ilene Bellovin, Ben Dewey, Bruce Gary, Barry Gruber, Bob Elliott, James 'Zeus' Fahey, Andrew Johns, David Kramer, Steve Lang, Jeff Leve, Bill Levenson, Mark Lewisohn, Virginia Lohle, Jim Marshall, Colin Newman, Bruce Pates, Bruce Pilato, Jenifer Polenzani, Faye Pridgeon, Diane Quintana, Peter Shukat, Joe Sia, John Stix, Brad Tolinski/*Guitar World*, Ken Voss, and Herbert Worthington.

Very special thanks to my editor, Michael Pietsch, for his patience, continued interest, and belief in this project.

I am especially grateful to Felix Carcano for his friendship and support. Kind thanks also to Chas, Madeline, and the Chandler family for their kind hospitality during our stay in Cullercoates, Newcastle.

Jeff Gold at Warner Bros. Records deserves special recognition, as he made every effort to assist this project. Kind thanks are due Steve Lang and the entire staff at the Warner Bros. tape library in Burbank, as well as Bill Levenson and Joe Palmaccio at the Polygram tape library in Edison, New Jersey. Eddie and I also wish to thank Mark Linett for making Your Place or Mine Studios available for additional tape research.

We welcome the support of Al Hendrix, Janie and Troy Wright, Yale Lewis, and Karen Wetherell.

Hours of interviews were transcribed by Geri Chapman. Special thanks to Kathy Lowe for the computer loan and overuse of her printer, Bill Abbate for the computer assistance, and Maura Griffin's Cut & Paste Technologies, Inc.

Noel Redding's detailed autobiography, *Are You Experienced?,* written with Carol Appleby, provided an invaluable assist. U.S. chart positions were drawn from Joel Whitburn's *Billboard Top LP's.* U.K. listings were taken from Paul Gambaccini, Jonathan Rice, and Tim Rice's *British Hit Singles* and *British Hit Albums.*

The book would not have been possible without the guidance of Peter Shukat and all of those at Shukat, Arrow, Hafer & Weber.

Kudos are due the many Hendrix archivists always eager to answer questions and volunteer articles, films, photos, tapes, and memorabilia to help improve this project. Bob Elliott, Barry Gruber, Jeff Leve, Bill Nitopi, Bruce Pates, Bruce Pilato, and Ken Voss went above and beyond the call of duty.

Thanks to all, including the McDermott family and those whose names we may have missed. Enjoy!